TIME
ANNUAL
2001

TIME
ANNUAL
2001

TIME ANNUAL 2001

32

42

104

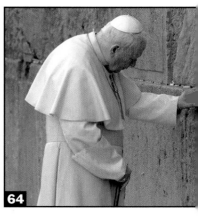

64

CONTENTS

126

Society

Sport

The Olympics

118

Science

Health

The Arts

The Best of 2000

Milestones

144

TIME ANNUAL 2001

MANAGING EDITOR	Kelly Knauer
DESIGNER	Ellen Fanning
PICTURE EDITOR	Patricia Cadley
RESEARCH DIRECTOR	Lela Nargi
PRODUCTION EDITOR	Michael Skinner
COPY EDITOR	Bruce Christopher Carr
TIME SPECIAL PROJECTS EDITOR	Barrett Seaman

TIME INC. HOME ENTERTAINMENT

PRESIDENT	Rob Gursha
EXECUTIVE DIRECTOR, BRANDED BUSINESSES	David Arfine
EXECUTIVE DIRECTOR, MARKETING SERVICES	Carol Pittard
DIRECTOR, RETAIL & SPECIAL SALES	Tom Mifsud
MARKETING DIRECTOR	Kenneth Maehlum
ASSISTANT DIRECTOR	Ann Marie Ross
ASSOCIATE PRODUCT MANAGER	Jennifer Dowell
ASSISTANT PRODUCT MANAGER	Meredith Peters
MANAGER, RETAIL & NEW MARKETS	Bozena Szwagulinski
COORDINATOR, RETAIL MARKETING	Gina Di Meglio
EDITORIAL OPERATIONS DIRECTOR	John Calvano
ASSISTANT EDITORIAL OPERATIONS MANAGER	Emily Rabin
BOOK PRODUCTION MANAGER	Jessica McGrath
ASSOCIATE BOOK PRODUCTION MANAGER	Jonathan Polsky
FULFILLMENT MANAGER	Richard Perez
ASSISTANT FULFILLMENT MANAGER	Tara Schimming
EXECUTIVE ASSISTANT	Mary Jane Rigoroso

THE WRITING OF THE FOLLOWING TIME STAFF MEMBERS AND CONTRIBUTORS IS FEATURED IN THIS VOLUME:
Charles P. Alexander, Harriet Barovick, Bernard Baumohl, Mark Bechtel, Lisa Beyer, Jay Branegan, Massimo Calabresi, Margaret Carlson, James Carney, Adam Cohen, Matthew Cooper, Howard Chua-Eoan, John Cloud, Jay Cocks, Adam Cohen, Richard Corliss, Andrea Dorfman, John F. Dickerson, Sally B. Donnelly, Tammerlin Drummond, Michael Duffy, Tamala M. Edwards, Daniel Eisenberg, Philip Elmer-DeWitt, Christopher John Farley, Andrew Ferguson, Sandy M. Fernandez, Michael Fitzgerald, Jaime A. FlorCruz, Nancy Gibbs, Frank Gibney Jr., Elizabeth Gleick, Frederic Golden, Dan Goodgame, Christine Gorman, Paul Gray, Karl Taro Greenfeld, John Greenwald, Lev Grossman, Anita Hamilton, Margot Hornblower, Walter Isaacson, Pico Iyer, James O. Jackson, Leon Jaroff, Daniel Kadlec, Jeffrey Kluger, Richard Lacayo, Tim Larimer, Michael D. Lemonick, Eugene Linden, Steve Lopez, Belinda Luscombe, Scott MacLeod, Ellin Martens, Dolly Mascarenas, J.F.O. McAllister, Johanna McGeary, Tim McGirk, Jodie Morse, J. Madeleine Nash, Kate Noble, Viveca Novak, Daniel Okrent, Michele Orecklin, Alice Park, Desa Philadelphia, James Poniewozik, Eric Pooley, Paul Quinn-Judge, Joshua Cooper Ramo, Romesh Ratnesar, Matt Rees, Edwin M. Reingold, Simon Robinson, Margot Roosevelt, Thomas Sancton, Bill Saporito, Richard Schickel, Elaine Shannon, Judith Shulevitz, Ian K. Smith, Joel Stein, Ron Stodghill II, Robert Sullivan, Chris Taylor, David E. Thigpen, Karen Tumulty, David Van Biema, Sarah Vowell, Douglas Waller, Steve Waterson, Daniel Williams, Richard Zoglin

SPECIAL THANKS TO:
Ken Baierlein, Sue Blair, Andy Blau, Dick Duncan, John Dragonetti, Linda Freeman, Arthur Hochstein, Ed Jamieson, Joe Lertola, Meghan Milkowski, Nancy Mynio, Rudi Papiri, Emily Rabin, Ken Smith, Michele Stephenson, Lamarr Tsufura, Cornelis Verwaal, Miriam Winocour

First Edition • ISSN: 1097-5721 • ISBN: 1-883013-74-7
TIME is a trademark of Time Inc.

We welcome your comments and suggestions about TIME Books. Please write to us at:
TIME Books • Attention: Book Editors • PO Box 11016 • Des Moines, IA 50336-1016

If you would like to order any of our hardcover Collector's Edition books, please call us at 1-800-327-6388.
(Monday through Friday, 7:00 a.m.–8:00 p.m. or Saturday, 7:00 a.m.–6:00 p.m. Central time).
Please visit our website at www.TimeBookstore.com

PRINTED IN THE UNITED STATES OF AMERICA

2000: Year of the Survivor

O N JAN. 1, 2000, AMERICANS JOINED PEOPLE AROUND THE WORLD IN A GRAND, rolling celebration of the new millennium. Partying our way out of the 20th century, we survived the Y2K scare nicely—good practice for the year to come, when surviving became something of a leitmotif. In March the highflying dotcom bubble burst, and we watched, fascinated, as last year's technomillionaires fought simply to stay in business. In the summer we embraced a silly yet strangely gripping TV program—*Survivor*—in which a group of voluntary castaways vied to become the last person standing on a South Pacific Island. But these exercises in persistence turned out to be mere practice rounds for the year's most enthralling, aggravating endurance contest: the unresolved presidential election that festered like an open wound and was finally decided not by popular vote but by the U.S. Supreme Court. Result: an electorate disillusioned with the voting process, a President without a mandate and a divided, diminished court. It isn't every year that TIME runs a cover showing the U.S. Constitution and the headline: "Yes, We'll Survive." This was such a year. Yet survive we did, and survive we will.

STEPHEN FERRY—LIAISON FOR *TIME*

DATE: November 11, 2000 • **PLACE:** Palm Beach, Florida • **PHOTOGRAPHER:** Stephen Ferry • **SCENE:** With the presiden

ngling by pieces of chad, Charles Burton, chairman of the Palm Beach County canvassing board, inspects a discarded ballot

Images

DATE: April 22, 2000 • **PLACE:** Miami • **PHOTOGRAPHER:** Alan Diaz • **SCENE:** Armed federal agents raid the home of Láza

onzález and seize Cuban refugee Elián González, 6, from Donato Dalrymple, one of the fishermen who rescued him at sea

DATE: October 5, 2000 • **PLACE:** Belgrade, Yugoslavia • **PHOTOGRAPHER:** Zeljko Safar • **SCENE:** Police fire tear gas i▸

...owds besieging the parliament building. The protesters demanded that Slobodan Milosevic surrender the presidency

Images

DATE: Sept. 30, 2000 • PLACE: Gaza City • PHOTOGRAPH: France 2 TV (video stills) • SCENE: Jamal Aldura tries to shie

s son Rami, 12, during a fire fight between Israeli soldiers and Palestinians. In death, Rami became a Palestinian martyr

Images

Deer take refuge in the Bitterroot River as wildfires ravage their habitat. In the summer Western states saw the worst fires in 50 years

FRANCIS SPECKER—NY POST—REX USA

DATE: October 22, 2000 • **PLACE:** Yankee Stadium, New York City • **PHOTOGRAPHER:** Francis Specker • **SCENE:** Yanke

...tcher Roger Clemens hurls a splintered bat at Mets catcher Mike Piazza in the Subway Series. Clemens was fined $50,000

CAMP DAVID SUMMIT

*While Clinton awaited the dove of peace
His unhappy campers longed for release*

TIM REIS FOR TIME

POPE JOHN PAUL II

*His burden is heavy; it only increased
When he payed a visit to the Middle East*

ANITA KUNZ FOR TIME

RUDOLPH GIULIANI

*The opera lover did time in the pillory:
Bad health, bad marriage . . . then Hillary*

THOMAS FLUHARTY FOR TIME

MARION JONES

*Of all track royalty, she's the most regal,
Too bad her man swills stuff that's illegal*

TIM O'BRIEN FOR TIME

PAT BUCHANAN

*Long ago, he coulda been a contender
Now Pat's old hat and just a pretender*

MARK FREDRICKSON FOR TIME

VICENTE FOX

*For Mexico's new boss, a neighbor vexes
Read my lips, said he: "No new Texas"*

MARK HESS FOR TIME

STEPHEN KING

*Double, double, e-toil and e-trouble
He was burned by the cyberbook bubble*

THOMAS FLUHARTY FOR TIME

BOBBY KNIGHT

*B-ball's top screamer at last is quiet,
He says he's a victim, but we don't buy it*

JOHN S. CUNEO FOR TIME

SUBWAY SERIES

*After the Mets vet met the damn Yankee,
Jeter was champ and Piazza was cranky*

JAMES BENNETT FOR TIME

BEN & JERRY

Hippies to the core, they bravely held out
But fed up at last, they finally selled out

ELIÁN GONZÁLEZ & DAD

It's playtime at last for Papa and Elián
So ends the tale of the Cuban chameleon

SHAQUILLE O'NEAL

In NBA combat the title he racked up
Now Lakers fans are happily Shaqqed up

THE WILLIAMS SISTERS

To put more thrills in our tennis arenas
Give us more Venuses and extra Serenas

BILL GATES

"What I have made a worldwide wonder
Please, let no court plan put asunder!"

WOULD-BE VEEP'S WIVES

Lynne and Hadassah paid double dues
Loyal No. 2s cheering loyal No. 2s

RALPH NADER

His quixotic race was torpid indeed
But for Gore, he was unsafe at any speed

CARLOS SANTANA

The veteran rocker's stature just grew
See, Bill Clinton? There is an Act Two!

TRENT LOTT

His Senate's divided! Watch him battle!
Poor Trent's lot: all hat—and no cattle

EXIT STRATEGIES

"Why can't I drop dead onstage? Lots of other people have done it."
ELTON JOHN, 53, on why he has not retired

"I have no intention of uttering my last words on the stage. Room service and a couple of depraved young women will do me quite nicely for an exit."
PETER O'TOOLE

"Do you know what it's like to have to walk around in high heels and sing 35 songs a night, to have to diet to get into those dresses?"
BARBRA STREISAND, on why she is on her final tour

"Once I was deflowered, they weren't interested in me."
BILL CLINTON, on throwing his le[s] at some monkeys during his trip to Indi[a]

"Hillary! You are so pretty!"
VIETNAMESE CROWDS, adoring the Senator-elect

"I reach high speeds. I especially love driving down a hill directly at a tree and swerving to one side at the last moment. That's my way to relax."
BORIS YELTSIN, former President of Russia, on driving his golf car[t]

"You don't have to get snippy about this."

AL GORE to George Bush, when Gore called on election night to retract his concession

"Pickup trucks, deer hunting, barefoot girls and boiled peanuts—that's what the flag represents ... nobody looks at it as a symbol of hate."
ERIC JOHNSON, Georgia state senator, on the state flag, which features a large Confederate X

"No, you are a lunatic."
J.K. ROWLING, Harry Potter author, recounting what she usually says to anyone who asks if her books are satanic

"It is the crown jewel of the prison system."
EHUD BARAK, Israeli Prime Minister, on barbed-wire-enclosed Camp David after peace talks there

"I've become mentally detached from it."
CLINT HALLAM, recipient of the world's first successful hand transplant two years ago, on why he now wants it amputated

"Start up blow-drying Teddy Koppel's hair, 'cause this game's done."
DENNIS MILLER, comedian, at the end of his debut evening as ABC *Monday Night Football* commentator

DUBYA SPEAKS

"I know how hard it is to put food on your family."

"I understand small-business growth; I was one."

"The most important job is not to be Governor, or First Lady in my case."

"The human being and the fish can coexist peacefully."

"I am so busy doing nothing ... that the idea of doing anything—which, as you know, always leads to something—cuts into the nothing and then forces me to have to drop everything."
JERRY SEINFELD, on how he's spending his time, on New York City radio station WFAN

WHITE POWER

"I woke up and spoke to my mother and scared us both to death."

BARRY WHITE, walrus of love, to students at Oxford, on how his voice changed when he was 14

"I don't make love to nobody's music, not least my own." BARRY WHITE

"Do we really want this kid raised by guys stupid enough to get into a hostage situation with Janet Reno?"

BILL MAHER, TV comic, on the Elián González situation

"He's very relaxed at the table, throwing his salad around willy-nilly. I didn't find him stiff at all."

MADONNA, on Prince Charles

"For the next few days, I'm going fishing."

WEN HO LEE, after a judge ended his controversial nine-month imprisonment

"He is not an absent-minded professor; he is a felon."

JANET RENO, on Wen Ho Lee, at a Senate hearing defending her handling of the spy case

"He once said he slept with every one of his leading ladies except one ... I know who that one is. What was I thinking?"

MARY TYLER MOORE, actress, on Elvis

ALTERNATE REALITIES

"My perky-elf days are over ... I'd love to play a hooker on *The Sopranos*."

KATHIE LEE GIFFORD

"When I became a doctor, I thought that was pretty prestigious, but I've got to tell you, you get a lot better treatment as a jerk from *Survivor*."

SEAN KENNIFF, *Survivor* survivor

"I'm cute in gym shorts! I'm slim and trim, and you'd be impressed—I've got good calves." LARRY KING

"My mom once said, 'Honey, you should marry a rich man.' I said, 'Mom, I am a rich man.'" CHER

"You dead yet?"

YOGI BERRA, to Whitey Ford, on news of Ford's recurrence of cancer

"It was neat, really neat."

RICK ROCKWELL, *Who Wants to Marry a Multi-Millionaire?* TV game-show groom, on his honeymoon with new wife Darva Conger

"It was very creepy."

DARVA CONGER, multi-millionaire bride

ELECTION FOLLIES

"Never, in times so complex and chaotic as these, have we faced two contenders who are boring and insipid."

FIDEL CASTRO, on George W. Bush and Al Gore

"We don't just have egg on our face—we have an omelet."

TOM BROKAW, after NBC and other networks changed their prediction on who would win Florida twice in six hours

"If you give people the impression you're a smarty-pants, that's no good for sure."

AL GORE, when asked if Americans want an intellectual as President

"I'll tell you one thing: when this Hillary gets to the Senate—if she does, maybe lightning will strike and she won't—she will be one of 100, and we won't let her forget it."

Senate Majority Leader TRENT LOTT

"I'll probably just vote whatever my mom or dad says."

BRITNEY SPEARS, before the presidential election

"Both of them, [so I could] knock both their heads together."

Minnesota Governor JESSE VENTURA, on whether he'd rather have a beer with George W. Bush or Al Gore

"Free hairdos for the poor."

JOHN WATERS, on what his campaign slogan would be if he ran for President

"The difference between rats and political consultants: there are some things that a rat just won't do."

BOB GARFIELD, *Advertising Age* columnist, on the possibility that the Bush campaign used a subliminal image of the word rats in an anti-Gore ad

George W. Bush pulls a Harry Truman, whistle-stopping through Michigan after the Republican Convention. During the war for Florida's electoral votes after the election, Bush kept cool by retreating to his Texas ranch

AMERICA'S WILD

The race for the White House ends in a standoff—and ignites a five-week skirmish for

RIDE
lorida's electoral votes

THE AMERICAN PEOPLE HAVE spoken," Bill Clinton said after the closest election in our history, "but it's going to take a while to determine exactly what they said." Did it ever. For 36 days, Democrats and Republicans battled for Florida's 25 electoral votes, while the Presidency hung in the balance. In a nation already riven by partisan poison, the war etched new fault lines that ran from Florida to the U.S. Supreme Court. In the end, the President was chosen not by the people but by the Justices of the court, whose house, like America, was split right down the middle. Still, in conceding, Al Gore reminded us: "That which unites us is greater than that which divides us." George Bush's task would be to prove those words were true.

A NIGHT FOR THE HISTORY BOOKS

Unpresidented! On a seesaw election night, Florida and the White House are undecided, Al Gore is undecided, and George W. Bush decides to get snippy

AS AMERICANS WENT TO THEIR POLLING PLACES ON Tuesday, Nov. 7, experts predicted a very tight vote, following a bland, by-the-numbers campaign in which neither Republican George W. Bush nor Democrat Al Gore emerged a likely winner. But no one expected a squeaker of historic proportions. Throughout the day Tuesday, the campaigns knew that turnout was huge in the battleground states: lines stretched around the block in Cleveland, Ohio; voters waited for hours in Nashville, Tenn.; and some precincts in Florida were reporting that 80% of registered voters had been to the polls.

Midafternoon, when the initial exit polls came in, the

BUSH "You're calling me back to retract your concession?"

GORE "Well, there's no reason to get snippy ..."

---

first hints of history in the making began to flicker through the nation's e-mail system, confirming what some Bush aides had feared—that their man had lost momentum in the closing days. Gore had hit Bush hard on not being ready to lead, on not even knowing that Social Security was a federal program. Bush and Cheney, who had promised to restore honor to the White House, turned out to have four arrests between them. The news of Bush's 1979 drunk-driving arrest in Maine, which broke on the last weekend of the campaign, was hurting, said a senior Bush adviser. "That's the only thing that changed in the last days of the campaign." Voters who had made up their mind in the closing days were breaking to Gore.

Shortly before 8 p.m. E.T., the networks announced that Gore had taken Florida. The battleground states of Michigan and Pennsylvania soon fell as well, and every anchor became a math teacher, showing how it was increasingly difficult for Bush to find the 270 electoral

votes he would need to win. All the networks were reading the results from the Voter News Service consortium and grinding them through their own analysis to try to be the first to declare a winner. What they didn't know was that VNS had a bad sample in Tampa, some faulty data in Jacksonville. Plus there were voters in Palm Beach who told the exit pollsters that they had voted for Gore when in fact their vote had been registered for Pat Buchanan.

George Bush had hoped to have a special dinner in Austin, the Texas capital, with his wife and parents and brother Jeb, cherishing the knowledge that the exit polls were telling them everything they wanted to hear. But when the news that Gore had captured Florida appeared on a TV screen in the restaurant, the mood turned to black. With tears in his eyes, Jeb apologized to his brother for letting him down. The Bushes went back to the Governor's mansion to watch and wait and wonder.

The Bush aides at campaign headquarters in Austin were furious that the networks would call Florida even before polls had closed in the more heavily Republican panhandle, in the Central time zone. Also, the raw numbers the Bush people were seeing were telling them they were slightly ahead of Gore statewide, not behind.

At 9:55 p.m., CNN took Florida back from Gore, and the other networks shortly followed, declaring it too close to call. The lobby of the Nashville Loews hotel, Gore headquarters, was suddenly empty. Campaign chairman Bill Daley was on his cell phone, and he looked sick.

By 1:30 most states had tumbled one way or the other, and both men had a total of 242 electoral votes. The counts were unimaginably, unbearably close. Florida was still undecided, but by 1 a.m. the Bush camp had more than a 200,000-vote cushion. But the margin kept shrinking. Around 2 a.m., 98% of the precincts were in, and Bush was ahead by more than 50,000 votes.

At 2:15 a.m. the networks gift-wrapped Florida once more, and this time handed it to Bush. At last, there was a winner. Virtually the entire staff in Bush headquarters left the building, forming a dance line along the eight blocks to the celebration site near the state capitol.

Gore was watching the final returns in the staff room on the seventh floor of the Loews. When the race was final-

ly called for Bush, there was a moment of stunned silence. Then as Gore stood and thanked his aides, they began to cry and hug one another. The Vice President made it clear he wanted to move with swift grace to say his goodbye to his waiting supporters and the country, even though his wife Tipper was ready to hold on a while longer, and so were some other aides. Nonetheless, Gore called Bush around 2:30 a.m. to concede. "You're a good man," Bush told him. He said he understood how hard this was, and gave his best wishes to Tipper and the children.

But the man who invented the Internet was suddenly saved by it. As Gore's motorcade splashed through the rainy streets to the Nashville war memorial for the concession speech, traveling chief of staff Michael Feldman's pager quivered. It was field director Michael Whouley, saying he needed to talk to Daley. "Changed situation here," Whouley said. He was in the boiler room, watching the Florida board of elections website, which, Daley says, "had the margin down to 900, and within minutes, it was 500, 200, slipping pretty quickly." By now the motorcade had arrived at the memorial. Daley told Feldman to grab the Veep and keep him from going onstage.

Daley called his counterpart in the Bush camp, Don

BUSH "[My brother] Jeb says I've won Florida ..."

GORE " Your younger brother is not the ultimate authority on this."

Evans, and said, "We may have a situation here." Under Florida law, a margin that slim triggers an automatic recount. Then, around 3:45, Gore got on the phone himself with the Governor. "As you may have noticed, things have changed," he said. If indeed the vote went to Bush, he'd be happy to concede and give him his support, but for now, "the state of Florida is too close to call," Gore said. Bush did not take the news well. "Let me make sure I understand," Bush said, stunned. "You're calling me back to retract your concession." The two fiercely competitive men had not become friends in the past year. "Well, there's no reason to get snippy," Gore said.

The Vice President had to repeat himself—it's too close to concede—a couple of times. But Bush was confident that this time the networks had called it right. His brother Jeb was right there, crunching the numbers for himself from the Florida website. "Let me explain it to you," Gore said. "Your younger brother is not the ultimate authority on this." The call ended abruptly. "Well, Mr. Vice President," Bush said, "you need to do what you have to do." When Gore put down the phone, he pumped his arm in victory, the aides around him burst into cheers, and they all began to applaud.

Before the motorcade had even made it back to the Loews, the Gore team was moving fast. Seventy lawyers and other operatives piled onto a chartered plane to head down to Florida. They would be on the ground within two hours. The rest of the world was dizzy. Foreign leaders had been sending Bush their congratulatory telegrams and then had to call and retract them. The networks had unfurled their fancy presidential script, "George W. Bush, 43rd President," only to roll it back up again. The New York *Times* had to stop the presses. And then Bush, Gore and the rest of us went to bed, unpresidented. ∎

WE WANT GORE! Palm Beach voters denounce the ballot whose poor design, they charged, made them miscast their vote

DIVIDED WE STALL

Welcome to Flori-duh, land of hanging chads, butterfly ballots and undervotes

AMERICANS WOKE UP WEDNESDAY MORNING, NOV. 8, not knowing who would be the next leader of the free world, not knowing when we would know, not knowing if the eventual winner would be able to govern with a Senate split down the middle and a teeny Republican edge in the House and a nation so neatly and evenly divided that it would take a pair of tweezers to find a mandate in the results. Neither side even tried.

The world's greatest economic powerhouse, cradle of the information age, was counting ballots by hand. One hundred million people had voted, and the outcome danced in the margin of error. There were murmurs from all over the country, not just in Florida, of broken voting machines and disappearing ballot boxes and intimidation and confusion, a growing conviction among true believers on both sides that the White House was about to be stolen. The 2000 presidential election looked as if it might be decided by one five-thousandth of 1% of the vote.

Nov. 8
In the early-morning hours, voters await victory celebrations in both Austin, left, and Nashville, right. Gore calls Bush at 2:30 a.m. with congratulations but—hearing that Florida is still up in the air—calls back to retract his concession, to Bush's dismay

AP/WIDE WORLD

Nov. 9
Florida state law mandates a machine recount, triggered by Bush's 1,784-vote lead. Result: Bush's lead is reduced to 327

Nov. 7-8
On election night, networks first declare Gore has won Florida, then say it's too close to call. At 2:15 a.m., they declare Bush has won

AP/WIDE WORLD

Nov. 8
Palm Beach voters file suit, charging that poor design of the "butterfly ballot" led them to vote for Pat Buchanan and not Gore

SILVER IMAGE

Al Gore seemed to have won a moral victory, but without Florida he would not win in the electoral college. His 222,880-vote lead in the popular tally was the fuel for his campaign's demand for a manual recount in some Florida counties, for time to register the outcome of the absentee ballots there and for the nation to show some patience. And so the end of one campaign marked the beginning of another. "The American people have now spoken," Bill Clinton declared, "but it's going to take a while to determine exactly what they said."

At first the fight centered on the confusing ballots in Palm Beach. Some 19,000 had been thrown out because voters had punched two holes for President; an additional 10,000 did not register any presidential choice. Pat Buchanan's total of 3,704 votes in the county was three times as high as in neighboring counties with different-style ballots. With Bush emerging from the initial count with a 1,784-vote lead, this could mean the margin of victory for Gore. When they looked closely as the recount was getting under way, Democrats noticed that in other counties with punch ballots, a disproportionate number had no vote for President. In Broward alone, which gave Gore 68% of its vote, there were 6,686 ballots that did not register a presidential vote. In Pinellas, election authorities figured out this problem and began removing the little hanging flap, or chad, from the punch cards, although they didn't catch all the faulty ballots before the full recount was completed. Nonetheless, Gore picked up 417 votes there, and now it became important for Democrats to press for a hand count—not just the machine recount automatically triggered by Florida law because of the narrow margin of Bush's lead. And it became just as important for the Republicans to stop the recount.

So the election war moved into a new phase that would last for weeks, one that tried the patience of all but the most devoted students of politics. As each day brought one or more court rulings, the loser absorbed the blow and moved on—and the winner didn't bother celebrating. There wasn't time. The lawyers were due in court, and the generals were due on TV. They were keeping an eye on the polls and the catcalling protesters; the bickering recount monitors; the flawed, human, sometimes heroic county election-board officials trying to do the right thing despite gale-force political winds and media glare.

For all the candidates' talk about core principles—

WE WANT BUSH! **Republicans scorn the "Sore Loserman"**

Gore's duty "to respect every voter and every vote," Bush's fealty to "the laws of the State of Florida"—it was clear from the start that both sides would say or do whatever it took to win. Bush's team was right when it said Gore wanted to count and count until he got the result he wanted. And the Vice President's camp was right when it said Bush was trying to short-circuit the recount and hang on to his slender victory. Which is why, amid the mind-boggling array of court filings and counterfilings and dueling press conferences that followed, there was really only one narrative line worth following: Bush's attempts to shut down the recounts, and Gore's efforts to keep them going at all costs. "As long as we're counting, it's not over," said a Gore strategist. A Bush aide put it this way: "We're trying to run out the clock; they're playing for delay."

The game didn't change as the battle moved up the judicial food chain. The Bush team's first line of defense was the Democrats' favorite new villain, Florida secretary of state Katherine Harris, co-chair of Bush's campaign in the state. When the heavily Democratic Florida Supreme Court overruled Harris and kept Gore's hopes alive, Bush appealed to the conservative-dominated U.S. Supreme Court to put the Florida court in its place.

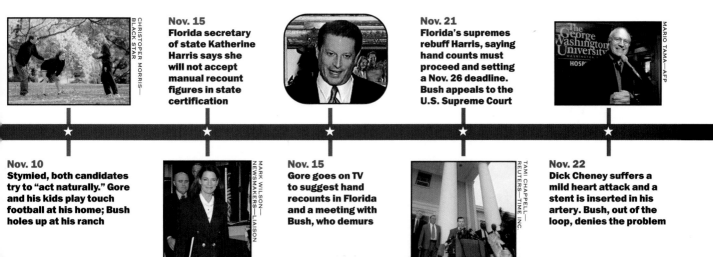

Nov. 15
Florida secretary of state Katherine Harris says she will not accept manual recount figures in state certification

Nov. 21
Florida's supremes rebuff Harris, saying hand counts must proceed and setting a Nov. 26 deadline. Bush appeals to the U.S. Supreme Court

Nov. 10
Stymied, both candidates try to "act naturally." Gore and his kids play touch football at his home; Bush holes up at his ranch

Nov. 15
Gore goes on TV to suggest hand recounts in Florida and a meeting with Bush, who demurs

Nov. 22
Dick Cheney suffers a mild heart attack and a stent is inserted in his artery. Bush, out of the loop, denies the problem

BIG AL'S PALS

WARREN CHRISTOPHER
To head up his team, Al Gore turned to Bill Clinton's first Secretary of State, who brought sharply tailored suits, a sharp legal mind and instant gravitas to the ugly brawl

DAVID BOIES
Now perhaps America's most renowned litigator (Microsoft, Napster), Boies supervised Gore's legal effort and argued *Bush v. Gore* before the Supreme Court

BILL DALEY
Gore's hardball campaign manager quickly took control on the ground in Florida. Republicans howled to see the son of Chicago's former Mayor demanding ballot recounts

DUBYA'S DUDES

KATHERINE HARRIS
Florida's secretary of state—and the woman Democrats loved to hate—was co-chair of the Bush campaign in the state and did her all to ram through certification

JAMES BAKER
He's back! Just as Gore turned to Christopher for ballast, Bush asked his father's Secretary of State to helm his struggle, bringing Baker into W.'s circle for the first time

JEB BUSH
The Florida governor, once viewed as a more promising politician than his older brother, was distraught when he didn't deliver a big win in the state for the Republicans

In Florida the Democratic legal team fought Harris as she issued new opinions and set new deadlines almost daily, and sometimes hourly, most of them designed to delay the hand recounts until they became moot. On Nov. 9 the circuit court in Palm Beach County granted a preliminary injunction that prevented state and county officials from certifying its election returns as final. On Nov. 10, Democrats formally requested a manual recount in three heavily Democratic counties: Miami-Dade, Broward and Palm Beach. That same day, the statewide computerized recount was concluded—and Bush's lead had dwindled to 327 votes.

On Wednesday Gore appeared live on the network news broadcasts to suggest a way out of the Florida swamp. He proposed either a hand recount in the disputed Democratic counties or a hand recount statewide; if Bush agreed, Gore would drop the legal challenges and abide by the result. The plan didn't take: Bush rejected it three hours later, believing that both of Gore's options would give the Democrat an advantage. But the effort made Gore look statesmanlike at a time when Bush was portraying him as an election stealer.

Shortly after Gore's TV appearance, Harris rejected the requests of Broward and Palm Beach counties that their recounts be included in the certification process; two days later, Judge Terry P. Lewis of the Leon County Circuit Court supported her. It seemed like the end of the Gore camp's hopes. But only hours later, as Democratic vice-presidential candidate Joe Lieberman was holding a conference call with 120 House Democrats to rally their spirits, Gore strategist Bob Shrum broke in with some startling news: the Florida Supreme Court had forbidden Harris to certify the vote on Saturday, pending a hearing on Monday. Lieberman responded with a gleeful bark: "All right!" It wasn't over yet.

Within two hours of the court's decision, the Vice

Dec. 2
Florida Judge N. Sanders Sauls hears arguments on whether to recount 14,000 undercounted ballots. On Dec. 4, he rules against Gore and such a recount

Nov. 26
Harris certifies Bush the winner by 537 votes, omitting the results of recounts from Palm Beach County. The act is moot, due to the Bush appeal to the U.S. Supreme Court

Nov. 24-25
Responding to pro-Gore protests led by Jesse Jackson, G.O.P. forces mount highly organized protests against the recount

Nov. 30
As the tally hassle in Tallahassee widens, disputed ballots are transported from South Florida to the state capital in a Ryder truck

President got more good news. The canvassing board in Miami-Dade County decided to begin a hand recount of its 654,000 votes. And a federal appeals court in Atlanta rejected Bush's plea to stop all manual recounts on constitutional grounds. But even as Gore supporters rallied over the weekend, Bush's lead in Florida moved back up to 930, as overseas absentee ballots were tallied.

What the court ruling did not do, however, was freeze the action on the ground. As the overseas absentee ballots were counted, Bush and Gore forces locked into another round of frenzied warfare over 1,000 overseas ballots, most of them from members of the armed forces, that were rejected mainly because they had not been postmarked. Democrats mounted a coordinated challenge against the military ballots because they would probably lean toward Bush. The trench war was threatening to escalate into a full-scale culture war. The Bush team charged that Gore was disenfranchising the fighting men and women he sought to command as President.

Hovering behind the generals and lawyers and foot soldiers on both sides were the principals, Gore and Bush. Their styles couldn't have been more different—Gore always on the offensive; Bush relying on staff and playing defense. Gore was binging on data and calling the shots from his high-tech battle station in the vice-presidential residence; Bush was holed up at his remote Texas ranch, clearing brush, far from the court battles and the ballot fights and the blizzard of chad.

In the meantime, the situation in Florida continued to fester. Jesse Jackson had been staging street protests in Florida since Election Day; now the G.O.P. struck back. Florida Republican legislators threatened to name their own set of electors to send to the Electoral College; an angry mob (directed by organizers with headsets and microphones) showed up to pound on the doors of the offices where Miami-Dade canvassers were meeting. The prolonged struggle grew even more surrealistic when Bush's running mate, Dick Cheney, suffered a mild heart attack and was hospitalized.

On Tuesday, Nov. 21, the Gore team scored a major victory: the Florida Supreme Court ruled that the hand counts could proceed, provided they were finished by 5 p.m. on Sunday the 26th. For the first time, the Bush camp felt some genuine dread. So they played the card that ultimately would bring them victory: they appealed the ruling to the U.S. Supreme Court. On Friday the court surprised just about every legal scholar on the planet when it said it would hear the Bush petition that the ongoing recounts were unconstitutional.

Sunday, Nov. 26, seemed like election night all over again. The halls were decked, the pundits were quacking, Democrats were saying Florida was still too close to call. By the 5 p.m. deadline, the counting still wasn't done, but in a dramatic signing ceremony at 7:30, secretary of state Harris certified George W. Bush the winner by 537 votes. But the Democratic faithful were primed to fight on—especially since Harris had decided to leave out the results of the hand count Palm Beach canvassers stayed up all night to produce.

In fact, the Sunday deadline had already lost its magic power to conjure a President, because by that time both sides had loosed upon the world armies that were hard to call back. Even as Gore fought on to continue the recount in Florida state courts, the action shifted to Washington and the U.S. Supreme Court—whose final split decision would at last make George Bush the President-elect. ■

AT LAST As Christmas neared, Bush called for reconciliation from the Texas capitol

Dec. 8
Florida Supreme Court, 4 to 3, orders a hand recount of 45,000 undervotes. On Dec. 9, the U.S. Supremes, dividing 5 to 4, halt the manual count, pending a Dec. 11 hearing

Dec. 13
In historic back-to-back speeches, Gore concedes at last and Bush strikes a note of reconciliation. Says Gore: "We will stand together behind our new President"

★　★　★　★

Dec. 4
After hearing Tribe and Olson, U.S. Supremes order Florida supremes to clarify their ruling extending certification

Dec. 12
The U.S. Supreme Court, in a 5 to 4 ruling along political lines, again says the Florida recount must end. The state's electoral votes—and the presidency—go to Bush

SUPREME SHOWDOWN

In the long election's decisive vote, Bush beat Gore, 5 to 4

SUPREME, INDEED: IN THE END, IT TOOK THE NATION'S highest court and its vast store of institutional prestige to end the 36-day electoral quagmire. When people like Katherine Harris, Florida Republican legislators and House majority whip Tom DeLay talked about ending the recounts and declaring Bush the winner, they were widely attacked as mere political partisans. But when five Supreme Court Justices did very much the same thing, Al Gore started drafting his concession speech.

Nothing came easy in this complicated saga: it took not one but two passes in the Supreme Court before the presidency was decided. On Friday, Dec. 1, the Justices heard Bush's appeal of the Florida Supreme Court's ruling extending the deadline for certification. Outside, more than 1,000 citizens were loudly exercising their First Amendment rights: Falun Gong members and Maryland high school kids, Republican mothers and Al Sharpton.

Inside the chamber, the American élite assembled for the arguments that most legal scholars had predicted wouldn't come. Bush attorney Theodore Olson, a stellar appellate lawyer who worked in Reagan's Justice Department alongside Kenneth Starr, argued that the Florida Supreme Court's ruling allowing new manual recounts amounted to the creation of a new law after the election— a breach of the federal Electoral Count Act of 1887, a law written in the wake of the Hayes-Tilden debacle of 1876.

The Gore team was led by Harvard law professor Laurence Tribe, a noted constitutional scholar. To Olson's argument, Tribe replied that the Florida justices weren't writing new code but merely interpreting conflicting Florida statutes. The Justices sliced into both sides with razor-like questions, and on Monday, Dec. 4, issued a unanimous, unsigned decision ordering the Florida court to clarify its recount ruling. The same day, Florida circuit judge N. Sanders Sauls found against Gore, refusing to overturn Bush's certified victory. Gore's chances seemed at their lowest ebb. But at the end of the week, a staggering one-two punch set up the endgame of the struggle.

On Friday, Dec. 8, the Florida Supreme Court, defying expectations, replied to the Justices in Washington with one of the nerviest decisions in the annals of American law. A bitterly divided court ruled, 4 to 3, that every single one of Florida's counties must recount its undervotes, those that hadn't registered a vote in a machine tally. The ruling was the first smashing triumph for Gore in weeks, and it had his partisans extolling America's independent Judiciary. But to the stunned Bush camp, the Florida justices were just liberal power grabbers, intent on overturning a certified election result.

Within 24 hours, just as the recount of the undervotes was getting under way, the U.S. Supreme Court roared back with a blockbuster of its own: a 5-to-4 order directing Florida canvassing boards to halt the recounts. Again the reaction was partisan, but flipped in a fun-house mirror: the Bush team thrilled, the Gore team staggered.

On Monday, Dec. 11—only one week after the U.S. Supreme Court first demanded that the Florida Supreme Court reconsider its manual recount ruling—the Justices in Washington heard arguments in the case that would decide the election. Its apt title: *Bush v. Gore*. This time, Gore asked David Boies, noted for his success in the Microsoft antitrust suit and Gore's lead lawyer in Florida, to argue for him; Olson again argued for Bush.

After the hearing, Americans waited for a decision— and waited. On Tuesday night at 10 p.m., TV networks cut into their programming to announce that a decision had been handed down. Then they cut live to their reporters at the Supreme Court building. Here was the money shot, the final score they had waited through five weeks of overtime to call—if only they knew what it said. Slowly,

ANTONIN SCALIA	RUTH B. GINSBURG
FOUND FOR: Bush	**FOUND FOR:** Gore
NAMED BY: Reagan; 1986	**NAMED BY:** Clinton; 1993
USUALLY VOTES: conservative	**USUALLY VOTES:** liberal

❝ [This] can only lend credence to the most cynical appraisal o

JOHN PAUL STEVENS	DAVID SOUTER	WILLIAM REHNQUIST	CLARENCE THOMAS	SANDRA DAY O'CONNOR	STEPHEN BREYER	ANTHONY KENNEDY
FOUND FOR: Gore	**FOUND FOR:** Gore	**FOUND FOR:** Bush	**FOUND FOR:** Bush	**FOUND FOR:** Bush	**FOUND FOR:** Gore	**FOUND FOR:** Bush
NAMED BY: Ford; 1975	**NAMED BY:** Bush; 1990	**NAMED BY:** Nixon; 1972	**NAMED BY:** Bush; 1991	**NAMED BY:** Reagan; 1981	**NAMED BY:** Clinton; 1994	**NAMED BY:** Reagan; 1988
USUALLY VOTES: liberal	**USUALLY VOTES:** liberal	**USUALLY VOTES:** conservative	**USUALLY VOTES:** conservative	**USUALLY VOTES:** swing	**USUALLY VOTES:** liberal	**USUALLY VOTES:** swing

they pieced together the flummoxing, unsummarized verdict: another 5-to-4 ruling, split precisely along the partisan fault lines of the court. The court's conservatives—Chief Justice Rehnquist and Justices Scalia and Thomas—had been joined by swing voters O'Connor and Kennedy in finding for Bush and shutting down the recounts. The court's four more liberal Justices—Stevens, Breyer, Ginsburg and Souter—dissented, strongly.

The court's decision—a tangle of six different majority, concurring and dissenting opinions—was every bit as controversial as the election it resolved. A sizable number of critics, from law professors to some of the court's own members, attacked the ruling as antidemocratic and politically motivated. Many said they were pained to see a court that once distinguished itself by removing barriers to voting—including racial prohibitions, poll taxes and literacy tests—stand in the way of counting valid votes. And Justice John Paul Stevens spoke for the disillusioned everywhere when he declared in dissent that the decision to stop the vote count and declare Bush the winner "can

only lend credence to the most cynical appraisal of the work of judges throughout the land."

But the court had ruled, and although Al Gore took a night to think over his opportunities, his staff announced the next morning that he would concede that evening. On Wednesday, Dec. 13, the Vice President offered his concession in a speech that was poignant, personal and dignified. Thirty minutes later, President-elect George W. Bush spoke from the chamber of the Texas house of representatives, a site chosen to symbolize bipartisanship, as Democrats hold the majority there. In a speech that also rose to the historic occasion, Bush praised his opponent and said, "I know America needs reconciliation."

After 36 days—after an election that showed America's voting process to be deeply flawed, after a split decision that left the nation's highest court open to charges of playing politics, after the presidency was awarded to a man who had won fewer popular votes than his opponent—after all this, Americans could at least agree on one thing: our long national nightmare was over. ■

he work of judges throughout the land.**"** —Justice J.P. Stevens

DIFFERENT BEATS,

A quartet of populists—a war hero, a former Senator, a consumer advocate and a

HOLY WAR In the South Carolina primary, McCain attacked the religious right, whose solid backing ensured a big Bush victory

PATRICK BUCHANAN

Amid the suspense over the deadlocked presidential vote, one aspect of the 2000 election escaped notice: it may have been the last hurrah for the Reform Party. The independent movement forged by Ross Perot, which garnered nearly a fifth of the vote in 1992, spent much of the year in chaos. After flirting with Minnesota Governor Jesse Ventura (its one major player in office) and New York real estate developer Donald Trump as potential candidates, the party split at its August convention in Long Beach, Calif. The majority faction chose pundit and former G.O.P. candidate Pat Buchanan, while the smaller group gave its nod to John Hagelin, a physicist and transcendental-meditation advocate. Buchanan got the spoils, $12.5 million in federal matching funds, and the conservative gadfly set off on a quixotic quest for the White House, barreling around the country in search of audiences and votes. Though he pulled only 1% of the national vote, Buchanan left a mark on the election: some elderly voters in Palm Beach, Fla. voted for him instead of Al Gore, baffled by the notorious butterfly ballot.

HOWDY! The happy warrior at work

BILL BRADLEY

His campaign for the Democratic nomination started hot, then cooled down—aimless events in New Hampshire, a botched debate in Iowa, sliding poll numbers just about everywhere—and matters didn't improve when Bill Bradley admitted in January that he had been experiencing recurrences of arrhythmia, the chronic (but not life-threatening) irregular heartbeat he'd made public a month before. Yet with supporters like Michael Jordan and Senator Daniel Patrick Moynihan—and a big war chest of donations—the former basketball star and New Jersey Senator gave Al Gore a scare in New Hampshire, where their battle turned ugly. In a petty and bitter TV debate, Bradley all but called Gore a liar, and Gore all but called Bradley a whiner and a fraud. But Gore found traction, won the state's primary by four points and kept on winning. In March, after losing every one of the Super Tuesday primaries, Bradley conceded. One problem: as the picture at right indicates, this was a politician who loved "the people"—just not one at a time.

DIFFERENT DRUMS

ght-wing gadfly—challenged George Bush and Al Gore in the run for the White House

JOHN MCCAIN

The one candidate who truly electrified voters in campaign year 2000 was Republican Senator John McCain of Arizona. The war hero, who endured 5½ years as a prisoner in North Vietnam, put a serious scare into G.O.P. front runner George Bush before dropping out of the primaries. McCain had a tough mission: he was a Beltway insider with a conservative record running as a maverick outsider on a centrist platform—against a likable guy his party had crowned months before the primaries began. But McCain's straight talk, unbuttoned demeanor and long-term commitment to campaign-finance reform touched a nerve with feisty New Hampshire voters: McCain stunned Bush when he won the first G.O.P. primary by 18 points. A spooked Bush played hardball in his "firewall" state of South Carolina, where a mail and phone campaign smeared McCain: Bush won big and went on to win most of the primaries that followed, as McCain ran out of cash. Although some had feared the two might never reconcile after their bitter duel, they did make up, and McCain campaigned for Bush.

EGO TRIP? **Critics were furious that Nader saw no difference between Bush and Gore**

SOLO **No gladhander, Bradley keeps to himself on the Puget Sound ferry**

RALPH NADER

The rumpled old consumer advocate, 66, ran as the candidate of the Green Party, touching a nerve with young people, environmentalists and anticorporate crusaders. The unpolitician's fans were enthusiastic: he drew crowds of 10,000 and more in Boston and Portland, Ore., and sold out New York City's Madison Square Garden. To the 2,702,648 who cast ballots for him—some 3% of the total vote—Ralph Nader was a hero. But in the end Gore supporters had another word for him: spoiler. Democrats charged that his candidacy became an egomaniacal crusade that failed in every one of its objectives: Nader did not get the 5% of the vote needed for the party to get federal funding; he splintered the Green Party; and his vote tally, while small, was just enough to steal certain victory from Gore. "He cost [Gore] the election," Delaware Senator Joseph Biden ranted, saying that enough of Nader's nearly 100,000 votes in Florida would have gone Gore's way to make him President. But Nader was unrepentant. "Well-intentioned cowards," he called his critics, whom he described as unforgivably tolerant of a poisoned system in which both major candidates dance on strings controlled by corporate villains.

SENATE STANDOFF

With Democrats picking up seats, the senior chamber will be more evenly divided than ever

NEW YORK **The First Lady celebrates her smashing victory over Rick Lazio**

CYNTHIA JOHNSON FOR TIME

HILLARY RODHAM CLINTON

The First Lady won the New York Senate seat vacated by Daniel Patrick Moynihan by an impressive margin. In hindsight, her victory made sense: New York has a 2 million-voter Democratic advantage; she had Al Gore's coattails to ride—and her popularity had taken off when her husband was under siege. Clinton made mistakes early on, like trying to pretend that her birthplace of Chicago was an outer borough of New York City. But she got lucky when her expected foe, New York City Mayor Rudy Giuliani, amid marital woes, dropped out of the race to fight prostate cancer. The G.O.P. Rottweiler was replaced by a puppy dog named Rick Lazio, a four-term Congressman from Long Island. While Lazio kept emphasizing that he wasn't a carpetbagger, Hillary worked hard upstate, dandling babies and mastering the arcana of dairy-price supports and economic revitalization. In the end, New Yorkers want someone bigger than life, and Little Ricky was no match for a vanity candidate like Hillary.

JEAN CARNAHAN

The most emotional victory in the battle for the Senate came when Missouri Governor Mel Carnahan, who was killed in a plane crash on Oct. 16, beat out Republican incumbent John Ashcroft. It was too late to remove Carnahan's name from the ballot, and his Democratic successor as Governor said he would appoint Carnahan's wife Jean, 66, to the Senate seat if her late husband won. "My husband's journey was cut short," she said after his death. "And for reasons we don't understand, the mantle has now fallen upon us." Some Republicans grumbled about her right to assume that mantle, but Ashcroft, gracious in defeat, said, "Missouri is a compassionate state, and I think, in a very special way, they have demonstrated their compassion."

ORLIN WAGNER—AP

MISSOURI **Tragedy sparks an upset**

VIRGINIA **Allen and wife hail the win**

AP/WIDE WORLD

GEORGE ALLEN

The amiable, tobacco-chewing son of a former Washington Redskins coach ran a penetrating offense to unseat two-term Virginia Democrat and onetime party phenom Charles Robb. Allen, 48, portrayed the wonkish and sometimes wooden Robb as ineffective during his Senate tenure and too liberal to defend "Virginia values." Both Allen and Robb are former Virginia Governors who galvanized their parties. Allen is a dyed-in-the-wool conservative who favors tax cuts and small government and opposes most gun-control laws (reversing his position, he later supported a federal ban on assault weapons). He has said he would allow abortions only if heartbeats or brain waves are undetectable in the fetus or in the case of danger to the health of the mother.

MARIA CANTWELL

And you thought the race for the White House was close: the makeup of the U.S. Senate hung in the balance until a recount in Washington State declared Democrat Maria Cantwell the winner over Republican incumbent Slade Gorton by a slim 2,229 votes. Cantwell, a three-term state legislator and one-term U.S. Congresswoman, lost her House seat in 1992, then grew wealthy as a computer software executive. Though her high-tech credentials might have seemed to make her the perfect representative for local bigfoot Microsoft, Bill Gates & Co. supported Gorton, a strong advocate for Microsoft in the nation's capital. Gorton, a populist who boasted that "schmoozing just isn't my strongest skill," had served in the Senate since 1988.

ANTHONY P. BOLANTE—REUTERS

WASHINGTON **Another photo finish**

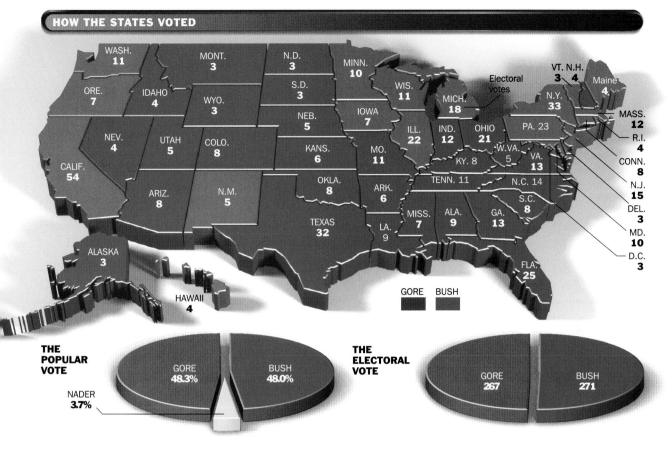

WASH. 11 · **MONT.** 3 · **N.D.** 3 · **MINN.** 10 · **VT.** 3 · **N.H.** 4 · **Maine** 4

ORE. 7 · **IDAHO** 4 · **WYO.** 3 · **S.D.** 3 · **WIS.** 11 · **MICH.** 18 · **N.Y.** 33

Electoral votes

NEB. 5 · **IOWA** 7 · **ILL.** 22 · **IND.** 12 · **OHIO** 21 · **PA.** 23 · **MASS.** 12

NEV. 4 · **UTAH** 5 · **COLO.** 8 · **KANS.** 6 · **MO.** 11 · **KY.** 8 · **W.VA.** 5 · **VA.** 13 · **R.I.** 4 · **CONN.** 8

CALIF. 54

ARIZ. 8 · **N.M.** 5 · **OKLA.** 8 · **ARK.** 6 · **TENN.** 11 · **N.C.** 14 · **N.J.** 15 · **DEL.** 3

ALASKA 3 · **TEXAS** 32 · **LA.** 9 · **MISS.** 7 · **ALA.** 9 · **GA.** 13 · **S.C.** 8 · **MD.** 10 · **D.C.** 3

HAWAII 4 · **FLA.** 25

GORE　BUSH

THE POPULAR VOTE

GORE 48.3% · BUSH 48.0%

NADER 3.7%

THE ELECTORAL VOTE

GORE 267 · BUSH 271

ONE NATION, DIVISIBLE

From the popular vote to the electoral college, the race was tighter than the skin on a snake

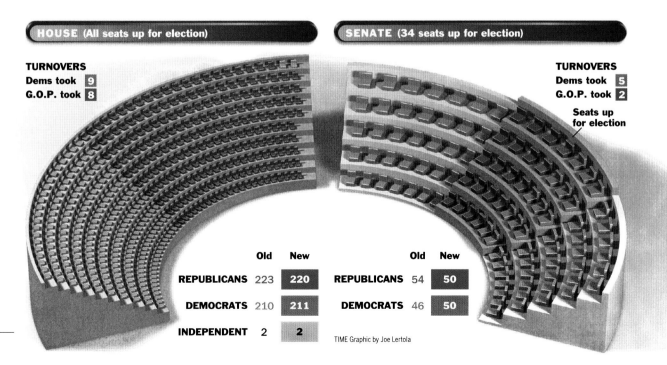

TURNOVERS
Dems took 9
G.O.P. took 8

TURNOVERS
Dems took 5
G.O.P. took 2

Seats up for election

	Old	New		Old	New
REPUBLICANS	223	220	**REPUBLICANS**	54	50
DEMOCRATS	210	211	**DEMOCRATS**	46	50
INDEPENDENT	2	2			

TIME Graphic by Joe Lertola

George W. Bush

FOR A PROUD SON OF A ONE-TERM PRESIDENT, COULD THERE BE A MORE humbling path to power? The candidate with the perfect bloodlines comes to office amid charges that his is a bastard presidency, sired not by the voters but by the courts. You could almost see the weight of it, the regret and relief and resolve, when George W. Bush, at last President-elect, stood in the Texas statehouse with tears in his eyes and promised Americans, "I will work to earn your respect." He was all but admitting respect does not just come with the job when you win this way. But could anyone possibly use this to greater advantage than Bush?

"I believe things happen for a reason," Bush said that Wednesday night, hinting at something his audience was still too bruised even to imagine. Does it take a war, a flood, to leave us no choice but to start all over again? Bush campaigned for a year against partisan politics—and that was before partisanship became so infectious that it polluted every institution of government. The man who talked less about what he would do than how he would do it finds that his bet has been called. You promise to be a uniter, not a divider? Here is a broken, cloven polity. You promise to change the tone? We can't bear to listen anymore to the rancor of the past five weeks, or eight years, or 13, if you extend this period of pitiless politics back to the confirmation hearings of Robert Bork.

But there's more. Bush staged the most inclusive G.O.P. Convention in memory, only to win a smaller percentage of the African-American vote than any Republican since Barry Goldwater. Bush himself admits that the greatest misconception about him is that he is not racially sensitive.

If the task ahead seems impossible given how the race ended, it is worth remembering how it began. Bush came to the field with less experience in public life than just about anyone in a century and took in more money in his first four months of campaigning than anyone had raised in two years; he confronted a sitting Vice President with the wind at his back and maintained a nearly unbroken lead for more than a year, even though more people agreed with the other guy's positions. He took on the suicide right wing of his party and made them roll over and play dead, threw the invisibility cloak over the congressional wing of his party and made them disappear. Stripped of all the winning G.O.P. issues—the cold war, crime, the economy—he proceeded to run on Democratic ones—education, health care, Social Security. Lampooned as a feckless frat boy, he ran a disciplined race, making his inexperience a virtue, his vagueness a shield, his admission of sins a sign of sincerity.

That was enough to keep him in the race far longer than many expected, if not enough to win him the most votes. But then came the second campaign, and the way he played the endgame told us even more about him. Through the five-week Florida prizefight, he showed what he meant when he kept saying he would hire the best people, give them their freedom and hold them accountable. He stood back, stayed out of the fray, since law isn't his field and he knows what he doesn't know.

Even some Democrats now say privately that Bush and his soft serums may be better suited to cure the disease that afflicts the capital. With a Congress almost perfectly bisected, Republicans thirsty for power and Democrats for revenge, Bush holds the needle and thread. He said he would reach across party lines, and now he has no choice: what began as a campaign promise has become a precondition for his presidency. He must go hunting for Democrats to join his cause and for issues with broad support, in hopes that some quick successes on the easy problems will yield the capital for the harder ones.

So the first election of the new millennium is finally over, and as the cast scattered and the chads were swept away, George W. Bush must have been looking forward to that January day when the characters would all come together one last time on a platform on the West Front of the Capitol: Bush, Cheney, the Justices of the Supreme Court, the Gores, the Clintons, the parents Bush, the winners, losers and refugees of the strangest election in more than a century. All through the campaign, Bush rehearsed this moment, the first act of a new President, when he put his hand in the air and swore to uphold the Constitution and the honor and dignity of the office, so help him God. This time it would be for real, the easiest part of the job and yet harder than he could have imagined, because while the office would at last have been won, the honor would remain to be earned. ∎

NOT THIS TIME: On election night, Bush was ready with an acceptance speech—but he waited five weeks to give one

Home on the RANGE

George Bush's ranch is the way he likes to see himself—plain, rugged and thoroughly Texan

BY JOHN F. DICKERSON CRAWFORD

GEORGE BUSH STEPS FROM ONE WET rock up onto another. "It gets even better over here," he promises, poking a boot into the mud for balance. We're climbing on a line of small boulders that form a joint down the middle of a gully as if they'd been rolled there like dice. "I'm gonna put a wooden walkway of some kind in here," he says, dodging a vine. Bush can look as if he's clanging around in a blue suit, but he doesn't look lost on the ranch in the Marlboro Man getup: worn black jeans, a blue work shirt and a mustard-colored barn jacket with stains and a corduroy collar. The breast reads, GEORGE W. BUSH, GOVERNOR.

Most politicians try to impress people by showing how smart, how engaged and how busy they are. Bush does the opposite. He likes to be underestimated, likes to pretend you're telling him something he didn't already know. And he likes to be seen as unflappable. No problem is too tough that it can't be licked with a little of the common sense that rules on his 1,600-acre property in Crawford, Texas. If that means people think he's not quite so clever as all these city folks he has working for him, all the better.

So part of this outing at the darkest moment of the 36-day postelection battle with Al Gore is almost a country-boy ruse. Of course he wants us to see him here. This ranch, which he bought just a year ago, is a rich Texas symbol of achievement—what kids from Midland dream of having.

SANCTUARY: Bush found postelection peace on his 1,600-acre retreat

Photographs for TIME by Brooks Kraft

And it wasn't handed down. That ranch is all that he sees himself to be: rugged, real, thoroughly Texan. But Bush's persona here is more than an act. He seems at peace in this place where he knows each tree and hollow.

A Secret Service agent slips as he tries to keep up. Bush's wife Laura stopped following a while ago, but her husband yells out anyway, "Be careful, Bushie." She calls him by the same nickname. "We're going to clear over there this afternoon," he says, pointing to a thicket of spindly cedar. Along the way he tries to stoke the suspense without giving the secret away. Bush wants us to discover whatever it is he's leading us to the way he did. The seam we've been following winds us around an outcropping of rock, and suddenly we're at the base of a limestone cavity. It rises up 60 ft., the color of butter-pecan ice cream, shaped as if the scoop has just scored it. Down the middle

I have driven the two hours from Austin to find out. And I have come at a bad time. The day before, the Florida Supreme Court resuscitated Gore by calling for a hand recount of the state's disputed ballots. They've given him votes too, so Bush's lead has shriveled up to 154. The new recount has already begun when I arrive. Bush has asked the Supreme Court to stop it. If it doesn't act in time, Gore could get ahead, changing the dynamic in an instant. Aides are the most worried they have been all campaign long that they could lose. The uncertainty should be driving Bush nuts—not just because it would irk any normal human, but also because he can be quite a fidget. Even when he is standing over food laid out for lunch, he starts to agitate. "Let's eat. Let's eat," he says. "Let's get after it."

So when I pull up outside his modest cottage, I'm not expecting much more than a high five. "Sorry, presidency

Ranger George knows every inch of his spread. He point

falls a modest line of water. Somehow the splash can only now be heard as we stand next to its blue-green pool. Bush calls this the amphitheater.

"I took Jenna out here," says Bush of one of his twin daughters. "Because when we bought the ranch she was like, 'Why?'" Bush knows a lot of others have been wondering the same thing. In photo ops the only part of the Crawford ranch the world can see makes it look like one of those dry, generic planets that Captain Kirk is always beamed down to on *Star Trek*. This place in central Texas, just 23 miles southwest of Waco, is Bush's sanctuary. Nearly every weekend of the campaign he came here; he has spent the major part of the postelection period here, away from the fishbowl of the Texas Governor's mansion. Why does he come here? What does he do here?

may be slipping away," I can imagine him saying. "You won't mind showing yourself out will you?" Why on this of all days would he want someone watching everything he does, drawing conclusions from what's on his walls, picking apart his syntax? Yet both Bush and Laura seem delighted to see me. He looks surprisingly relaxed, considering he spent the lengthy drive from Austin that morning being briefed on the Florida recount. He told his advisers, "I'll be at the ranch. Let me know."

We'll see how long he holds off before he calls for an update. The morning is crisp and sunny, and the sky is filled with specific clouds. We head out for the tour of the homestead. "Get a chance to practice my drivin'," says Bush. As he pulls up to the first gate, he asks the Secret Service agent, "You seen that stag come by here?" A male deer has slipped through the extra-high fences of a near-by exotic-game farm and found its way among the property's gently lolling cows. Well, most of them are lolling anyway; a bull a few yards away has picked this moment to mate. "Putting on a show," Bush murmurs out of the side of his mouth. Then the stag shows up. It's a taxidermist's dream, with massive forelegs and a rack that should need cantilevering. "He's going to jump the fence," says Bush, and then, on cue, the stag easily does just that, loping toward the southern portion of the property.

Ranger George knows every inch of his acreage. His arm shoots out to point at the different kinds of oaks, the elm and the hackberry. There's an overwhelming brownness as you look out over large portions of his land, which has the texture of a worn brush. He stops the truck to show us a rare cottonwood and make sure we can all see

But it's cedar that is vexing him now, the clotting underbrush that chokes the majestic old oak and elm hardwoods. "When it is cleared, you'll have the full effect of the amphitheater," he says, sweeping his hand across the long ridge of limestone that leads to the waterfall. "I'm making the case for my cedar-eradication project."

It is a truth about Bush that he prefers to guide by the big picture and the bottom line. While Gore enjoyed playing at the molecular level, Bush is annoyed by it. Every aide tells you this is the key to understanding his leadership approach. And it is the way to understand how he rules the ranch too. The stuff has to be cleared to get the broader view, cleared so that you can see from the land on top of his property down into the greener valley. We stop at an overlook he has just thinned out so that he can show Laura. Each night they take a walk before sunset; now

ut the different kinds of oaks, the elm and the hackberry

the white-tailed deer hiding in the trees. "Motts are what they call those groupings of oaks," notes Bush. He catalogs every stream crossing, every canyon and the precise number of cows, bulls and calves that he lets graze on his land. There's Ophelia, his gray Texas Longhorn. Some of the oak trees look like old villagers, wrinkled and stooped, as if they have fought hard for every inch of growth.

His descriptions have none of those elongated pronunciations he's prone to; he serves up none of the verbal jambalaya he's known for on the stump. His accent has no thickener the way it might if he were trying to give the Disney version of the tour. And he doesn't go the other way either, trotting out 10¢ words like sylvan or making wide detours to talk about Teddy Roosevelt. His voice is as easy as he is. Meanwhile, the recount continues.

they will have a clean lookout down to the Rainey Creek, more than 100 ft. below. Bush has torched his conifer hackings all over the ranch, leaving black burn circles that look as if there's been fireworks testing. He's got plans: wildflowers over there, maybe a feeder to attract some wildlife. Laura is growing a patch of native grasses. Bush is quick to point out, though, that more than enough cedar has been left for the golden-cheek warbler and the black-capped vireo, which use its bark for their nests.

Chopping cedar is his ultimate escape. When he gets aboard one of his John Deere "Gators," a hybrid golf cart–tractor, and heads off into the brush, it's not unlike those jaunts his father used to take in the speedboat up at Kennebunkport. "It does just all fall away," says Bush, stepping under a canopy of trees. "I could give a damn

WESTERN WHITE HOUSE **Bush is building a limestone house set in a nest of old oaks, with a good view of his fishing hole**

about the Supreme Court. Well, of course I do care, but you forget ... " There's a little defiance and exasperation in his voice. He has stopped the truck this time to show off the "cathedral," a column of limestone steps that were carved by water but look handmade. A nearly perfect arch of branches roofs the long aisle. "I told my daughter, 'This is where the audience will sit,'" says Bush about some imaginary wedding in Jenna's future. "The audience will stand there. You and I will stand here, and the preacher will stand here."

Bush doesn't needle his visitors as they follow him through every hollow and over each slippery rock. He would in other settings, where his humor is often less witty than it is withering. But here in God's country there are no macho frat-boy tests. He seems eager to help people see what he finds so particular about this place. But in one case, he can't resist having a little fun anyway. "Can you drink this?" asks a guest reaching down to the water. "Sure," says Bush, watching the fellow taking a handful to his mouth. "Except for the cow s___." The spit-take follows in perfect order.

The two-hour tour of the grounds ends at the new house the Bushes have been building. Made of limestone from Lampasas, Texas, less than a two-hour drive from here, it has long rectangular bricks of a dusty putty color with the texture of little mountain ranges. Designed to wind around a series of old live oaks, the compound has an old oak spread out over the front as its focal point. The single-level home's 10,000 sq. ft. are nearly finished, but the high-ceiling rooms take up only a third of that space.

The limestone porch takes up the rest, circling the house like a moat.

The builders are from a religious community in Elm Mott, Texas. The women finishing the cabinetry are dressed in full-length cotton dresses with simple patterns. "They have the most lovely countenances," says Bush, stepping from the driver's seat. As he tours past the well-turned joints and solid doors they have carved and walks into a room, the dozen or so workers there break out in smiles. A carpenter he calls by name is so excited he does a little hop.

"That's the whining pool," he says, pointing to the nearly finished swimming pool, which was built as a sop to his teenage daughters. "If you whine loudly enough, you get a pool." A 10-acre man-made pond built and stocked with 5,000 bass has been designed around the oak trees, and one oak sits at the tip of a little peninsula. The view looks like a national park, and Bush, as grounds keeper in chief, leaves no detail unsmoothed. He tells of how irked he was by a dead tree's breaking the water's surface, how he took off in his bass-fishing boat, a gift from his uncle William T. Bush, wielding a chainsaw. "I was out there in Uncle Buck's bass-fishing buggy, and the wind was blowing from the north, and I was standing there, nearly got blown over," he remembers. The mission was unsuccessful.

Until the construction is completed, the Bush family is staying in the property's original cottage. The sage exterior color is repeated inside, where the rooms are plain. The front door opens into a sitting room with a folk-art three-dimensional rendering of the White House jutting

DEEP IN THE HEART OF TEXAS **Each evening they're here, Bush and wife Laura take a long walk around the ranch**

out from the back wall. Its bulky columns look as if they're made of toilet-paper cardboard. Other walls have a few touches of humor: a framed likeness of President Bush dressed as an oil sheik greets you as you walk out of the bathroom, and a set of three Chinese revolutionary posters exalt Chairman Mao. The bookshelves are in the dining room, packed with baseball tomes, novels (including non-Republican writers like Gore Vidal and Nora Ephron) and some histories. There are two televisions, one with rabbit ears. There's no cable, but the CIA did install a secure phone recently.

When we reach the kitchen, lunch is already out on the center counter. "What is it you tracked in here?" says Bush to Spot, the spaniel who has left prints all over the dark hardwood floor of the kitchen. He moves quickly for the heart-shaped mop to clean up the mess while Laura slices the tomatoes for lunch. Our host doesn't check in with Austin or Tallahassee. Gore could easily have taken the lead in the hand count by now, but Bush doesn't look distracted. The meal is simple: tuna salad with eggs, sliced tomatoes and a vegetable tortilla soup. The Governor needs more fuel for his cedar chopping later in the day, so he fixes himself one of his favorite sandwiches, peanut butter and honey.

At the worn maroon dining table, the conversation changes from the landscape of his ranch to that of his possible new presidential future. He is more curious about things than he appears in public, and talk ranges from Chad (in Africa) to the kind of rampant sucking up that White House staff members engage in. He has seen from his father's days how people censor themselves once they cross that Oval Office threshold, squashing their formerly strong opinions. When he talks politics, he focuses less on ideology than on the particular power relationships, individual motivations and how they can be used to get things accomplished. The meal ends with chocolate-chip cookies and milk.

In a short car ride before I leave, he laughs off a question about pardoning Clinton, instead telling a story. "When Laura and I were at the Cardinal O'Connor funeral, and it came time for the handshakes of peace … I see this huge hand reaching across five bodies, and it's Clinton, and he roars, 'Peace, Governor!'" Bush's Clinton accent is thick like pudding. He, like the rest of America, loves to do the Clinton voice. His cell phone rings. He fishes into a cavity in the dashboard and finds it. After a minute or so he says, "That's great news. Terrific." The Supreme Court has just halted the count.

Bush steps out of the car to finish the conversation in private. "That is good news," he says, showing only the slightest new enthusiasm. As I stand to leave, he starts playing fetch with Spot. Using a purple tennis racquet, he hits a tennis ball, brown from slobber. If I hadn't been there, maybe he'd be on those phones, pacing, torturing the TV's rabbit ears to get clearer reception. But instead he starts talking about Yale. "I must admit that I thought some of them thought those of us from the South didn't get it," he says, swatting the ball. "That was just fine with me." *Thwack* goes the racquet. The rancher says he's going to go clear the cedar, and I leave. He walks inside and calls Jim Baker. ∎

On Veteran's Day 2000, President Clinton joined former Senator Bob Dole to break ground for the World War II Memorial on the National Mall, scheduled to open in 2003. This architect's rendering shows the controversial site of the memorial, centered on the Mall's long axis

Courtesy American Battle Monuments Commission

LITTLE BOY LOST

Home or exile? Rescue or nightmare? Cuban or American?
A six-year-old refugee falls through a crack in the Caribbean

HAPPIER DAYS Inset, Elián with his
mother before their flight from Cuba

ELIÁN GONZÁLEZ WAS HAVING TROUBLE SLEEPing. The 6-year-old boy kept climbing out of his little race-car bed and going into the living room, where his great-uncle Lázaro lay on the white leather couch. The child had been watching his relatives fight over him ever since a group of fishermen from Miami had rescued him from the sea on Thanksgiving Day, 1999. They had fished him from the water following the sinking of a small craft that was carrying Elián, his mother and other refugees from Fidel Castro's Cuba to join relatives in America.

Only Elián had survived, and in the months that followed, he had become the centerpiece in an international tug-of-war that pitted the U.S. and Cuban governments—which claimed the boy should be returned to Cuba in the care of his father Juan Miguel—against the fanatically anti-Castro Cuban émigrés of the Miami area, who demanded that Elián remain in America, as his mother had wished.

This Friday before Easter Sunday had been another long day. Elián snuggled next to Lázaro, who stroked the boy's hair. "I'm afraid. Are they coming for me?" Elián asked again and again. Lázaro tried to comfort him, explaining in a calm voice that everything would be O.K. "Relax," Lázaro said in Spanish. "Relax, Eliáncito."

Donato Dalrymple was dozing on another couch nearby, still dressed in his jeans and polo shirt. One of the fishermen who rescued Elián, the former missionary had practically moved into the González house these past few days, convinced that he had a calling to protect this kid, no matter what. When he heard the pounding and the screaming, he thought it was a dream.

As Dalrymple tells it, when the Immigration and Naturalization Service agents stormed into the house just after 5 a.m., he grabbed Elián and fled to a bedroom, locking the door and then trying to duck into a closet. But the closet was crammed too full of clothes, and they could not close the folding doors. "Help me!" Elián cried. "Help me!"

The INS agents, armed with 9-mm MP5 submachine guns, looked first for Elián's cousin Marisleysis, 21, who had become his surrogate mother in America, assuming she would be the one to lead them to Elián. "Where the f___ is the damn boy?" Marisleysis says they shouted at her. She begged them to hold off, she says. "I will give you the boy; just put the guns down!"As they raced through the rest of the house, the agents knocked over a statue of the Virgin Mary and a huge picture of the Sacred Heart of Jesus in the living room. Finally, they kicked their way into the bedroom, breaking the door in half.

They found Dalrymple and Elián clinging to each other. "No, no, no!" Elián screamed. But they grabbed him and gave him to Betty Mills, an eight-year INS veteran who spoke to Elián in Spanish as she covered him with a blanket and raced out the

SURROGATE Elián's cousin Marysleysis cared for the boy

door to a minivan. As pepper spray wafted outside the house, bystanders heard the agents shouting the code meaning that they had possession of Elián: "Bingo! Bingo! Bingo!" Mills told Elián that it was O.K., that he was going to see his "papa" and that he was going to take his first airplane ride—not, she said, a boat ride, the stuff of the boy's worst nightmares.

Lázaro González ran into the front yard and collapsed. Dalrymple screamed, "Bastards!" as he, too, ran to the front yard and hurled plastic milk crates at the agents. "It was a horror show," he says. As the motorcade drove off, agent Jim Goldman called INS headquarters to report

For Elián's Miami relatives, the morning was a kind of death, after five months of hope and power and fame and the satisfactions of righteous rage. For Juan Miguel, the pain of Saturday morning was an awful means to a joyous end. For those who had come to view the Miami Cubans as well-meaning kidnappers, the raid by INS agents was nothing more or less than a rescue mission—unavoidable, long overdue and mercifully quick. The images were wrenching, but the outcome was a relief.

By the end of the day, both sides had the picture they wanted. An intrepid AP photographer captured a federal agent holding a submachine gun as the fisherman held the terrified child (*see* Images). Within hours came the counterattack, the photo of a grateful father holding his smiling son. In the end, what you made of the passion play depended on which picture stayed with you longer, and whose version of the story had the ring of truth.

For months Janet Reno had been trying to solve the crisis in her own lonesome way. She tried to play every role herself: Attorney General, family shrink, hostage negotiator and grandmother manqué. It meant assuming that everybody involved would behave rationally and put the child's interest first. And she believed above all that

Cuban Americans saw a passion play whose Miracle Child was Elián

that Elián was scared and shaken but safe. Goldman said he was stroking Elián's back, while Mills told him of his coming reunion with his father, who had come to America to retrieve his son. "This is one tough little kid," Goldman marveled. "I was shaking. He was not."

But Elián was crying again as the U.S. Marshals' plane took off from Homestead Air Force Base. Hoping to ease his fear, INS officials handed him a toy plane and showed him a map of the plane's route, then gave him a watch and showed him how much time would pass before he would see his father. They raised the shades and showed him the dawn sky. "He became completely enthralled in the pretty colors," said an INS official. Elián spent most of the flight sitting in Mills' lap, sometimes sleeping.

When the plane landed at Andrews Air Force Base in Washington, Juan Miguel González left his entourage and climbed aboard to be alone with his son. Five minutes later and teary eyed, he came down the steps with Elián in his arms, the boy's legs wrapped tightly around his waist, and headed into a base residence. Later Juan Miguel, who was divorced from Elián's mother and had remarried, invited agents Mills and Goldman to join his family, to thank them for taking care of his son. Elián, they said, was playing on the floor—"like any six-year-old boy."

For the residents of Miami's Little Havana, however, Elián was far from an ordinary boy. His saga had been, from the start, a passion play. Elián was the Miracle Child, delivered from the sea for a sacred purpose, and so it was no surprise that when they awoke the morning before Easter to news of his seizure, the exiles arrived in force, one man carrying a crucifix with a bloody doll nailed to it, and accused Attorney General Janet Reno of playing Pontius Pilate.

she could wait out her rivals in Miami and absorb hit after hit about her go-slow approach, certain that the law was on her side, even if nobody else was.

Then even the courts seemed to abandon her. When a federal appeals court in Atlanta ruled on April 19 that Elián might be able to decide his future for himself, Reno

GOTCHA! INS agent Betty Mills takes Elián to a minivan

ENRAGED Cuban Americans rioted in Miami's Little Havana steets after the raid and staged a general strike three days later

found herself, as a lawyer on the case put it, "in a deep, dark hole." Having promised Juan Miguel two weeks earlier that she would return his son quickly, Reno was now looking at months of legal wrangling and no guarantee that Elián would ever be reunited with his father, much less his homeland. By the Thursday before Easter, White House dismay with Reno's endless patience was quietly rising; that afternoon, Reno huddled with Bill Clinton and agreed to make a move soon.

Thanks to widespread leaking, just about everybody in Washington and Miami woke up Friday morning confident that Reno was ready to move. But instead, in a last-minute twist, the Attorney General was in her cavernous fifth-floor office at Main Justice, on the telephone with a group of fellow Miamians, led by University of Miami president Tad Foote, who thought they could still persuade the relatives to turn the boy over to his father. She pursued the plan until it collapsed at 3 a.m. Saturday morning. Within the hour, Reno gave the order for the federal agents to enter the house and take the boy.

As they watched the constant replay of the raid on the networks, staff members back in Reno's office were troubled, but they had no regrets. "It was a very sad thing to see," said Deputy Attorney General Eric Holder. "I was disappointed that people who indicated they cared most for the boy were unable to do the simple things that would have prevented what happened from occurring."

The Miami relatives and their supporters were on the air instantly, telling their harrowing story and denouncing the government. Said Marisleysis: "Bill Clinton and Janet Reno betrayed this country—not just my family, but this country!" As news of the raid spread, the crowds began to grow, and Miami police worked to maintain some order while allowing angry residents to express their fury at the sudden turn. Miami Mayor Joe Carollo denounced the government's actions. "What they did was a crime," he said. "These are atheists. They don't believe in God."

In Havana the reaction was subdued; the government cautioned Cubans that the fight for Elián wasn't over yet. (Legal appeals may continue for years.) Even those who had fought to return Elián to Cuba didn't like the idea of handing Fidel Castro a prize. Nevertheless, Fidel thanked Clinton, Reno and "American public opinion." He added, "The child may have cried for five minutes, but at least he's now spared from crying the rest of his life." Echoing Little Havana's piety, Cuban citizens like Virginia Sotolongo, 42, said, "The Virgin of Charity has done this miracle. I always believed that the child would be with his father." And so he was, thanks to the Virgin of Charity—or Janet Reno. ■

PAPA! Reunited, Elián and his father embark for Cuba

In the Fury of The Flames

Fire fighters battled raging infernos as some of the worst wildfires in 50 years rampaged across a dozen states

NATURE SOMETIMES ENTERTAINS SUICIDAL IMPULSES. In the year 2000 in the American West, it set itself on fire—fire's version of *The Perfect Storm,* a convergence of dry summer lightning, blast-furnace air and millions of acres of tinder.

Forest fires come and go. But this year's were among the worst in a half-century; they may prove to be the worst ever recorded. The grim tale can be traced in this snapshot of a single week in mid-August: 86 major wildfires were raging in a dozen Western states, from Arizona and California up through Colorado and Wyoming to Montana, Oregon and South Dakota. Five million acres of land had already burned, more than double the annual average for the past decade. More than 20,000 fire fighters, assisted by military troops and prisoners, were battling the blazes. Canada, Mexico, Australia and New Zealand sent fire fighters to America to lend a hand. Among the hardest hit states were Idaho, where 22 separate fires burned across 293,000 acres of forest, and Montana, where 25 fires devoured 385,000 acres.

Meanwhile, sparks were still flying over a late-spring wildfire that devastated Los Alamos, N.M., an important nuclear research site. On May 4, the superintendent of the Bandelier National Monument, six miles southwest of Los Alamos, began a controlled burn of 330 acres as a fire-prevention measure. And for the next week the fires would not stop, first consuming dry grass, then Ponderosa pines, then gobbling up hundreds of homes and singeing buildings at Los Alamos, birthplace of the atom bomb. The fires never came close to a building that holds drums of transuranium mixed waste and a metric ton of plutonium. No disastrous explosions occurred, but the air was monitored for radioactivity. Meanwhile, noxious fumes wafted from the lead paint, rubber and plastics in burning cars and buildings. Some 20,000 people were evacuated from the Los Alamos area. Roy Weaver, the Bandelier superintendent, was put on paid leave. He said he was not aware of a National Weather report advisory warning of perilous fire conditions, but the Weather Service, disputed his account. The General Accounting Office is investigating the incident.

The fires were quenched by fall, but not the questions they raised. Were they nature's work—or man's? Were they a once-in-a-half-century phenomenon—or would they rage again next year? Above all, how can we better protect the nation's patrimony of forests for the future? ■

FIRE! Clockwise from top left: in California, convicts were enlisted in the fight; smoke surrounds part of the Los Alamos National Laboratory; a crew lights a backfire in the Big Horn National Forest in Wyoming; flames engulf a tree and house in Los Alamos; livestock is threatened at a ranch in Darby, Mont. Center: A satellite view of the smoke plume from a single fire

CLOCKWISE FROM ABOVE LEFT: E.P. ZAMORA—FRESNO BEE—CORBIS SYGMA; JAKE SCHOELLKOPF—AP/WIDE WORLD; RICHARD SENNOTT—MINNEAPOLIS STAR TRIBUNE;
STEVEN G. SMITH—THE ALBUQUERQUE TRIBUNE—AP/WIDE WORLD; WILLIAM CAMPBELL FOR TIME. CENTER: NOAA—NESDIS—AP/WIDE WORLD

People

Mystery of Los Alamos

In September the U.S. government's case against nuclear scientist Wen Ho Lee came crashing to a halt when the Justice Department dropped 58 of 59 charges against the Chinese American once accused of stealing the "crown jewels" of U.S. nuclear defense. A top FBI agent recanted some of his testimony against the 60-year-old Los Alamos engineer; the New York *Times,* which had first put the spotlight on the case, questioned its own coverage.

Neighbors in White Rock, N.M., just down the road from Los Alamos, put out flags to welcome the man who

LEE **Was he a victim—or a traitor?**

had been denied bail and held in jail for 278 days, some 150 of them in solitary confinement. But for all the sympathy he earned, Lee still had a lot of explaining to do. He won back his freedom only after pleading guilty to a single felony count of mishandling national-defense information. Lee admitted he downloaded the equivalent of 400,000 pages of classified data about the U.S. nuclear-weapons program onto an unsecured computer system and then put them on high-volume cassettes.

Lee had refused to spell out why he spent an estimated 40 hours over 70 days downloading all those data or why he tried repeatedly to enter a restricted area after losing his security clearance—once, around 3:30 a.m. on Christmas Eve. As part of his plea agreement, Lee promised to explain everything to investigators.

UNITED **A gay couple ties the knot**

A Win for Gay Marriage

At the direction of Vermont's supreme court, which ruled that same-sex couples are entitled to equal rights, the state's legislators passed the the most sweeping gay-union legislation in the U.S. in the spring. The new law met with a firestorm of protest. Critics charged it would destroy the foundation of marriage and promised court challenges; gays hailed what they called a symbolic and practical victory.

The bill extended spousal rights to areas covered by state law: inheritance, medical decisions, insurance coverage, child custody and family-leave benefits. To be eligible, gay couples had to obtain a license from the town clerk and have their union certified by a justice of the peace, judge or clergy

member. Couples that later split up would have to file for dissolution. In the meantime, 30 states have passed legislation expressly refusing to recognize same-sex unions sanctioned elsewhere.

Who'll Police the Police?

A pair of high-profile cases involving police tactics roiled New York City and Los Angeles in 2000. In late February an Albany, N.Y, jury acquitted four white New York City cops, Sean Carroll, Kenneth Boss, Richard Murphy and Edward McMellon, in the murder of Amadou Diallo. Seeking a rapist in 1999, the cops had fired 41 bullets at the unarmed young African immigrant as he stood in the vestibule of his apartment building in the Bronx; they thought he was reaching for a gun. Prosecutors brought six alternate charges against each of the cops; none of them stuck—not murder, not manslaughter, not homicide, not reckless endangerment.

In the days and weeks afterward, protests and public outrage consumed the city, while in Los Angeles, the FBI joined an investigation into allegations that antigang cops acted like gangsters themselves— lying, stealing and shooting people with no cause.

JUSTICE! **Daily protests decried the cops' acquittal in the death of Diallo, inset**

Images

HE'S OUT James Dale can't be a Scout

A Loss for Gay Scouts

While Vermonters argued over gay marriage, questions on gay rights bedeviled the Boy Scouts. On June 28 the U.S. Supreme Court ruled 5-4 in favor of the Scouts in the case of *Boy Scouts of America v. James Dale,* finding that the Boy Scouts did not have to permit openly gay men to lead their troops. The Scouts contended that hiring openly gay leaders would interfere with their First Amendment right to express the view that homosexuality is wrong and would violate their First Amendment freedom to associate, or not, with whomever they please.

Dale's attorneys argued the issue isn't a group's right to exclusivity: it is whether a group like the Boy Scouts, which generally welcomes every boy, can claim that being anti-gay is part of its core values. It proved a Pyrrhic victory for the Scouts, who found themselves losing donation monies and the use of private meeting rooms in the wake of the controversial decision.

Death-Penalty Doubts

There was a time when only a few liberals and clergymen fretted over the fairness of the death-penalty system. But ever since famed defense lawyer Barry Scheck and his Innocence Project gained national exposure with their successes in freeing death-row inmates with DNA evidence, a number of prominent conservatives (though not George W. Bush) have expressed doubts about the reliability of the judicial process. In January, Illinois Governor George Ryan, a Republican, imposed a moratorium on executions in his state after no fewer than 13 death-row inmates were freed when new evidence cast doubt on their guilt. Religious broadcaster Pat Robertson called for a national moratorium. A majority of voters still support capital punishment, but the number is down to 66%, from a high of 80% in 1994. And 92% of those polled support making DNA testing available to those who were convicted before its widespread use.

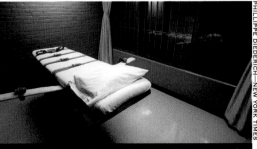

TEXAS The pace of executions here is two a month

COMMUNIST PARTY: When U.S. Secretary of State Madeleine Albright visited North Korea in October, she was treated to an old-fashioned spectacle. In May Day Stadium, as 100,000 spectators looked on, a 25,000-person card section created displays of military might while soldiers drilled on the field

Frederic J. Brown—AFP

BACK TO THE BOMBS

Hatred and violence consume the Middle East, as Jews and Palestinians battle in the streets and dreams of peace expire

A S THE YEAR 2000 ENTERED ITS last three months, the world was beginning to feel like a safer place. The centuries-old ethnic strife roiling in the Balkans was apparently being transformed by the miraculous power of democracy. The gunpoint tension on the Korean peninsula was being dissipated by the democratic reformer Kim Dae Jung in the South and his unlikely partner in the North, Kim Jong Il. And the unholy

struggle in the Middle East looked, even after a stalemated U.S. summit meeting, as if it were being narrowed mainly to semantic nuances about control and sovereignty over a mere 35-acre mount of land in Jerusalem.

Then came the explosions and mutilated bodies. In the span of a few hours on Oct. 12, Middle East rioting, gun fighting and their bastard cousin terrorism burst back into our lives with split-screen bulletins and double-deck headlines that hammered home again both the volatility of that region and the vulnerability of the entire world. It was a reminder that the horror facing the 21st century will be the one left unresolved in the 20th: after the end of the great confrontations between shifting alliances of nation-states, we are still faced with the bloody terrors wrought by ethnic, religious and tribal hatreds.

The Middle East violence began with skirmishes after Israeli superhawk Ariel Sharon visited a disputed holy site in old Jerusalem, escalated with the gut-wrenching televised death of a 12-year-old Palestinian boy shot as his father tried to shelter him (see Images) and then erupted when seething Palestinians (whom Yasser Arafat seemed at first unwilling and then unable to control) murdered

DEFIANCE In Ramallah, flash point of the early stages of the fighting, a Palestinian hurls a Molotov cocktail at Israeli soldiers

WORLD 53

CHRIS GERALD—AFPS

FRENZY A Palestinian in Ramallah rejoices, his hands steeped in Jewish blood

to Muslims than any place except Mecca and Medina, the Mount is the single most holy spot for Jews as well. At Camp David, Barak proposed that Arafat get control over the mosques, but not sovereignty.

Arafat wanted sovereignty to boost his status with Muslims, so he rejected the proposal, ending the summit and alienating Barak. Angry and isolated, Arafat prepared to send a message Barak couldn't ignore. He held a series of midnight meetings in late September with the leaders of his Fatah party's Tanzim, an armed militia bossed by local warlords, ordering them to prepare for violence.

The stage was set. And when Ariel Sharon, 72, a leader of Israel's right-wing Likud Party, visited the holy site on Sept. 28 in a bid to boost his political support and reassert Israeli rights to the land, Arabs saw it as an act of such breathtaking arrogance that it could only trigger an outburst. In what Arabs call the "Aqsa *intifadeh*"—the uprising of al-Aqsa Mosque on the Mount—at least 80 people were killed and nearly 2,000 injured, mostly Palestinians, and mostly young.

The violence stunned Israelis, whose troops faced widespread gunfire from Palestinian police and militia. Upon hearing the calls of their imams to defend the sacred compound, Israel's Arab citizens answered with rioting throughout the Galilee. Further unrest developed deep in Palestinian territory at the site of the Israeli-controlled Joseph's Tomb at Nablus. Barak pulled his soldiers out, supposedly with an agreement that the site would be guarded by Palestinian police. The next day those police joined with rioters in tearing down the historic tomb.

and mutilated two Israeli soldiers. Prime Minister Ehud Barak ordered a military retaliation, which halted his lonely quest for a comprehensive peace. The same afternoon, suicidal terrorists on a small boat crept up to an American destroyer refueling in Yemen and set off an explosion that killed 17 crewmen *(see following story)*. Death by death, the violence ratcheted up, each brutal deed hurtling the region farther from peace.

T HE SEEDS OF THE VIOLENCE WERE PLANTED OVER the summer. At a U.S.-sponsored summit meeting at Camp David in July, the Israelis made an unprecedented offer concerning the sacred, disputed 35 acres in Jerusalem the Jews call the Temple Mount and the Arabs know as Haram al-Sharif, or the Noble Sanctuary. To Jews, the site is revered as the location of the temples built by Solomon and Herod, the latter of which was destroyed by the Romans in A.D. 70. Even before that, it was sacred. At its center is the tip of Mount Moriah, where God tested Abraham by demanding the sacrifice of his son Isaac. That rock is where some scholars believe the Ark of the Covenant sat. But it also lies beneath the golden Dome of the Rock, the spot where Muslims believe the Prophet Muhammad ascended into heaven and back. The main mosque in the compound is al-Aqsa, some 1,300 years old. More sacred

But it was the disaster in the West Bank Palestinian city of Ramallah that elevated the crisis to calamity. The incident began when Israeli reserve soldiers Vadim Norzich, 35, and Yossi Avrahami, 38, made a wrong turn as they drove to their army base in the West Bank. In Ramallah they came upon a funeral procession for a 17-year-old boy shot the day before by Israeli troops. Identifying the

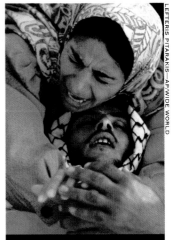

LEFTERIS PITARAKIS—AP/WIDE WORLD

TEARS A Palestinian mourns

two as Israelis, the impassioned crowd went after them. Palestinian police took the two reservists into a nearby station and held the mob at bay. But some of the vigilantes entered through a second-floor window. Through the opening, TV crews filmed them stabbing and pummeling the Israelis inside. One of the attackers returned to the window to proudly show the jubilant crowd his blood-soaked hands. Moments later, the body of one of the soldiers came flying out of the window onto the ground, where the mad crowd danced, beat it some more, then paraded the corpse through the streets. Palestinian police handed over the other soldier, badly mutilated, to a nearby Jewish settlement just before he died.

THE KILLINGS WERE ABOUT AS RAW A DISPLAY OF atavistic inhumanity as one could imagine. Worse atrocities than the Ramallah lynchings had been committed before in the conflict, on both sides, but never on camera. Barak ordered a fast Israeli retaliation, sending Cobra attack helicopters to bomb five carefully chosen security sites, one of them close enough to rattle the Gaza headquarters of Arafat. Four Palestinians were injured in the raids, but none were killed.

The spiral of violence was under way. For the first time, Israeli Arabs, fed up with years of discrimination, joined in neighbor-to-neighbor mayhem within the confines of Israel itself. Tanzim forces launched a full-fledged shooting war on Israelis at night. And Israel went from assertive riot control with rubber bullets to aggressive military operations using helicopter gunships, tanks and rockets. The world once again grew accustomed to a daily Middle East body count. Nov. 2: two Israelis killed in a car-bomb attack ... Nov. 9: Israeli helicopters kill a Palestinian military commander and two others ... Nov. 13: Four Israelis killed ... Nov. 16: Israeli helicopters strike Palestinian sites in retaliation.

Frantic efforts by Bill Clinton, Kofi Annan and others to stem the violence failed. In the blink of an eye, the Middle East had gone from a region pregnant with hopes for peace—building since the 1993 Oslo accords—to a place where proponents of the peace process were all but discredited. On both sides of the great divide, hardliners were riding high. When former Israeli Prime Minister Shimon Peres managed to broker a cease-fire with Arafat, Palestinians derailed it with the Nov. 2 car-bomb attack, heightening fears that Arafat was unable to control the Palestinian militias. In Tel Aviv, Barak's government was under extreme pressure. Amid the violence, Israel's opposition Shas Party gave Barak a one-month "umbrella" of political support, a temporary reprieve from domestic political pressure. But on Nov. 28, Barak declared he would call early elections after Jan. 1.

As body counts mounted on both sides, the greatest casualty was the peace process itself. Between them, the Palestinians and Israelis had killed the fragile trust each side had so grudgingly come to place in the other. And no one could imagine how it might be resurrected. ∎

WHY ARAFAT REFUSED A DEAL

The return to violence in the Middle East was sparked by the failure of the two-week Camp David summit meeting in July. Yasser Arafat did not want to be there: aging and in uncertain health, he was tired of compromising principles he held sacred, given his earlier concessions. His people were fed up with a process that had won them only the shards of an independent state. But President Bill Clinton had a legacy to secure before leaving office, and Israeli Prime Minister Ehud Barak needed to fulfill his promise of peace to stay in power.

Arafat balked when he saw that the "best offer" Barak was making did not give the Palestinians true sovereignty over their sacred sites in Jerusalem. Arafat had reason to anticipate something more

DEAD-END STREET The leaders' talks failed over the issue of Jerusalem

daring: in an informal plan dating from 1995, both sides would have their capital in greater Jerusalem, residents of East Jerusalem would be Palestinian citizens, and the Temple Mount would be declared by Israel to be "extraterritorial." When Barak proposed a good deal less, Arafat felt cheated. What looked impossibly generous to Israelis looked impossibly meager to him. In his mind, he was guardian of the Holy City for all Arabs, even all Muslims. Indeed, when he refused the plan and returned from Camp David, crowds hailed him as "the Saladin of this generation!"

But to non-Muslims, Arafat was cast as the intransigent spoiler. Clinton publicly lavished praise on Barak for his flexibility and chided Arafat for his lack of it. So the Palestinian leader sat in Gaza brooding on his next move, frustration building up among his people—and recalling that a judicious level of violence had wrung Israeli concessions before. Soon he was huddling with the bosses of the Tanzim militia. They were not talking peace.

Terror at Sea

A bomb in Yemen kills 17 U.S. sailors and raises new fears about America's vulnerability

BLINDSIDED The bomb blew a gaping 40-ft. by 40-ft. hole in the U.S.S. *Cole,* one of the Navy's most advanced ships

THE 300 MEN AND WOMEN ABOARD THE U.S.S. *COLE* had been at sea for two uneventful months when their vessel arrived in the harbor of Aden in Yemen on Oct. 12. Unrest in the region and the *Cole's* upcoming six-month mission with the Navy's Fifth Fleet in the Persian Gulf, where it would enforce the international oil embargo against Iraq, had upgraded the ship's Threatcon to "bravo," the Navy's second-highest state of alert. So as the *Cole* steamed into Aden Harbor just before noon, moving close to an off-shore mooring station where it could refuel, crew members were on deck, armed and at attention. But they missed the threat. Several small boats approached to assist in attaching the *Cole's* thick 5-in. lines to fixed buoys. At 12:15, a small harbor boat mingling among the moorers pulled alongside. Two men stood upright, at attention, and the boat exploded.

The blast tore a 40-ft. by 40-ft. hole in the port side of the *Cole,* shoving one of the ship's decks upward and destroying an engine room and an adjoining mess area. Sailors not maimed by the explosion and flying shrapnel had only an instant to scramble to safety before water rushed into the gaping hole and engulfed them. As the *Cole,* a $1 billion destroyer armed with an assortment of high-caliber machine guns, surface-to-air missiles and advanced radar equipment, listed sickeningly to port, crew members worked furiously to keep the ship afloat. Damage-control teams mustered and rushed to the scene of the explosion to seal hatches and contain the leak. A makeshift medical station was erected to handle first aid. Engineers struggled to assess the damage and the risk to the ship, and to restore power and communications, cut by the blast. A military attaché from the U.S. embassy provided the lifeline to the outside world: his cell phone. It was the only way the ship could alert Fifth Fleet command in Bahrain that they had come under attack.

The attack killed 17 sailors and injured 38 more. The message it seemed to carry, that America might face a

SOLEMN RITUAL **The remains of a *Cole* bombing victim are borne by an honor guard at the U.S. air base in Ramstein, Germany**

reckoning of its own for the collapse of Middle East peace, echoed nearly as loudly as the blast itself. President Clinton vowed to "find out who was responsible and hold them accountable." The numbing familiarity of his statement betrayed a sense of dread about America's exposure to terrorist attacks. The *Cole* disaster ranks as the most deadly terrorist assault on U.S. forces since the 1996 bombing of the Air Force barracks in Saudi Arabia—a crime for which the U.S. has yet to bring anyone to justice.

The Pentagon's efforts to explain how the attack could have taken place offered little comfort. The size of the blast, the perpetrators' ability to conceal the bomb and their advance knowledge of the *Cole's* plans suggest the attack was plotted weeks, even months, in advance. Said Admiral Vernon Clark, the Navy's Chief of Operations: "It would be extraordinarily difficult … to do anything about this kind of situation and to have stopped it."

But the fact is, Pentagon brass have received warnings about the vulnerability of Fifth Fleet warships since at least 1996. More fallout may emerge from probes into why the *Cole* was refueling in Aden in the first place. An Administration official said the U.S. was aware of "a general uptick in activity" in the previous month among rogue groups hoping to use Arab-Israeli tensions as a justification for mischief. Yemen is a fertile staging ground for such trouble; the country is wretchedly poor. One of America's chief nemeses, Osama bin Laden, has ancestral roots there and boasts a following among militants.

A team of counterterrorism experts, including 100 FBI investigators, accompanied by a protective force of U.S Marines and diplomatic security agents, flew to the scene, but they were bedeviled by uncooperative Yemeni officials. President Ali Abdullah Saleh refused to acknowledge that the *Cole* bombing—and a grenade attack on the British embassy in San'a that soon followed—might be the work of terrorists. Indeed, he went so far as to declare, "Yemen does not have any terrorist elements." The sailors of the U.S.S. *Cole* might not agree. ∎

REVOLT
In Yugoslavia

Discovering people power, the Serbs end
the brutal reign of Slobodan Milosevic

FREEDOM! Vojislav Kostunica's first words electrified his countrymen: "Good evening, dear liberated Serbia," he said

VERY REVOLUTION HAS A MOMENT OF COMBUSTION. Yugoslavia's came on Wednesday, Oct. 4, in the persons of three elderly men on a tractor. Hundreds of President Slobodan Milosevic's dreaded special police had swept down on the hard-bitten diggers at the Kolubara coal mine in Serbia's heartland. The miners had stopped work, intent on crippling the country's electric power grid, after Milosevic refused to concede his loss in the nation's presidential election. Trying to break up the 7,000 striking workers, security troops first surrounded the complex and blockaded a key bridge with police buses. But the miners stood fast, broadcast for help on radios and cell phones, and 20,000 pugnacious cit-

izens converged on the mine. As the huge throng approached the barricaded bridge, those three old men plowed their tractor straight into the police blockade, shoving the buses aside and opening the way for thousands to break through. The security men melted away. Armed with the revelation of its own strength, a grass-roots revolt had begun, and from then on nothing could stop it.

The next day that delirious display of people power was repeated over and over in the capital of Belgrade as hundreds of thousands of Serbs stormed the bastions of Milosevic's oppression, and these too gave way. First the parliament building, seat of Milosevic's political apparat, went up in flames as protesters tossed the autocrat's doctored ballots out the windows. Then state television, main prop of the regime, went black as protesters broke through the front door while police fled out the back. Then the official news agency switched its allegiance to Vojislav Kostunica, the unassuming constitutional lawyer whose election Milosevic was trying to steal. Riot police doffed their helmets and threw down plastic shields to join the insurrection. Army troops sat quietly in their barracks. By nightfall, Milosevic had nothing left to sustain his rule.

YEARS OF PENT-UP FRUSTRATION UNDER MILOSEvic's blighting misrule had finally erupted in a tumultuous showdown, as each new success taught Serbs that they had the power to change their future. Just like that, the Serbs took back their country and belatedly joined the democratic tide that swept away the rest of Eastern Europe's communist tyrants a decade ago. The West gloried in the fall of the man who had fueled savage European conflicts for a decade and cost his enemies so much in money and blood.

In an astonishing moment Friday night, the strongman who had ruled so long by controlling the media stood stiffly before a camera he no longer owned, his jaw trembling as he said he would step aside. But ever defiant, he warned he had no intention of bowing out altogether.

For bone-weary Serbs, though, it was enough that he was gone now. The euphoria of freedom surged across the country. The Serbs had surprised themselves with their own empowerment, feeling an exhilaration so strong that no fears about the future could quench it. They filled up the capital again the following Saturday to see their democratically chosen leader sworn in.

NATO's leaders rejoiced that their campaign to unhorse the Serb autocrat had been won. They promised Kostunica an end to economic sanctions—even if Milosevic, indicted for war crimes by an international tribunal, had yet to be brought to justice. And they put on hold any worries that Kostunica might prove a prickly partner. He told TIME the week after the revolt that "there were war crimes committed by NATO last year," but he moved to restore full ties with the U.S. and other NATO countries in November.

Milosevic had unwittingly set his fate in motion during the summer when he tampered with the constitution

A Professor Leads a Peaceful Revolution

Yugoslavia's new President, Vojislav Kostunica, 56, is a former law professor who founded his tiny Democratic Party of Serbia eight years ago. The taciturn scholar—no admirer of the U.S.—didn't want events to be settled in the streets, but when the revolt began, he ensured that it was bloodless. To push for reforms, he will rely heavily on the Democratic Opposition of Serbia, a conglomerate of 18 squabbling parties, and he will have to work with former Milosevic supporters. He said he wouldn't serve out his five-year term but would call for new elections in 18 months.

and called an election nine months early to buff up his democratic veneer. Voters didn't like that, but when Serbs went to the polls Sept. 24, even they suspected the rushed ballot would cement his presidency in place for another four years. When the opposition declared a runaway victory on Sept. 25, claiming Kostunica had got 52.4%, compared with Milosevic's 38%, the Serb autocrat hung tough. He first tried to have his cronies rig the count, then settled on proposing a second round of voting to buy time.

But Milosevic didn't know how bitterly Serbs blamed him for the accumulated woes of niggardly salaries, four lost wars, the NATO bombing that ruined the economy, the bitter years of sanctions and international opprobrium. Repression and self-serving propaganda had reached critical mass, draining away the last vestiges of his once genuine popularity. When Kostunica resolutely refused to participate in the Milosevic-ordained runoff and insisted he was already President-elect, the people stood behind him. At last the long, brutal reign of the Butcher of the Balkans was put to an end, by his own people.

Kostunica urged his countrymen to conduct a "non-violent, wise, civilized, democratic revolution." So far, they have. But the lesson of people power is that it's harder the second day. The Serbs' road will be difficult, but they will be supported by enemies of tyranny everywhere. ■

LOSER **Milosevic's plans to overturn his defeat failed**

BENEATH THE SEA,

After a mysterious accident, 118 sailors perish aboard a nuclear-powered Russian

FLAGSHIP **The *Kursk*, one of the Russian navy's newest subs, in 1999**

A SILENT TRAGEDY

bmarine, and divers find a sailor's last message: "None of us can get to the surface"

FOR CAPTAIN GENNADI LYACHIN AND NEARLY A SCORE of others crowded into the control room of the nuclear submarine *Kursk*, Saturday, Aug. 12, was to be a day of pride and triumph. The vessel, one of the Russian navy's newest and most powerful cruise-missile submarines, was at periscope depth during the second day of a 30-ship exercise in the Barents Sea, about 90 miles northeast of Murmansk. These were the biggest Russian naval maneuvers in several years, and it was a rare opportunity for Lyachin to put his ship through its paces with a full-scale task force—so rare that five high-ranking Northern Fleet staff officers were aboard to observe the exercise.

By noon, the new sub had successfully concluded a torpedo-firing run and was preparing for another. Lyachin, 45, one of Russia's most experienced submarine officers, radioed the task-force commander for permission to fire. The transmission was monitored by the American surveillance ship U.S.N.S. *Loyal,* lurking about 186 miles west-northwest of the *Kursk,* as was the commander's "permission granted." But instead of the sounds of torpedoes being blown from launch tubes, sonar operators aboard U.S. submarines working with the *Loyal* heard two explosions, one short and sharp, the second an enormous, thundering boom. A Norwegian seismic institute also recorded the explosions and said the second carried the force of two tons of TNT, registering 3.5 on the Richter scale.

GRIEF As loved ones wept, Putin kept mum

YURI TUTOV—CORBIS SYGMA

Evidence later obtained from underwater cameras shows that the blast tore open the entire double-hulled forward section of the 505-ft.-long vessel, an area the size of a school gymnasium. Seawater would have slammed into the torpedo and cruise-missile compartments, instantly killing the men on duty there. In the control room just aft of the shattered weapons compartments, Lyachin, the five staff officers and the dozen or so petty officers manning the ship's controls would have had no time to react before the combined power of the blast and seawater tore through, destroying the gleaming arrays of switches,

computers and video screens that constitute the "brain" of a submarine. All would have been killed outright or quickly drowned. From there, the water is likely to have cascaded through passageways and doors into the "sail," the conning tower above the control room, and into communications spaces and living quarters just aft of the sail. At that point, the floodwaters were probably thwarted by thick, watertight bulkheads guarding the twin VM-5 pressurized water reactors powering the submarine.

Even so, there would be no salvation for the men whose duties placed them in the reactor control rooms and the turbine and machinery spaces behind the reactors. The flash flooding in the forward part of the *Kursk* would have caused the bow to drop, pitching the 14,000-ton boat into a steep dive with steam turbines still delivering power to its twin screws. In seconds, the sub would have pounded into the seabed some 350 ft. beneath the storm-driven surface of the Barents Sea with a shock that would have hurled survivors against equipment and bulkheads. Finally, as the vessel settled onto the ocean floor, openings along the keel would probably no longer have been able to draw in the seawater needed to cool the reactors. Automatic systems would then have "scrammed" the reactors, pushing control rods into the core and shutting it down. The *Kursk,* its shattered bow shoved into a furrow of sand and heeling to port, lay silent, without power or heat or light or hope, its 118 souls either dead—or doomed to die soon.

"The majority of the crew was in the part of the boat that was hit by the catastrophe that developed at lightning speed," said Ilya Klebanov, Deputy Prime Minister and head of a commission investigating the sinking. It was all over, he said five days later, "in the space of two minutes, more or less." Perhaps: reports of the tapping out of SOS signals in Morse code suggested that some crew members had survived for a time in the stern sections of the boat, but Admiral Vyacheslav Popov, commander of the Northern Fleet, said on Aug. 18 that no tapping had been heard from the sub since Aug. 14, two days after the accident.

Those who did survive the initial flooding would have come to envy the dead. Dying always seems more gruesome when it is in slow motion, and slow-motion submarine deaths are perversely compelling because they happen in shallow water within reach of rescuers. Men who have been trapped in stricken submarines say the crew of the *Kursk* would have suffered from cold as temperatures fell to 41°F and from severe headaches as levels of carbon dioxide rose in the smothering atmosphere. They would have suffered too from fear and hopelessness as rescuers repeatedly tried, and failed, to save them. "Those guys can hear the minisubs," said a U.S. Navy officer. "Listening to that for any length of time as you're slowly suffocating would drive anyone nuts." By the end of the week, any men still alive would have steadily been sliding toward death. As the carbon-dioxide levels rose, their brains would have slowly turned off, as if on a dimmer switch; consciousness would have ebbed to coma, and reality would have faded to black.

What caused the loss of the *Kursk* remained unclear. Russian officials fell back on old, Soviet habits of secrecy and confusion during the first days after the disaster. They made no announcement for two days, then issued a bland statement that there had been a "technical fault" and the ship was on the sea bottom. After the seriousness of the accident became clearer, Defense Minister Igor Sergeyev declared there was "incontrovertible evidence" that the sub had collided with another vessel while cruising at periscope depth. In past years Soviet and U.S. vessels have had near collisions while spying on each other. The Pentagon firmly rejected any notion that U.S. submarines were involved, but some Russians clung to a collision scenario.

Other Russian officials dropped the collision claim and blamed an explosion in the weapons area, a theory supported by some Western experts, who said it could have come from a torpedo or missile or a high-pressure air tank used to blow ballast water when surfacing. Some

U.S. defense officials advanced the theory that the *Kursk* was in the process of firing an antisubmarine rocket that jammed in the tube. Its flaming engine might have set off the first blast, while the warhead's detonation would have accounted for the second. According to *Jane's Fighting Ships*, the *Kursk* normally carries 24 cruise missiles able to deliver 1,650 lbs. of high explosives or a nuclear warhead a distance of 300 miles, plus as many as 28 torpedoes with similar warhead capability (although the Russians said the *Kursk* was carrying no nuclear weapons, hewing to an agreement with the U.S. that neither side will deploy tactical nuclear weapons).

Whatever the direct cause of the disaster, the *Kursk* was doomed as much by underfunding, insufficient training and incompetent military management as by collision or high explosives. Since the end of the cold war, the Russian navy has declined from 613 ships of all types to around 95 today, a drop of 84%, compared with a shrinkage of around 40% for Western navies. Of the few ships remaining in the Russian inventory, only about 10% are considered by Western experts to be seaworthy. One reason is that the bulk of Russia's dwindling defense budget goes to fight the war in Chechnya. That means little money for maintenance, and the result can be seen in naval bases all around Russia, where ships lie in rusting rows, crewed by unmotivated and often unpaid sailors.

"Because of poor maintenance levels across much of the fleet, the fleet can't put to sea very often, so personnel are less well trained," says Joanna Kidd, naval analyst at the London-based International Institute for Strategic Studies. The *Kursk*, one of the newest and most important vessels in the fleet, would have received enough to keep up maintenance but probably not enough to ensure vital sea-time training for navy men. "It's speculation, but their reactions might have been slow," says Kidd. Similarly, the initial rescue efforts may have suffered owing to lack of training. The exercise in which the *Kursk* was lost reflected

TIME DIAGRAM BY JOE LERTOLA. SOURCE: FEDERATION OF AMERICAN SCIENTISTS. NOTE: SUB'S INTERIOR NOTIONAL

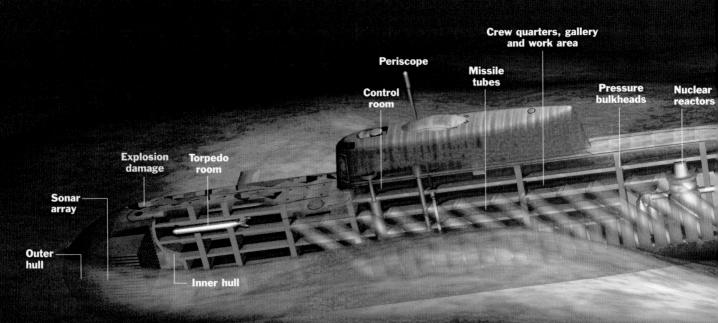

Sonar array

Outer hull

Explosion damage

Torpedo room

Inner hull

Periscope

Control room

Crew quarters, gallery and work area

Missile tubes

Pressure bulkheads

Nuclear reactors

President Vladimir Putin's declared intention to rebuild the navy at least to the levels of the French and British fleets, if not to the size and might of the U.S. Navy. It was intended as a dress rehearsal for a show-of-force cruise of the eastern Mediterranean later in 2000 to be led by the aircraft carrier *Admiral Kuznetsov* and the battle cruiser *Peter the Great*. Losing the *Kursk* was a major setback for these plans and for Putin's naval ambitions. "He has aligned himself personally with the revival of the navy's fortunes," said Kidd. "This is a big humiliation for him."

Perhaps that's why Putin had so little to say as the magnitude of the disaster unfolded. He surprised observers by leaving for his vacation retreat on the day of the accident, sending no messages of condolence to the fleet or to the families of the missing men, who grew furious over his silence. His officially published schedule told of phone conversations with foreign leaders but made no mention of briefings, consultations or expressions of concern about the *Kursk*.

On the Wednesday after Saturday's disaster, dressed casually and looking fit, Putin met with visiting academics to discuss at length problems of science, research and the brain drain. After the meeting, in response to journalists' questions, he reluctantly acknowledged that the situation with the *Kursk* was "critical" and said, "All necessary and possible efforts to save the crew have been carried out."

Not quite. For crucial days, Russian officials had rejected Western offers of help, including the dispatch of U.S., French, British and Norwegian rescue equipment. On Wednesday, Putin finally ordered the navy to accept help. The Russians promptly invited Norway and Britain to send equipment, but shortly before the British team arrived on Saturday, a full week after the accident, the Northern Fleet commander said, "The critical line of survivability has been closed."

Condemned from all sides for the coolness of his response, Putin finally met with the families of the *Kursk's* crew on Aug. 22, in the northern Russian city of Murmansk. Said Putin: "The grief is immeasurable; no words can console. My heart is aching, but yours much more so." His government announced that the families of the deceased would receive an average compensation of 194,000 rubles ($7,000)—equivalent to 10 years of a sailor's wages.

On Oct. 9, divers from Russia, Britain and Scandinavia left a western Norway port aboard the *Regalia*, a rig normally used by the offshore oil industry, on a grim mission to recover the bodies of the crew. In early November the rescue team managed to enter the craft, after five days devoted to the painstaking work of cutting holes in its 2-in.-thick inner steel hull with an instrument that sprayed pressurized water mixed with diamond dust. As they began recovering the bodies of the crew, the divers found a note left by one survivor proving that some of the men had lived through the catastrophe. The writer was Lieut. Dmitry Kolesnikov, the commander of the *Kursk's* turbine section. "All the crew from the sixth, seventh and eighth compartments went over to the ninth. There are 23 people here. We made this decision as a result of the accident. None of us can get to the surface," he wrote. "I am writing blindly." The note shed no light on the cause of the accident.

The divers ultimately recovered the remains of 12 of the 118 crewmen. But weather conditions in the frigid seas 300 miles above the Arctic Circle, combined with the difficulty of clearing debris within the hulk, forced the rescue team to suspend its operations. The Russian government announced it would consider mounting an effort to raise the entire *Kursk* in 2001. On Nov. 6, Russian and Norwegian divers cast a wreath on the arctic waters above the undersea mausoleum and headed for home. ∎

British LR5 rescue submersible

Russian ARS rescue mini-submarine

ssian ng bell

Propulsion

Escape hatch

Water temperature 39 F (4 C) 20 list

Ballast tanks

Steam turbines

Images

PAPAL PILGRIM It may have been Pope John Paul II's 91st international trip, but his journey to the Holy Land was one of his most memorable, even if only 1% of the region's citizens are Roman Catholics. In seven days the Pope visited Bethlehem; saw not one but two spots where Jesus may have been baptized; offered Mass from the site of the Sermon on the Mount and at the Church of the Holy Sepulcher; prayed at Gethsemane, where Jesus was betrayed; and placed a petition in the Western Wall, right, Judaism's historic sacred site.

Sayonara, Fujimori

For years some Peruvians have accused President Alberto Fujimori of running a brutal and authoritarian government. But in 2000 Fujimori's regime morphed from a monolith into a weird, militarized soap opera that concluded with his resignation. The drama began in mid-September, when the President's shadowy secret police chief, Vladimiro Montesinos Torres, was caught red-handed paying a bribe. Two days later, Fujimori declared that just months after winning a third term in an election international observers described as unfair, he would call new presidential elections for July, 2001. He also vowed to disband the secret police. Meanwhile, Montesinos left Peru for Panama, seeking asylum, only to return and go into hiding. In November, Fujimori, in Japan on a diplomatic visit, declared he would resign immediately, plunging Peru into a period of political turmoil.

FUJIMORI Rallying his supporters

THE ODD COUPLE Albright meets the new Kim

A Surprise in North Korea

Maybe his longtime honorific, "Great Leader," is on target after all: North Korea's Kim Jong Il, 58, emerged from isolation to reach out to the world. Gone was Kim the mysterious, cloaked in rumors of hedonism and buffoonery. In was Kim the peacemaker, who was even observed poking fun at himself.

In June Kim and South Korean President Kim Dae Jung met in Pyongyang to discuss mutual cooperation. In September athletes from the two long-estranged nations of the Korean peninsula marched under a single flag at the opening ceremonies of the Olympics in Sydney. And in October U.S. Secretary of State Madeleine Albright traveled to North Korea to become the first U.S. official to meet Kim.

Adieu to the Concorde?

The world's only supersonic passenger jet has been grounded. On July 25 an Air France Concorde crashed on takeoff from Paris' Charles de Gaulle Airport, killing 113 people. Horrified onlookers, including French President Jacques Chirac, watched the craft's left engines burst into flames before it crashed into a nearby village. British and French authorities concluded that the accident was set in motion when the Concorde's left tire was pierced and ruptured by a strip of metal that had apparently fallen onto the runway from an earlier, Continental Airlines plane. The tire exploded, sending bits of rubber into the huge air intakes in the Concorde's wings. Aviation authorities grounded the planes until their tires could be made safer.

TRAGEDY **The Concorde in flames**

Global News Briefs

• **The Philippines:** In November President Joseph Estrada, a former movie heartthrob, was impeached by Congress on grounds of corruption involving millions of dollars in paybacks from illegal gambling.
• **Sierra Leone:** In May United Nations peacekeeping forces were overwhelmed as they attempted to quell a brutal civil war in Sierra Leone, after a U.N.-brokered truce with merciless rebel leader Foday Sankoh unraveled. Four Kenyan peacekeepers were killed, and more than 300 others were held hostage. When order was restored, the U.N. pulled out the peacekeepers.
• **Uganda:** In March leaders of an

obscure Christian sect set fire to a building, killing 400 members of the cult, including many children.

Moderates Win in Tehran

The most freely elected parliament in Iranian history convened in May in a marble-sided edifice in downtown Tehran. In the biggest boost for reform since President Mohammed Khatami's victory in 1997, Iranians in February ousted conservatives and handed Khatami control of the 290-seat Majlis-e Shura. The mullah count in this new, moderate parliament is down from 53 to 33. But the struggle to reform Iran is still daunting: one strong Khatami supporter was shot in the head by hard-liners; dozens of other moderates are in jail.

KHATAMI **Walking a thin line in Iran**

People

21st Century Fox

On the night of July 2, Mexico finally became a democracy. The enormous participation of the Mexican people in orderly and overwhelmingly honest elections put an end to a political relic—a system born in the days of silent film that had survived into the era of the Internet. The Institutional Revolutionary Party (P.R.I.), a combo plate of corruption, authoritarianism, paternalism and state largesse, lost its 71-year hold on the presidency. After years of crime, drug wars and faltering currency, Mexico garnered worldwide respect for the elections.

The man behind the stunning revolution was Vicente Fox Quesada of the National Action Party (P.A.N.), who took office on Dec. 1. Fox, 58, is a former Coca-Cola executive who brought to Mexican politics a new, effervescent tonic—change. Everywhere he campaigned, the charismatic candidate, 6 ft. 5 in. in his cowboy boots, met shrieking enthusiasm. He promised a "peaceful insurgency" that would improve education and health care while keeping the economy stable.

Fox told TIME that the nations of the hemisphere needed long-range vision: "Mexico, the U.S. and Canada should decide where we want to be in the year 2030, as partners, neighbors and friends." Perhaps a new aphorism is in order: Poor America—so close to Mexico, so far from Fox.

Business

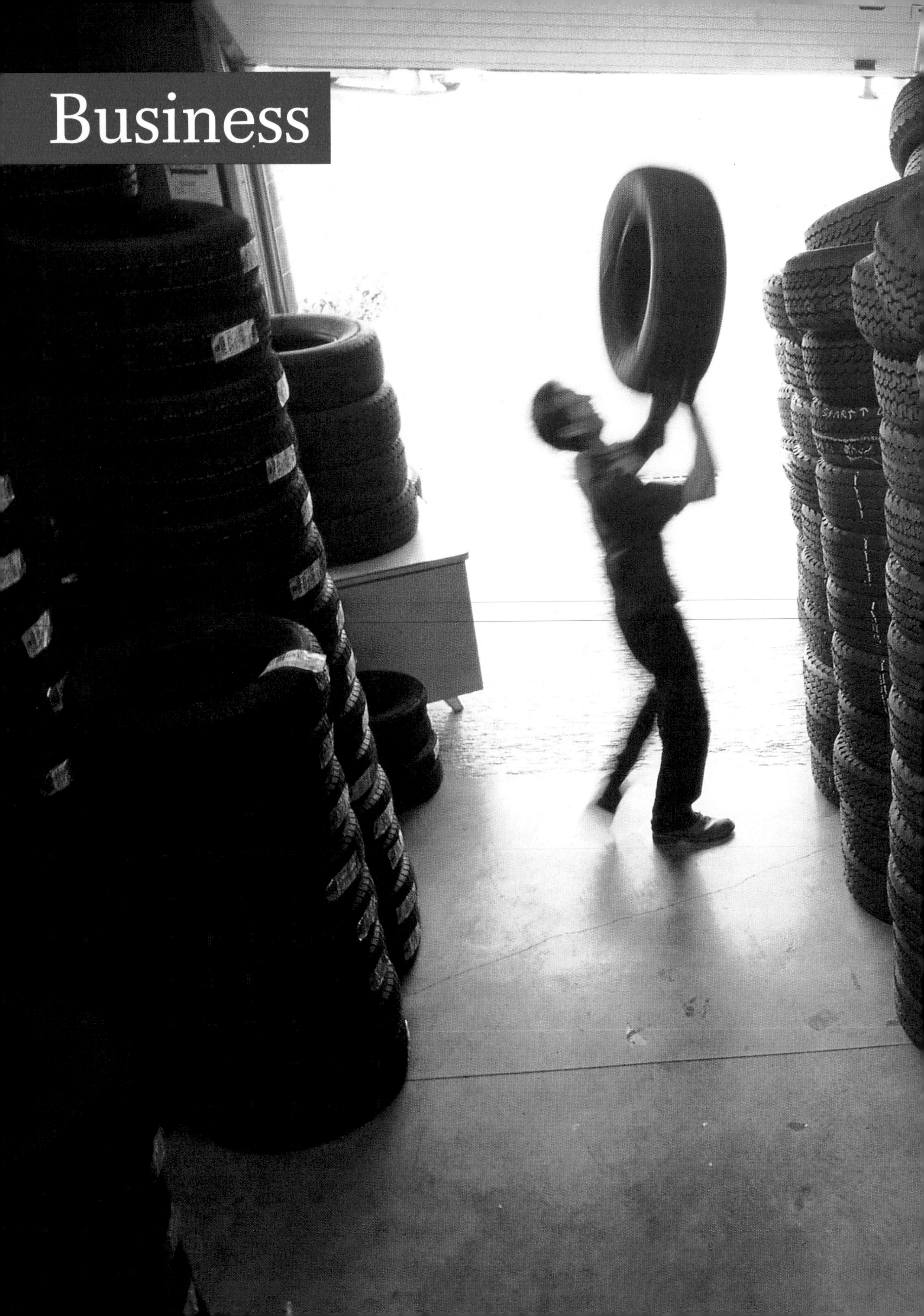

RETIRED: A warehouse fills up with recalled Firestone tires after the Japanese-owned company began recalling 6.5 million potentially lethal tires from Ford vehicles

Dan Habib—Concord Monitor—Saba

When Tires Kill

After a chain of fatalities, Firestone recalls millions of its tires

CRACKING THE FORTRESS Jim and Kathy Taylor's daughter Jessica died in a 1998 SUV accident. Their suit against Firestone, led by lawyer Randy Roberts, background, helped reveal that the problem affected tires across the nation

ESSICA LEANN TAYLOR, 14, A JUNIOR HIGH SCHOOL cheerleader, was bound for a football game outside her hometown of Mexia, Texas, on Oct. 16, 1998. A friend of Taylor's mother was at the wheel when the tread on the left-rear Firestone ATX tire allegedly peeled off like a banana. When the Ford Explorer SUV veered left and rolled over, Jessica died in the crash.

As most tire companies have successfully done in court over the years, Firestone denied any problem with the tires from the start. But the Taylors' attorney, Randy

Roberts, secured a crucial victory when a state judge ordered Firestone to hand over any complaints and other documents, as well as employee depositions from prior lawsuits, concerning its ATX and Wilderness tires nationwide. In addition, the judge permitted Roberts to share the information with lawyers involved in similar legal battles.

The judge's ruling was only one breakthrough in a cascade of revelations that climaxed on August 9, when Firestone, owned by Japan's Bridgestone Corp., voluntarily recalled 6.5 million of its most widely used products. The action targeted Firestone tires on Ford SUVs and pickups that eventually were implicated in as many as 101 traffic deaths and roughly 300 accidents in the U.S.

The action hit Firestone and Ford where they live—in the companies' best-selling models—and in their credibility with customers. The huge recall was scheduled to take up to 18 months to complete nationwide. But nervous motorists from all points of the compass flooded Ford and Firestone dealerships with requests-cum-demands for new tires, immediately. Many were turned away at first: there were no replacement tires to be had. Meanwhile, Ford and Firestone issued conflicting instructions for inflating the tires due to be replaced. While Ford recommended a pressure of 26 to 30 p.s.i., Firestone insisted on 30 p.s.i. "It just burns you up," said Sue Gorski, a Chicago dental assistant who drives a '98 Explorer. "It feels like driving a car with a ticking time bomb underneath."

To free up 70,000 more tires, Ford temporarily shut down three U.S. truck plants and Firestone airlifted replacements from Japan. But that wasn't enough to satisfy government officials, Firestone owners and consumer advocates, who demanded to know why it had taken so long for the recall to start. After all, injured motorists or their families had brought more than 100 suits against Ford and Firestone since 1992, including at least 10 complaints about tread separation that the companies had settled. The National Highway Transportation Safety Administration had been hearing complaints about the tires since 1991 but didn't act until May 2000, when the numbers spiked following an investigative report by Houston TV station KHOU. More red lights had flashed in the Middle East and South America in 1999 when treads began to peel off Ford Explorers sold in Saudi Arabia and Venezuela; Ford had quietly recalled the vehicles and replaced some 50,000 high-mileage Firestone tires.

As questions mounted following the recall, the crisis exploded. It turned out that State Farm, the nation's largest car insurer, had alerted the government and Firestone to an unusually large number of claims for the bad

TIRE TROUBLES

6.5 million recalled because they have been linked to 46 deaths and nearly 300 crashes

Treads peeled off, usually associated with underinflation, highway speeds and warm climates

Steel belts

Liner

Ply

Bead

Firestone recall
- 3.8 million Radial ATX and ATXII tires
- 2.7 million Wilderness AT tires

TIME Graphic by Lon Tweeten

tires as far back as 1997. And former workers at Firestone's Decatur, Ill., plant gave depositions that their supervisors put quantity ahead of quality. Many of the suspect tires were made there. Firestone described the tiremakers, who had been replaced by nonunion workers during a 1994-96 strike, as disgruntled employees. Meanwhile, Bridgestone said its profits in the first half of the year had fallen nearly 50% as a result of the recall—and its U.S. p.r. firm quit.

In September Senate Commerce Committee chairman John McCain summoned both Ford boss Jacques Nasser and Firestone CEO Masatoshi Ono to sweat under the nasty glare of Capitol Hill scrutiny. In sharp contrast to the carefully scripted performance of Nasser—who would later pin the blame squarely on Firestone's tires—Ono was visibly uncomfortable, expressing regret on one hand, denying any tire defect on the other. The reserved Japanese executive had spent the better part of the past decade propping up the sagging fortunes of Firestone, the U.S. company Bridgestone paid $2.6 billion for in 1988. His watered-down apology incited a harsh response. Senator Richard Shelby, Alabama Republican, summed up the general sentiment by asking, "What does it take to put a company on notice that perhaps they've got a defective product out there?" Ford may come out of the pileup dented by a few hundred million dollars, but the 100-year-old Firestone brand could be completely totaled. ∎

UNDER PRESSURE
Firestone CEO Ono, left, faced the heat on Capitol Hill as lawmakers probed why the decision to recall took so long. Ford boss Jacques Nasser, above, blamed the Japanese company

NOW MEET THE NEW
NEW ECONOMY

Dotcoms become dotbombs, but the New Economy isn't dead: it's driving powerful change in older companies

STARTING OVER **Erin Meek in the spartan offices of Medsprout, a new kind of dotcom that lives on the cheap**

VERY REVOLUTION EVENTUALLY ARRIVES AT THAT bitter moment when the flag waving has to stop, the grand social theories have to adapt to reality, and a large number of the revolutionaries have to board the tumbrels for a ride to the guillotine. For the e-commerce companies that were so proudly marching in the vanguard of the Internet revolution, that moment arrived in April 2000—Bloody April. When the carnage was over, the dotcoms were looking like dotbombs, and the New Economy banner they had unfurled was evolving into … well, call it the New New Economy.

It was fun in the spring of 2000, watching those bratty dotcom billionaires … oops … millionaires … uh … thousandaires … squirm as their cyberpriced stocks came screaming back to earth and their e-dreams disappeared overnight. But by the fall, something else dawned. It wasn't just kids from Stanford taking it on the chin. It was us. Suddenly, warning lights were flashing. By late November, everyone from mighty chipmaker Intel to housewares seller Home Depot to computer maker Gateway had signaled a sharp drop in profits, leading nervous investors to pummel their stocks.

To that growing disquiet add the recurrence of warfare and terrorism in the Middle East, plus an elec-

AMAZON.COM

| January 3 | $89.5 (price per share) |
| December 1 | $24.5 |

tion that never seemed to end. Result: a full-fledged retreat on Wall Street. By the time the rout ended, both the Dow Jones average and the tech-heavy NASDAQ index were reeling. Americans who had grown accustomed to a supercharged rate of return on their Wall Street investments suddenly began to sense that the economy might be a Ford Explorer speeding along on Firestones. Welcome to the new millennium!

Much of the sinking feeling stemmed from concerns that the thing that got us here—the vaunted New Economy—was looking like a big Sony Betamax that had promised a revolution it could not deliver. The New Economy is supposed to be frictionless, tied as it is to the ultra-productive cyberworld of computers, broadband networks and the Internet, and cosseted by low inflation and low interest rates. But nobody told that to OPEC, which sent gas prices soaring in the summer. Or to Yasser Arafat. And if the New Economy is rewinding, what will become of the economic expansion that had already started grinding down after an unprecedented 10-year run?

The economic risks in 2000 were the greatest in recent years. If the U.S. is unlucky, rising inflation, higher interest rates and slower spending could whip up what economist David Wyss calls "a perfect storm" that could turn the soft landing the Federal Reserve is try-

GATEWAY

| February 24 | $73 |
| December 1 | $19 |

ing to engineer into an outright recession sometime in 2001. Wyss, chief economist for Standard & Poor's, still expects a gentle slowdown that would lower growth from nearly 5% at present to a more sustainable 3.5% in 2001. But he also sees a 1 in 4 chance of a slump. "Bad things," he warns, "can happen to new economies."

Fed Chairman Alan Greenspan declared that U.S. economic fundamentals were solid, and his voice always carries authority. Fed vice chairman Roger Ferguson told TIME in October, "The economy is cooling from its unsustainable pace of earlier this year, but recent data certainly don't suggest a dangerous slowdown."

Yet if things were so good, why was Wall Street doing so poorly, especially now that America has become a nation of stock traders? An explanation is that Wall Street has exchanged its traditional role of follower of economic trends for that of economic pacesetter. Consider the way that dotcom mania showered wealth on every jaunty entrepreneur with the gleam of a good idea but not a clue about earnings. In the past, the stock market would rarely show its checkbook to a start-up sans profits. And now that Wall Street has been burned, the fear is that the current stock pullback could leave even companies with real potential starved for cash—thereby stifling innovation. Some experts claim the economy could spiral into a harrowing free-fall.

But that's not very likely. The U.S. appears to be witnessing something richer and more varied than either New Economy enthusiasts or dotcom alarmists have envisioned: the rapid—if still painful and uneven—merging of the old and new economies. "What we're seeing," says Garth Saloner, a professor of e-commerce at Stanford's business school, "is the diffusion of technologies that were popularized by the dotcoms into traditional companies."

Viewed in that fashion, the New Economy is nothing more than a fancy term for the basic infrastructure that allows consumers and companies across the globe to shop, work and play at Internet speed. In New York City, for example, travel agencies routinely farm out chores like updating frequent-flyer miles to online boutiques as far away as India. The payoff, according to economists, has been a boom in productivity that has raised America's once tiny gains in output per hour of work to a robust 5% in 1999. That helped the economy

PRICELINE.COM

| March 13 | $96 |
| December 1 | $2.5 |

BEZOS A survivor, for now

to grow at an unbelievable 8.3% annual pace in the final quarter of 1999, while inflation stayed comfortably below 3%.

And that efficiency includes funding new businesses and laying waste to those that disappoint. So the bursting of the speculative tech-stock bubble of the late '90s was a reckoning much overdue, even desirable. In the frenzy, the market had awarded astronomical valuations to dotcom companies that had never made a dime—and paid an unheard-of 100 to 200 times earnings for true New Economy leaders like Cisco or Amazon (led by TIME's Man of the Year 1999, Jeff Bezos), whose stocks have since plunged, some as much as 50%.

April was the cruel month when the dotcoms' dreams gave way to reality. When the dust cleared, countless e-commerce companies were history. FORTUNE magazine ran a major story on "Dotcom Fever" in January; by June the business book was running a "Dotcom Deathwatch" feature. Among the casualties: Boo.com, Craftshop.com,

iVILLAGE

| March 16 | $26 |
| December 1 | $1 |

RedRocket.com, HomeWarehouse.com and Toysmart.com. As Wall Street let the dogs out, Foofoo.com went belly-up and—alas!—decaying with the roadkill on the info highway was the engaging sock-puppet spokespuppy who had pitched Pets.com.

The relentless setbacks left normally ebullient e-businesses dazed and chastened. By July cyberspace start-ups were exercises in frugality: at Medsprout.com, a New York dotcom that provides online information for doctors, the conference room was also the bottled water room and the CEO shared his office.

It's no small irony that even as Silicon Valley suffers, much of the heartland still basks in the good times the New Economy has made possible. Throughout the Midwest, consumers shrugged off the downturn in stocks and took out home-equity loans to finance remodeling, or a new car or a European vacation. "There's not a chance this boom is over," said Diane Swonk, chief economist for Bank One in Chicago. "Consumer attitudes are high in the face of high oil prices, stock-market volatility and even election rhetoric. Most Americans live on Main Street, not in Silicon Valley."

DELL

| March 22 | $58 |
| December 1 | $18.5 |

Heartland America is where the new and old economies are melding, and the ultimate winners will be those companies that can do it best. K Mart and fellow Midwest giants Sears and Target have been leading the online parade of bricks-and-mortar retailers. K Mart, which is expanding its BlueLight.com line from 150,000 to 500,000 items, jump-started the site by offering free Internet access to customers.

To see how far a company can go in transferring its brand to the Internet, take a look at General Electric. Every GE business has an e-commerce strategy, and most include self-help sites that show users how to repair and maintain GE products. Builders and architects can use Web-based programs to design kitchens and lighting systems with GE wares. Want prompt delivery of that new refrigerator? Punch in your order at a Home Depot, and GE will deliver the appliance straight from its warehouse. GE even offers insurance, loans and mutual funds online through a financial website.

The New Economy has created faster growth with less inflation than anyone would have thought possible only five years ago. Yet none of that makes U.S. prosperity bulletproof. "The fact that the New Economy is here doesn't mean that you can't have a new recession," warns Standard & Poor's economist Wyss. "All it means is that we can grow faster than in the '70s and '80s." Quite so. And since the new and the old economies are on the road to becoming virtually synonymous, we may all be better able to withstand whatever risks may lie ahead. ∎

LOOKING Two veterans of the late firm APBNews.com hunt for new jobs

SHAUN BEST—REUTERS—ARCHIVE

CLASH Despite a few ugly scenes, most "Seattle Two" protests were peaceful

Big Merger, Long Wait

It was a marriage made in media heaven—assuming for argument's sake that such a place exists. In January publishing/movie/cable/TV giant Time Warner (parent of TIME) agreed to be acquired by cyberspace bigfoot America Online. Time Warner head Gerald Levin and AOL boss Steve Case hailed the monster merger as a perfect marriage of Old Media and New. But federal regulators, responsive to charges by competitors that the merger could restrain Internet access, stopped the big match from proceeding in 2000.

ALAN TANNENBAUM—CORBIS SYGMA FOR TIME

PARTNERS? Case and Levin

Takin' It to the Streets

Sequels work for Hollywood—why not for protesters? In an action they dubbed "Seattle Two: The Sequel," tens of thousands of foes of global capitalism took to the streets in the nation's capital in April during meetings of the International Monetary Fund and World Bank. The objects of their concern: everything from globalization and the environment to Third World debt relief. Though there were a number of tough moments, police and protesters avoided the rolling riots that inflicted millions of dollars of damage on downtown Seattle in '99.

More Smiles per Hour

The latest chapter in America's love affair with the automobile is Chrysler's PT (for personal transportation) Cruiser: a sleek, small, tall car with broad hints of pre–World War II models and a whiff of hot rods from the '50s and '60s. Inspired by Volkswagen's successful New Beetle, Chrysler gave it sloe-eyed headlights, an undershot bull-dog snout of a grille and an almost vertical rear. A swooping wedge of sleek, subtle curves, it was an instant hit.

CRUISER A retro fantasy from Chrysler

People

Chicanery Amid the Chintz

Going, going … the reputations of the world's two leading auction houses were all but gone in the spring of 2000. Following a three-year Department of Justice investigation, auctioneers Sotheby's and Christie's, which between them control some 90% of the $4 billion world market for early wardrobes and late Warhols, pleaded guilty in a commission-fixing scam going back to 1992.

Three weeks after Christie's won "conditional amnesty" by turning over information to the feds, Sotheby's chairman, real estate developer A. Alfred Taubman, and his hand-picked

MARINA GARNIER—CORBIS SYGMA

ABASHED Brooks and Taubman

CEO, Diana ("Dede") Brooks, resigned. On Oct. 5, Brooks, 50, a graduate of Miss Porter's School and Yale University, pleaded guilty to taking part in an illegal conspiracy. But her testimony seemed to promise that the final gavel had yet to fall. Brooks stated it was "at the direction of a superior at Sotheby's" that she had engaged in the price-fixing plan. She had but one boss at the firm: Taubman.

DAIMLER CHRYSLER

Technology

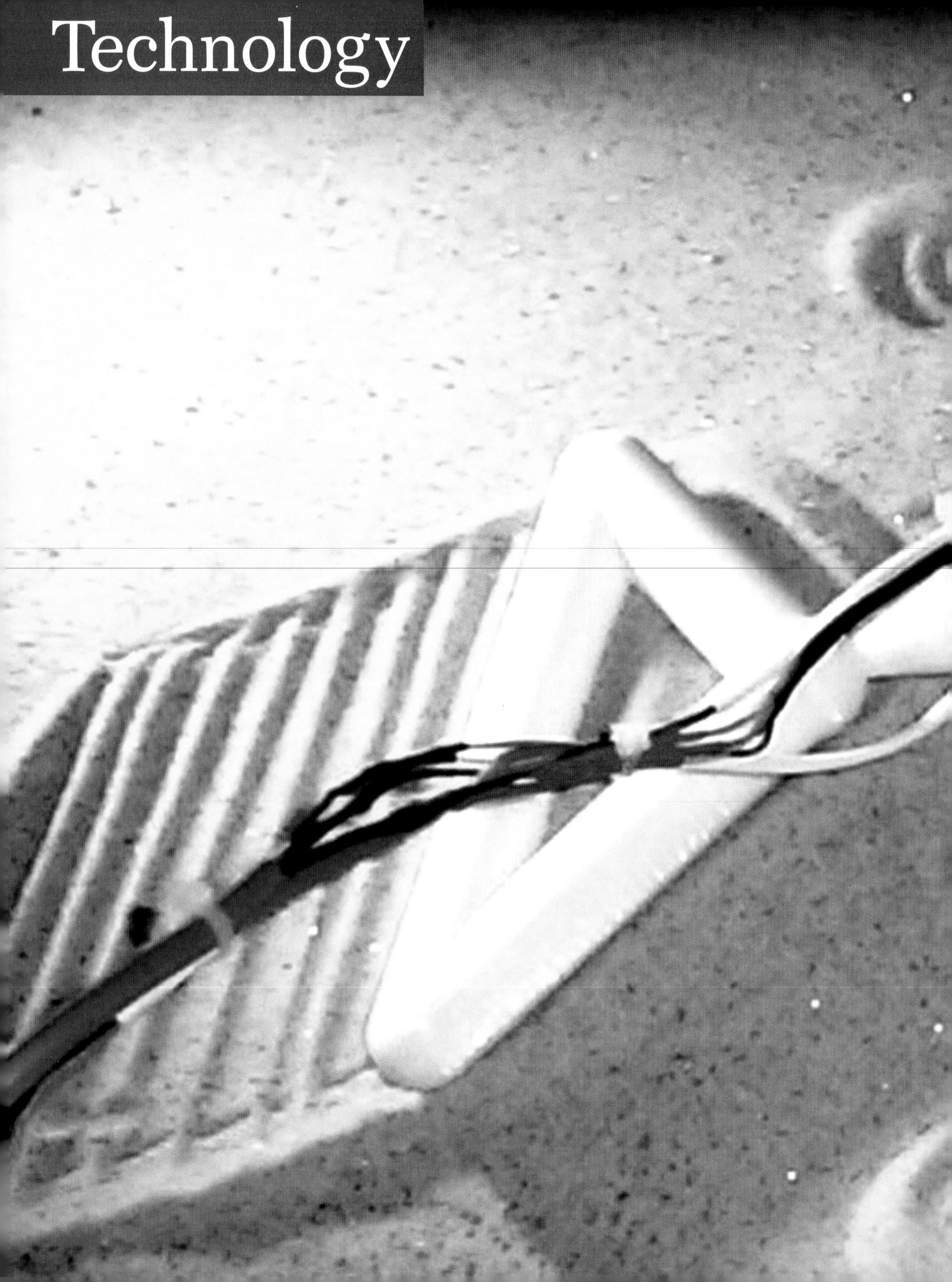

BABY STEPS: First a Brandeis University computer designed the small robot crawler above. Then the computer was hooked up to a plastic-model-making machine that produced it. Finally, the computer tested and refined its creation through repeated generations

Brandeis University

MEET THE

How a college dropout's brainsto

GEEK CENTRAL Fanning's sudden fame hasn't changed his laid-back ways

NAPSTER

olutionized the music business forever

S HAWN FANNING ONLY DIMLY RECALLS THAT TIME in mid-1999, when he wrote the source code for the music file-sharing program called Napster. He can't remember specific months, weeks or days. The 18-year-old college dropout was just hunched over his Dell notebook, writing the software and crashing on his uncle's sofa in Hull, Mass. Then he'd shake off fatigue, scarf a bowl of cereal and sit back down. He worked feverishly, sure that someone else had the same idea, that soon some software company or media conglomerate would be unveiling a version of the same application, and then his big idea wouldn't be his anymore.

And he believed in it because his idea was so simple: a program that would allow computer users to swap music files with one another directly, without going through a centralized file server or middleman. He'd heard all the complaints about how frustrating it was to try to find good music on the Net, how so many of the pointers on websites offering current (which is to say copyrighted) music seem to lead only to dead ends. But Fanning figured that if he stuck to it, he could bypass the rats' nest of legal and technical problems that kept great music from busting out all over the World Wide Web. All he had to do was combine the features of existing programs: the instant-messaging system of Internet Relay Chat, the file-sharing ease of Microsoft Windows and the advanced seeking and filtering capabilities of various search engines.

But there was a huge leap of faith involved. Nearly everyone he mentioned the idea to believed it wasn't workable. "It's a selfish world, and nobody wants to share," snorted his older, more experienced buddies. Fanning, an inarticulate teenager at the time, couldn't adequately explain himself. He insisted that people would do it, because, like … well, just because.

What he was thinking was that this would be the application that would finally unleash the potential of the Web, the viral growth possibilities of the community, the transgressive power of the Internet to leap over barriers and transform our assumptions about business, content and culture. He just couldn't spit out the words to convince his friends that his idea could change the world.

Yet love it or hate it, that's what Napster has done: changed the world. It has forced record companies to rethink their business models and record-companies and recording artists to defend their intellectual property. It has forced purveyors of "content," like Time Warner, parent company of TIME, to wonder what exactly content will mean in the near future.

Napster and Fanning have come to personify the bloody intersection where commerce, culture and the First Amendment are colliding. On behalf of five media companies, the Recording Industry Association of America sued Napster in December 1999, claiming the website and Fanning's program were facilitating the theft of intellectual property. Most likely the blueprint for the future of the entertainment industry will be drawn from this ruling. And most likely—no matter what lower courts may rule along the way—the dispute will finally be resolved by the Supreme Court.

ATLAS HUGGED **Fanning and Middelhoff pose like buds**

whole wave of start-ups dedicated to what has become known as P2P, or peer-to-peer, client-based Internet software. Among Napster's revolutionary qualities is that it allows computer users to exchange files directly, avoiding server bottlenecks. Only Napster's index and directory reside on a central server; the files are actually transferred via various protocols directly from user to user. That means that no copyrighted material is ever in Napster's possession, as its lawyers are happy to remind you.

There are myriad—and totally legal—possibilities for P2P applications, from swapping dense technical files through a local-area network (something scientists at the Centers for Disease Control and Prevention are looking into) to replacing corporate servers with P2P systems for business applications. The fledgling network offers a new space for creating ideas and transferring them faster, more freely, more widely than ever before.

But what if someone owns the right to that fast-moving content? That's the issue behind the legal proceedings that will determine the future of digital music and perhaps the future of all industries that trade in intellectual property. Attorneys for the record industry have subpoenaed Fanning's e-mails and taken depositions from him, his uncle and other early Napster employees. The plaintiffs contend that Napster is guilty of something called tributary copyright infringement, which means Napster is being accused not of violating copyright itself but of contributing to and facilitating other people's infringement.

Which really means that if consumers are not guilty of breaking the law, then Napster cannot be found guilty. The issue may come down to what Napster lead attorney David Boies, who successfully prosecuted the Department of Justice's case against Microsoft, describes as "the definition of commercial or noncommercial uses." It is perfectly legal for consumers to copy music for their own (noncommercial) enjoyment. Congress has even declared, in the Audio Home Recording Act of 1992, that it is legal to make

Legal issues aside, Fanning's program already ranks among the greatest Internet applications ever, up there with e-mail and instant messaging. In terms of users, the Napster site is the fastest growing in history: it passed the 25 million mark after less than a year of operation. And, as Fanning predicted, his program does everything a Web application ought to do: it builds community, it breaks down barriers, it is viral, it is scalable, it disintermediates (removes the middleman)—and, oh yeah, it may be illegal.

For its users, Napster has become another appliance, like a toaster or washing machine. Call it the music appliance: log on, download, play songs. The simplicity of the program is part of its genius: a happy accident, since Fanning took only three months to write the source code. He says he didn't have time to make it more complicated.

The pressure he felt came from a pent-up demand for digital music in the late '90s that was going largely unsatisfied. Before Napster, downloading music was so cumbersome it was mostly relegated to college students with access to fast pipes and techno geeks sufficiently driven to search the Net for the latest Phish bootlegs. The digital-music standard MP3 made it possible to take songs from a CD and "rip," or convert, them into MP3 files, usually in violation of copyright. But even in the mid-'90s, when faster computers and high-bandwidth connections to the Internet made it possible to seek and find MP3 files, ripping CDs was a tedious process.

Then, as if everyone had just been waiting for it, Napster—some kid's big idea—appeared. In creating Napster, Fanning not only transformed the music business but also helped launch a new programming movement—and a

> ## Suddenly we could all become music pirates—because it was just so easy to swap the files

recordings and lend them to others, provided it is not done for commercial ends. It is unlawful, of course, if it's done for profit. "The law does not distinguish between large-scale and small-scale sharing or lending," insists Boies.

The record labels certainly disagree, and they sought an injunction to shut down Napster, which U.S. District Judge Marilyn Patel granted in July. Although it was immediately stayed by federal appeals judges, the same injunction will be ruled on by a federal court, and then, most observers believe, by the Supreme Court.

The criterion for granting an injunction is, among other things, that the plaintiff should be able to prove that irreparable harm is going to occur between now and the completion of the case. That may not be so easy. Although Napster might seem to be taking sales away from the record companies, CD sales have actually increased since Napster began—by $500 million in 2000 alone.

Then, just as Napster was tied up in court, Fanning complicated the issue by deciding to hitch his wagon to the star of one of the world's biggest media giants. In early November Napster announced it would partner with Bertelsmann, the German behemoth that began 150 years ago as a religious-hymnal publisher. No matter how it benefits (or maybe damages) both sides, the deal vaulted the global entertainment industry into a new arena, where the game may well be played by the freewheeling rules of the Internet, not by those of media companies.

UNDER THE AGREEMENT, NAPSTER SAID IT WOULD develop a business model that would resolve the dispute over intellectual property by paying record companies and performers for their music. To help the tiny company (53 employees) overcome the hurdles involved, Bertelsmann opened a $50 million line of credit for Napster. The Germans agreed that once the new model is in place, Bertelsmann's subsidiary BMG Entertainment would make its music catalog available online and drop out of the copyright suit. Bertelsmann's boss Thomas Middelhoff worked the phones to persuade his counterparts at major record lables to make similar deals.

Napster resides in the bloody intersection where commerce, culture and free speech collide

As for Fanning, he had reached a level of fame unprecedented for a young man who is neither a sports hero nor a pop star. He appeared on the cover of FORTUNE, *BusinessWeek*, *Forbes* and the *Industry Standard*. He introduced Britney Spears at the MTV video awards. But he has been few fans among musicians: rockers like Metallica virulently scorned the software guru as a New Age thief.

Meanwhile, there is another big idea he is dying to work out, another program he has been tinkering with that, he says, could be bigger than Napster. He dreams of recapturing those days back in Hull. Back then, he thought he would just write the application and set it free—his name would be embedded deep in the source code and known only to other hackers (and to old friends who knew him by his childhood nickname, Napster, for his curly hair). He misses that simple time, before magazine covers and TV interviews and Britney Spears and having to put on a goofy black suit and necktie to appear in court. ∎

KEN HIVELY—LA TIMES—RETNA USA

METALLICA **The hardcore band is an outspoken opponent of Napster, but some artists have embraced its swap-meet vibe**

The Love Bug

It came, it flattered—and then it broke your computer's heart

ANNE GUEPIERE WORKS IN THE HONG KONG OFFICE of a large U.S. company. At about 4 o'clock on a Thursday in May, she received an e-mail. It seemed innocuous enough. The subject line read ILOVEYOU. With it came an attached file labeled LOVE-LETTER-FOR-YOU.TXT.VBS. How nice. Just a couple of clicks, and her curiosity would be satisfied.

Too late. "I didn't even read the 'ILOVEYOU' part," recalls Guepiere, whom history would record as, if not Patient Zero, then surely one of the earliest victims in a global pandemic. "Only when I opened [the attachment] did I realize there was a problem." Indeed, it was a bigger problem than anybody, probably even its mischievous creator, could have imagined as computers everywhere tumbled like so many dominoes. Once again that scourge of the Internet age—a computer virus—had struck. Silently, lethally, without even a hint of a warning fever, it raced around the world at light speed, clogging communications and bringing both commerce and politics to a halt.

Because of its implicit, fatally attractive message—Oh, just give me a glance; I bear friendly tidings from a loving admirer!—headline writers immediately (and irresistibly) nicknamed it the Love Bug. But there was nothing lovable about it. Before it spent itself—in its first incarnation, it was truly a 24-hour virus—it would affect tens of millions of computers, eventually ring up a toll as high as $10 billion in lost work hours and reopen troubling questions about the safety and security of our vital electronic lifelines. By almost any measure, it was the most damaging virus ever, with at least three times the byte—as more than one punster put it—of Melissa, 1999's electronic femme fatale.

Like a real Asian influenza, the virus first emerged in Hong Kong. From there it sped westward with the sun, lying silently in wait in corporate e-mail accounts until unsuspecting office denizens punched in, logged on and double-clicked on the file. On the other side of the world, in the offices of the German newspaper *Abendblatt* in Hamburg, system administrators watched in horror as the virus gobbled up 2,000 digital photographs in their archives. In Belgium ATMs were disabled, leaving citizens cashless. In Paris cosmetics maker L'Oreal shut down its e-mail servers. As much as 70% of the computers in Germany, the Netherlands and Sweden were laid low. Even Microsoft, whose software was the Love Bug's special target, got so badly battered that it severed outside e-mail links at its Redmond, Wash., headquarters.

NOTHING LOVING ABOUT THIS BUG

Disguised as a friendly e-mail message proclaiming ILOVEYOU, a computer virus or worm raced around the world in May, creating havoc estimated at as high as $10 billion. Replicating as it went, the Love Bug infected untold millions of computers, erased data, including precious photo and music files, and paralyzed electronic communications for countless people, from members of Britain's Parliament to offices on Capitol Hill, to major corporations like Ford and Lucent.

TIME Diagram by Joe Lertola and Ed Gabel

1 First discovered in the files of an Internet service provider in the Philippine city of Quezon, the virus appeared successively in Asia, Europe and the Americas

Sent: Thu 5/4/00 John Doe
From: Jane Smith
To:
Subject: ILOVEYOU
Kindly check the attached LOVELETTER

The virus is believed to have spread westward from the Philippines

THE PANDEMIC

■ **Hong Kong** businesses are hit by a sweeping virus attack, crippling communications

■ **In Europe**, as many as 70% of Germany's computers are hit, including those at electronics giant Siemens

■ **In London** the House of Commons shuts down its e-mail to halt the bug

■ **The virus sweeps** Washington, hitting the Pentagon, State Department and NASA. Bush headquarters are bitten by the bug

HOW IT SPREAD
Within hours, the virus hit thousands of computers around the world, attacking their systems as soon as users opened their e-mail

Governments too felt the pain. In London, Parliament shut down its servers before the Love Bug's assault. The Yanks didn't do any better. On Capitol Hill, crippled e-mail systems forced an atypical silence in the halls of Congress, as well as some unusual scrambling. The bug infected 80% of all federal agencies, including both the Defense and State departments, leaving them temporarily out of e-mail contact with their far-flung outposts. The virus corrupted no fewer than four classified, internal Defense Department e-mail systems.

Fiendishly created, the Love Bug struck with a one-two punch. Once you clicked open that fatal attachment and activated its deadly code, the virus either erased or moved a wide range of data files. It singled out in particular so-called http://.jpgs and MP3s—digital pictures and music—and, like a natural virus, replaced them with identical copies of itself. Then, if it found the Microsoft Outlook Express e-mail program on your computer, it raided the program's address book and sent copies of itself to everyone on that list. (The more innocent Melissa grabbed only the first 50 names.) Technically, this two-pronged approach made the Love Bug both a virus and a worm; it was a virus because it bred on a host computer's hard drive and a worm because it also reproduced over a network.

As these replicated messages spread, they created monumental jams, slowing Internet traffic to a crawl. And they quickly attracted the attention of virus hunters around the world. Their first challenge: nailing the bug's digital fingerprint. The second challenge: identifying the perpetrator. Clues weren't hard to find. Embedded in the virus' code—or blueprint—were the alias "spyder," an e-mail address and the words "Manila, Philippines." The code also yielded a short sentence in broken English that provided at least the shadow of a motive: "I hate go to school." Was the world facing a cyber-Columbine? By 4:30 a.m. Eastern time, the virus fighters had linked the Love Bug to a website hosted by Sky Internet, an Internet-service provider based in Quezon, the Philippines. They persuaded the ISP to close down the site, but the Love Bug kept on spreading.

Within a week, the criminal Cupid came forward. A skinny 23-year-old Filipino computer student, Onel de Guzman, came out of hiding for a press conference at which he came close to admitting responsibility for the Love Bug. Did he unleash the virus? "It is possible," admitted de Guzman, who sported dark glasses and covered his face with a handkerchief. In late June, Philippine authorities arrested de Guzman and charged him with theft and fraud, saying he had stolen the passwords that allowed him to upload the bug. But the alleged instigator skated in August, when the case was dismissed for lack of evidence.

The Love Bug may be history—but what kind of future is there for an Internet so fragile that a cobbled-together program can bring it to its knees? Clearly, the Internet is still not ready for prime time—and the next outbreak could be worse. Imagine what a well-designed Love Bug could do when we have become even more dependent on computer networks and those networks are wireless. An Internet outage could keep us not only from sending e-mail but also from gassing up the car or depositing our paychecks.

The medium may be new, but human nature hasn't changed: whatever firewalls the virus hunters come up with, virus writers will always find a way around them. What the Love Bug attack teaches us is that if we want to become a connected society, it is not enough to defend our own backyard (i.e., our own PC). We have to clean up the streets and build an Internet in which it is safe for us to stay as intimately linked as we clearly want to be. ■

2 Arriving at a computer as an e-mail message, the virus announces itself with the words ILOVEYOU with an attachment. Click twice and it is activated on your system

3 The bug begins a series of actions that can cripple your computer. If you have Outlook Express e-mail, it will replicate itself every time you send new mail or go online

INSTALLS ITSELF ON COMPUTER'S HARD DRIVE
Infects the operating system and settings that run Windows, becoming active every time the computer is restarted

REPLACES FILES WITH A COPY OF ITSELF
Scans the infected disk looking for particular files, like photos (.jpg) and music (MP3), and overwrites them

Pict.jpg   Pict.jpg.vbs

MODIFIES INTERNET EXPLORER START-UP PAGE
Creates a new home page for the browser with a program that will steal passwords and e-mail them to the virus writer

WHY IT ONLY AFFECTS PCS
The popularity of Microsoft Windows, which runs on 9 out of 10 computers, makes PCs particularly inviting targets

SENDS COPIES OF ITSELF VIA E-MAIL AND CHAT ROOMS
Hijacks Outlook addresses and sends them infected e-mails. It can also relay the virus when you enter a chat room

COURTESY HAWORTH

ON A ROLL The Drift workstation and tricycle desk from design firm Haworth aim to organize your work better while you roam

The Office Gets a High-Tech Face-lift

As the workplace enters the future, technology merges with the furniture

MILLIONS OF TELECOMMUTERS DON'T HAVE OFFICES in the old-fashioned sense: they set up quarters wherever they set down their laptops. "Today's office is an aging concept, 150 years old, that people have been hanging on to," argues Stevan Alburty, who runs WorkVirtual, an office-consulting shop. It's only a matter of time, telecommuting true believers claim, before city skyscrapers and suburban office parks are abandoned altogether, left as archaeological curiosities for the future.

Well, don't start your dig just yet. PCs may be great for solitary pursuits. But as long as co-workers need to brainstorm, bat around ideas and just plain gossip, they will always return to the water cooler, choosing a little face-to-face time over e-mail and the Web.

Clueless corporations, which in the past have approached the office as a storage site for people and paper, are only just starting to think outside the cubicle, imagining workspaces that foster interaction, not isolation. Soon the standard-issue, gloomy maze of hallways and bullpens of today may be replaced by a wide range of office setups

that, just like the New Economy, stress customization over mass appeal. Employees should be able to personalize their workspaces and constantly reconfigure their surroundings to suit their changing needs.

So what might this workers' paradise look and feel like? Well, for starters, technology will be "invisible but unavoidable," as Bob Arko of industrial designer IDEO puts it. The tangled cables that snake through today's offices will disappear, replaced by wireless systems that zap voice, data and video through the air. Smart materials could make any surface or gadget feel like wood one day and metal the next. Intelligent chairs might conform to your posture, offering a much needed back rub in the process.

The harsh right angles and rigid grid layout so despised by hapless cubicle-ites are also likely to vanish. Instead, workers might find themselves in a tentlike structure with a retractable roof, pitched right in the middle of a vast, open commons area. Screens stretching from poles could shift from transparent to opaque, depending on your mood and need for privacy. Don't worry about the noise from your next-door neighbor; acoustics technology can block that out. And don't fret about fighting for a window office either; with walls of flat-screen monitors raining down images and data from all directions, you will be able to enjoy any number of stunning virtual views from your cockpit. To chat with a co-worker a continent away, just call him or her on a lifelike, 3-D videoconferencing system. If you need to get busy on a project with a few of your colleagues, simply fold up your movable workstation—and get both yourself and your ideas rolling. ∎

READING, WRITING AND RAM **Laptops appear to be powerful tools for learning**

An Apple for the Student?

Should grade schools buy laptop computers for every kid? Don't laugh: when a Connecticut school tried it, disciplinary suspensions went down 80%, while scores on state achievement tests went up 35%. In April the New York City board of education voted to create an educational Internet portal, which they said would make money by selling ads and licensing e-commerce sites, reaping profits that would help buy laptops for each of their system's 87,000 fourth-graders. Within nine years, all city students in Grades 4 and higher should have their own computers.

Sony Plays the Grinch

The game of the year? Sony's PlayStation2, if you could get one. Sony rolled out 500,000 of the $299

PARK **Taking the Net to the street**

black boxes in stores across the U.S. in October—mysteriously down from a promised one million. Sony has sold a mind-boggling 75 million first-generation PlayStations, and the PS2 is the first salvo in a high-stakes platform war with Microsoft, Sega and Nintendo to dominate the next generation of electronic games. The glitchy rollout (or demand-builder?) was a cruel blow to parents who had promised Junior a new PS2 for the holidays.

**PLAYSTATION2
Gotta have it!**

A Dotcom that Delivers

Here's a fantasy: you order a book on the Web, and an hour later it's delivered to your door by bicycle messenger. Yet that's not a fantasy for 300,000 customers in 12 cities who use Kozmo.com, a one-hour urban delivery service that lets people place orders online and receive them by messenger—with no delivery fee. The brainchild of Joseph Park, left, Kozmo started strong, but as the New Economy began to founder, the company posted a loss of $26 million in 1999 and later laid off 10% of its 3,300 employees. Park, 28, claims that Kozmo's outlook is just fine—but in his biz you're always spinning.

People

Long Live the e-King

It was a horror show for the Gutenberg types: Stephen King brought instant mass respectability to the world of online publishing in March by premiering his new story, *Riding the Bullet,* exclusively on the Net. The experiment caused a near meltdown of the servers that delivered the $2.50, 66-page novella to more than 400,000 people the first day.

Flush with his success, King went on to publish another new work, *The Plant,* only on his own website. The book was released in installments, each of which could be downloaded without any special software. The author was counting on readers to pay him $1 per installment using the honor system. "My friends," King boasted on the site, "we have a chance to become Big Publishing's worst nightmare." But he toned down the Tom Paine rhetoric when the number of fees proffered for the story didn't come close to matching the number of copies downloaded.

Even so, Big Publishing was soon riding with the King on the accelerating e-book bullet. Time Warner and McGraw-Hill created e-book divisions, and Simon & Schuster announced plans to publish an entire lineup of original e-books from authors as diverse as former President Jimmy Carter and gonzo scribe Hunter S. Thompson. E-gad!

KING **Weaving wicked on the Web**

Johnny Allen Wade

Kathy Cagle Leinen

Doris Higgin

John A. Youngblood

Class

Claudette (Duke)

These bronze-and-glass chairs are part of a grouping of 168 chairs that honors those who died in the bombing of the Alfred P. Murrah Federal Building in Oklahoma City on April 19, 1995. The memorial, created by the Butzer Design Partnership, opened in April

Steve Liss for TIME

OBB COUNTY, GA. MAY 11, 2000. IT'S A THURSDAY morning, and 18-year-old "Karen" and five pals decide to go for it. They skip first period and sneak into the woods near their upscale high school. One of them takes out six rolls—six ecstasy pills—and they each swallow one. Then they're back to school, flying on a drug they once used only on weekends. Now they smile stupid gelatinous smiles at one another, even as high school passes them by. That night they will all go out and drop more ecstasy, rolling into the early hours of another school day. It's rare that anyone would take ecstasy so often—it's not physically addictive—but teenagers everywhere have begun experimenting with it. "The cliques are pretty big in my school," Karen says, "and every clique does it."

Grand Rapids, Mich. May 1997. Sue and Shane Stevens have sent the three kids away for the weekend. They have locked the doors and hidden the car so no one will bug them. Tonight they hope to talk about Shane's cancer, a topic they have mostly avoided for years. It has eaten away at their marriage just as it corrodes his kidney. A friend has recommended that they take ecstasy, except he calls it MDMA and says therapists used it 20 years ago to get people to discuss difficult topics. And, in fact, after

Rave New World

Ecstasy, the "hug drug" that powers all-night raves, is giving pop culture a jolt

tonight, Sue and Shane will open up, and Sue will come to believe MDMA is prolonging her marriage—and perhaps Shane's life.

Suddenly people all over the country are talking about "ecstasy" as if it were something other than what an eight-year-old feels at Disney World. Occasionally the trickle from the fringe to the heartland turns into a slipstream, and that seems to have happened with the heart-pulsing, mildly psychedelic drug called ecstasy, or "e".

Law enforcers are coming across gigantic stashes of ecstasy in places where it was rarely seen. In January 2000 some 30 people were arrested in New Orleans for distributing the drug. In March in Providence, R.I., a seven-month investigation into ecstasy dealing ended with the arrest of 23. In bigger cities, the trade has exploded. In December 1999 the U.S. Customs Service discovered 100 lbs. of ecstasy shipped from France through the FedEx headquarters in Memphis. The agents followed the drug's intended trail to Los Angeles and found a staggering 1.2 million tablets, worth $30 million.

The busts have had little effect. Nationwide, customs officers seized ecstasy at a much faster rate in 2000 than they had in 1999; in 1997, they seized just 400,000 hits. In a 1998 survey, 8% of high school seniors said they had

GLOW WITH THE FLOW A dancer with glow sticks, one of many sensory stimulants ravers favor

SCOTT HOUSTON—CORBIS SYGMA FOR TIME

tried e, up from 5.8% the year before. In New York City, according to another survey, 1 in 4 adolescents has tried ecstasy. So much e is coming into the U.S. that the Customs Service has created a special ecstasy command center and is training 13 more dogs to sniff out the drug.

Simple reasons lie behind the drug's popularity among sellers and users. E is cheap to make, easy to distribute and consume—no dirty syringes or passé coke spoons needed, thanks—and it has a reputation for being fun. E's euphoria may be chemically manufactured, but it feels no less real to users.

 IS CALLED THE HUG DRUG BECAUSE IT FOSTERS gooey, rather gauche expressions of empathy from users. Students at Northern Arizona University in Flagstaff reminisced to TIME about melting into "cuddle puddles"—groups of students who massage and embrace on the dance floor. The skin feels tremblingly alive when caressed. "Feathers, toys, lotions, anything," gurgled "Katrina," then 23, and a student at N.A.U. "A guy touching your skin with a cold drink. It's delicious."

Though often cut with other drugs, ecstasy pills are at least intended to be a substance called MDMA (and known to chemists as methylenedioxymethamphetamine). MDMA is pharmacologically related to amphetamines and mescaline, but it doesn't produce the nervy, wired feeling that can accompany speed or the confusion of a purer psychedelic like LSD. It doesn't generate addictive cravings. Treatment admissions for drugs of its type still account for less than 1% of the total of such cases.

In fact, e's popularity is largely due to its lack of noticeable downsides. It's possible to overdose on ecstasy, but even police agree that the drug isn't like heroin or crack in terms of short-term dangers. Most problems are attributable to dehydration among novices who don't drink water. However, another club drug, GHB—which is also known as "Liquid X," though it's chemically unrelated to ecstasy (sometimes called "x" as well as e)—can easily cause coma and death.

MDMA was first synthesized in 1912, but the big experiments with it didn't begin until the 1970s, when a group of psychologists rediscovered it as a tool for therapy. By the early '80s, the drug—still perfectly legal—was sold openly in bars and clubs. But at the time a scientific debate had begun—and continues today—about whether MDMA can cause long-term brain damage. In 1985, on the basis of preliminary data about its harmfulness, the DEA used its discretionary power to outlaw MDMA. A group of therapists sued, but after a three-year court battle, the DEA won the right to ban the drug permanently.

So why is it upon us again? Partly because the debate about MDMA's harmfulness has never been resolved. Johns Hopkins neurologist George Ricaurte has concluded in several animal studies and one human study that MDMA can damage a particular group of brain nerve cells. But he wants more research. Ricaurte says his work has never shown that the damage to the affected cells has any visible effect on "the vast majority of people who have experimented with MDMA." The debate has now found its way onto the Web, where the old therapist crowd behind MDMA has become active. The sites are populated mostly by young users, however, "rave" kids who blindly praise the drug and the blissful high it induces.

And what is a rave? Simply defined, it is a party—often an all-night-long party—at which some form of elec-

Suddenly people all over the country are talking about "ecstasy" as though

"THE NOD" Dancing at an all-night rave in Washington

tronic, or "techno," music is played, usually by a deejay. A rave can be as small as 25 people or larger than 25,000. And while raves have been around for a decade, the rituals, visuals and sounds associated with raves have recently started to exert a potent influence on pop music, advertising and even computer games. Films about raves include the comedies *Groove* and *Human Traffic* and the documentaries *Better Living Through Circuitry* and *Rise*, a study of the rave scene in New Orleans.

Raves have traditionally been held in venues without permits or permission, giving them an outlaw allure. Today, however, an increasing number of raves are legal ones, and places like Twilo in New York City specialize in re-creating the rave feel in legitimate clubs. "The New York club scene was not about music until Twilo opened," says Paul van Dyk, a popular deejay who specializes in trance—a soft, transporting form of techno and one of the genre's many, many offshoots.

KIDDIE CORPS Ravers are often entranced with doodads from childhood; pacifiers and plastic beads are popular gear

ere something other than what an eight-year-old experiences at Disney World

RAVERS OFTEN WEAR LOOSE, WIDE-LEGGED JEANS that flare out at the bottom. Knickknacks from childhood, like suckers, pacifiers and dolls, are common accessories. Dancers, sweating to the music all night, often carry bottles of water to battle dehydration, which can be aggravated by ecstasy. Attendees sometimes dress in layers so clothes can be stripped off if the going gets hot, and flexible glow sticks are popular. One sound you will hear if the party's going right: a communal whoop of approval when the deejay starts riding a good groove. In the movie *Groove*, the filmmakers refer to that connection between deejay and dancer, between promoter and satisfied raver, as "the nod." Many rave promoters and deejays don't do it for the money. They do it for the nod.

First we had the Beat Generation; now we have the Beats-per-Minute Generation. Rave iconography is already being co-opted by Madison Avenue, which has learned all about digging up the underground and selling the dirt. TV ads for Toyota's Echo have the trippy look and feel of rave flyers; Coke commercials show flipped-out dancers and urge us to "enjoy" (cola, we presume, rather than ecstasy). Rave fave Moby, a deejay turned electronic musician, got Madison Avenue's nod: every track on his popular album *Play* was licensed, popping up in ads for *Party of Five*, movies like *The Beach* and commercials for Nissan's Altima sedan and Quest minivan. Donna Karan's DKNY label plans to use deejay John Digweed's song *Heaven Scent* to promote a fragrance.

Rave on: in the first year of the new millennium, Americans are in love with ecstasy. "New York used to be a meat-and-potatoes drug town—heroin, coke and pot," says John Silbering, a former narcotics prosecutor who works for the Tunnel, a big New York City nightclub. "Today we no longer find coke or heroin among the young. It's always ecstasy." ■

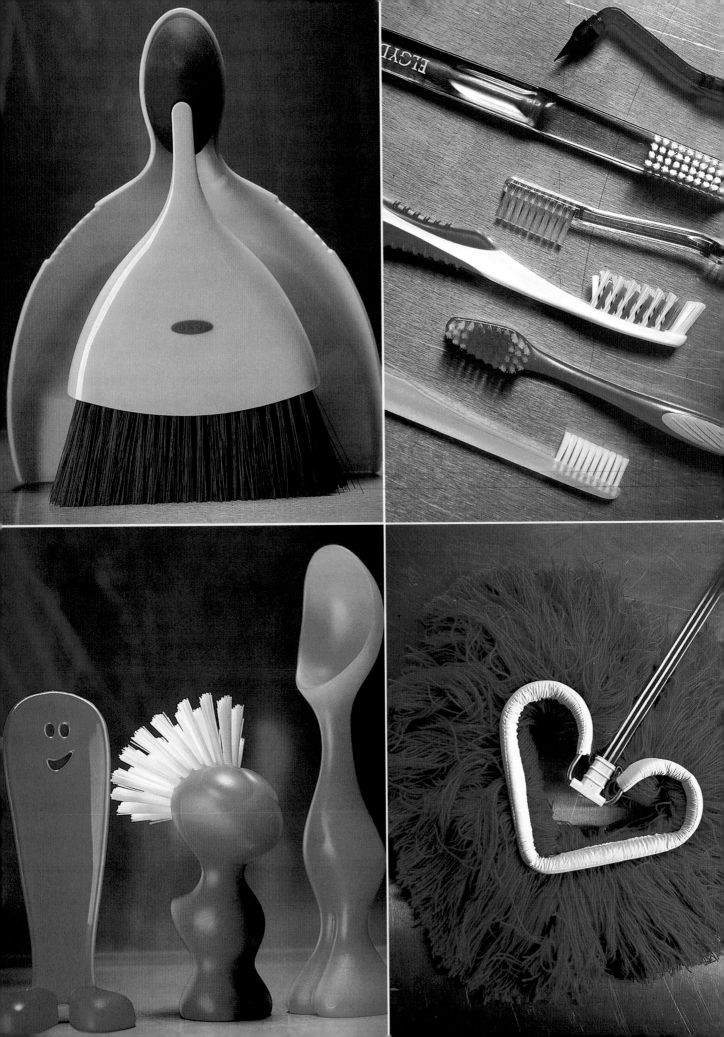

B ACK IN 1960, A DUTCH CULTURAL CRITIC NAMED Constant Nieuwenhuys predicted that someday we would all become architects. Stuck in a world where everything looked the same, he argued, we would be so alienated from our environment by technology that we would constantly redesign the space around us just to recover the joy of living.

Nieuwenhuys was wrong about only one thing. We're not alienated at all. Here we are, roaring into the 21st century, powered by the longest economic boom in U.S. history, wired to the Web and to one another, thirstily consuming new technology even before we know how to use it. In this frenzy of perpetual motion, we want to re-create the space around us, not only as our joy but also because we can, and because that way it's our space. We're snapping up translucent blueberry-tinted computers, bubble cars and little chrome cell phones as fast as they can be produced. We're fully employed, and we want something to show for it, even if we're not Internet billionaires. So where design used to be considered vaguely precious, the province of the Sub-Zero-owning élite, it's now available to all—from the crowd that shops at Target

instance, not only helped save Apple but also has inspired a raft of whimsically styled, low-cost personal computers from firms like Dell, Gateway and Compaq. The new Beetle rescued Volkswagen's image and became a catalyst for change in the auto business. Carmakers are finally putting a premium on how their products look because they know that otherwise we won't buy them anymore.

So it is with makers of just about everything. "When industries are competing at equal price and functionality, design is the only differential that matters," says Dziersk, echoing the credo first spouted in the '30s by Raymond Loewy, father of industrial design. Loewy was the man who gave America the Lucky Strike pack and the sleek Greyhound bus, and when he added a flourish to the Coldspot refrigerator, to make it look a little more streamlined than its 1934 competitors, Sears' sales skyrocketed.

Loewy used to say the most beautiful curve was a rising sales graph, and that notion has driven design since he was in shorts. Good design married commerce during the Great Depression, and Loewy's career took off then because he made products irresistible at a time when nobody had the means to pay for anything. In the '50s,

HAUTE DESIGN

Function is out. Form is in. From radios to toothbrushes to cars, Americans are discovering the delights of "commodity chic" and embracing a new wave of style

to those aesthetes who can pick out an Enzo Mari at 20 paces. If we learned anything from the barbaric old '80s, we learned that more is not enough. We want better—or at least better looking.

Meet the new design economy—the crossroads where prosperity and technology meet culture and marketing. These days efficient manufacturing and intense competition have made "commodity chic" not just affordable but also mandatory. Americans are likely to appreciate style when they see it and demand it when they don't, whether in boutique hotels or kitchen scrub brushes. "Design is being democratized," says Karim Rashid, designer of the Oh chair by Umbra and winner of a 1999 George Nelson award for breakthrough furniture design. "Our entire physical landscape has improved, and that makes people more critical as an audience." And more willing. Says Mark Dziersk, president of the Industrial Designers Society of America: "This is the new Golden Age of design."

Make that the Platinum Age. Suddenly, design has become big Big Business. Nobody is quite sure how big, but just consider that Americans spent some $6 trillion on goods and services last year, and roughly one-fifth of it went into buying stuff for their homes. The stunning success of the colorful (read: No more beige!) iMac, for

Charles and Ray Eames led a cohort of Californians who used postwar manufacturing capacity to create sleek, efficient domestic environs. In the '60s, however, industrial design seemed to lose its way and ended up in the mire of an American consumer sensibility that simply wanted more products for less money, from which it began to emerge only in the '90s.

Now, instead of one Raymond Loewy, the design world is humming with an eclectic mix of impresarios and entrepreneurs intent on earning a living from making the beautiful things in your life. There are big corporate players, like Sony and Ford and Philips, the European electronics consortium. There are architects and designers—iconoclasts like Philippe Starck and young upstarts like Jasper Morrison or Marc Newson. And of course there's Martha Stewart, who has parlayed her sense of style into a billion-dollar role as America's spokeswoman for taste. Martha's line of home furnishings helped wipe the red ink off the bottom line of the discount chain K Mart.

America's housing-construction boom has reached historic proportions, and people need to fill those new homes with stuff that defines who they are. An expensive designer couch used to confer status; now it's important to have something that's personal, whether it's from the

SMILE! An Alessi bottle opener works with a grin

flea market or B&B Italia. Like the Mosquito Table, which looks like an aircraft wing. Or the Conrad chair, made from something called Bora Bora bark.

Entrepreneurs are thriving on people's delight in design. The clothes may have made the man in ancient times, but now the man carries an iBook, a magnesium-encased Sony Vaio or a sleek black Apple G3. It's in our tools too. Do you use the cool new Husqvarna mower or Fluke Corp.'s i410 clamp meter? And your bathroom: one of the hottest current pieces of furniture is the all-stainless-steel toilet (yes, including the seat) designed originally for use in prisons.

Ironically, the design revolution has been given a leg up by not-so-special stores like Pottery Barn and Ikea, which descended on Middle America in the mid-'90s. Beginning with the premise that you didn't have to be an aficionado or hire an interior designer to have a good-looking life, they made do-it-yourself decorating safe. Neither too expensive nor too outlandish, these stores offered a way to dodge those thorny design decisions ("Can I like a black leather couch and Shaker armchairs?") and still have a space that wasn't bland. Chains like Pottery Barn, which accounted for two-thirds of parent Williams-Sonoma's sales growth in 1999, raised the bar on good design. If any fool could put together a stylin' home at his local mall, what excuse could you have for owning such a lame-looking couch? More important, why should a cool-looking couch cost so much?

The answer to that question is right down the road, at one of the new Target stores springing up around the country. The champion of America's new design democracy used to be style-blind. Then Target's executives recognized that competing just on price with the likes of Wal-Mart was a losing proposition. So the store was re-invented with a simple formula: get a big-name designer to do $20 knockoffs of the same stuff he or she designed for the SoHo sophisticates. Thus Michael Graves, known for his work for upscale design firms like Italy's Alessi, is supplying Target with stainless-steel teakettles, blocky

wood patio furniture and plump-handled spatulas. The chain has enjoyed double-digit sales growth since Graves' products hit the store. Now Graves has been joined by the doyen of design, Philippe Starck, another Alessi regular. Says Dziersk: "This is the principle that began with the Bauhaus: everyone should have access to beautiful things."

We have technology to thank for that access. Computerization and new materials have made production of just about anything cheaper and more efficient, and quality easier to maintain. The combination means that form no longer has to follow function for a product to be profitable. Toyota can afford to gamble on a quirky-looking car like the new Echo, jam it with extras and sell it for less than $10,500. Sony miraculously rescued its

ROBERT CLARK FOR TIME (2)

SAY CHEESE! A streamlined camera for the digital age

personal-computer business with the ultra-slim Vaio, a silver-and-purple beauty that does little more than any other laptop; it just looks and feels better.

Nothing highlights the technological revolution better than plastics, which were long viewed as cheap and ugly. Not since the early–20th century popularity of Bakelite has plastic been so loved. Polypropylene, for instance, a plastic dating from the '50s, can be molded so smooth it is almost sensuous, and it takes dyes like silk.

Corporate demand for these new design strategies is surging. General Mills is re-examining cereal boxes, Kodak has ditched the black-box camera, Swingline has streamlined its standard stapler. Pharmaceutical companies have released a plethora of toothbrushes—ridged, twisted, tapered, with bands, dots and swirls. The same philosophy applies to dozens of products long regarded as banal—garbage cans, toilet brushes and cheese graters. They're cute, they're cheap, and they're disposable.

The question now is whether the design economy can be sustained or whether, when America's wave of prosperity recedes, we'll all edge back to plain-vanilla functionality. If he were around, Raymond Loewy would remind us that he got his start during the Great Depression, so perhaps the real design revolution is still to come. If so, Constant Nieuwenhuys is looking more prophetic than ever. ■

RALF-FINN HESTOFT—SABA FOR TIME

VROOM Ford's coy, retro-futuristic concept car

ANDREW LICHTENSTEIN—CORBIS SYGMA

FAD OF THE YEAR **A scooter-powered kid displays the new art of urban surfing**

Small Wheels, Big Deal

Rollerblades are old news—they reek of the 20th century. Citizens of the new millennium like to get mobile with an alternate mode of self-propulsion. Scooters, those nostalgic vehicles of 1950s suburban youth, were updated and repackaged in 2000 and soon were embraced by everyone from metropolitan commuters to thrill-seeking teens to those who occasionally found walking too great an inconvenience. Without question, it was the year's hottest fad.

In its essentials, the new scooter is much like the old: a board on two wheels, steered with handlebars and propelled by foot. The new versions, however, are made from lightweight metals, sport faster and more shock-absorbent wheels, are narrow enough to thread through congested sidewalks and have collapsible steering columns for portability. The top-selling Razor, retailing for around $119, weighs about 6 lbs.; folded, it can fit into a backpack. Unlike a bike, it requires no lock or parking space and incurs no hostile stares when crammed on a commuter train at rush hour. Ah, simplicity.

Justice in Birmingham?

The bombing of the 16th Street Baptist Church in Birmingham, Ala., in 1963 was one of the most horrific crimes of the civil rights era: it killed four black girls at Sunday school. For years no one was charged in the case, until Robert E. Chambliss was convicted of murder in 1977. He died in jail in 1985. In May Alabama took a long stride toward justice when Bobby Frank Cherry, 69, and Thomas E. Blanton Jr., 61, both former Ku Klux Klansmen long suspected in the crime, were indicted by a grand jury for helping Chambliss commit the crime. Both men maintain they are innocent.

AP/WIDE WORLD

RUINS **After the church bombing in 1963**

The Stories of O

Alas, poor Oprah! She has fewer and fewer worlds left to conquer. The doyenne of daytime TV dazzled the magazine world in 2000 with the splashiest debut since ... well, no one could recall its like. *O: The Oprah Magazine,* a joint venture of Oprah's Harpo Entertainment Group and Hearst Magazines, hit newsstands in the spring, and it is an Oprah experience from start to finish. In a personal guarantee of the brand, Oprah graces every cover. The pages are a literary experience consistent with her TV show: heartfelt, improving and mysteriously able to transform the commercial exploitation of bathos into a unique blend of self-

WINFREY **Print's new princess**

help spirituality, pop feminism and Ben Franklin optimism.

Tale after tale records the triumphs of ordinary women over poverty, traumas and racism. Not content to proffer mere voyeurism, *O* is also a workbook. Some pages have blank spaces for writing down things you'd like to change about yourself; others contain postcards with sage aphorisms, perforated and thus refrigerator-ready.

Not for everyone, perhaps, but *O* was a smash. By fall, already on its second editor (Oprah, a demanding boss, ran the New York City–based mag long-distance from Chicago), it was selling a whopping 2 million issues a month. Next stop? Well, if Hillary's a Senator ...

Sport

SHAQUILLE FOR REAL: Finally paying off on his promise, 7 ft. 1 in., 330-lb. Shaquille O'Neal, 28, powered his Los Angeles Lakers to the NBA championship over the Indianapolis Pacers and was a slam dunk for the league's MVP honor, winning by the largest margin ever

ALONE AT THE TOP

Racking up the greatest single season in the history of golf, Tiger Woods proved his only rival is Jack Nicklaus' record

J UNE 18, PEBBLE BEACH, CALIF. TIGER WOODS wins the U.S. Open, running away from the field by a record-breaking 15 strokes. In his four rounds of 65-69-71-67—a record-tying 272—Tiger led virtually from wire to wire. He had no three-putts—not one in 72 holes. When he hit a triple-bogey on Saturday, he immediately erased the mistake with three birdies.

July 23, St. Andrews, Scotland. At the Old Course, birthplace of golf, Tiger Woods wins the British Open to complete his career Grand Slam of golf's major tournaments at age 24. His 19-under-par score topped the field by eight strokes. Bulletin: Tiger three-putted one hole.

August 20, Valhalla Country Club, Louisville, Ky. In one of the most dramatic finishes in golf history, reigning champion Tiger Woods retains the PGA's Wanamaker Trophy, beating gutsy journeyman Bob May in a thrilling three-hole play-off. On the last hole of regular play, May had sunk a 15-ft. birdie putt to pull ahead of Woods. But Tiger immediately responded by nailing a tough six-footer to tie the score.

On the first hole of the play-off, Tiger drilled a 20-ft. putt for a birdie that May couldn't match.

Not a bad summer's work. But to take the measure of Tiger Woods, you have to look beyond his performance in 2000 and go back to his victory at the 1997 Masters. After conquering Augusta, Tiger studied videotapes of his play: blasting 300-yd. drives, hitting crisp iron shots right at the pins, draining putts from everywhere. And he thought, as he later told friends, My swing really sucks.

Now let's put that in perspective. Woods had joined the pro tour only seven months earlier, at age 20, and captivated the game and its fans as no rookie ever had. He had won four of the 15 PGA Tour tournaments he entered, earning $1.8 million in prize money and some $60 million in endorsement contracts from the likes of Nike and Titleist. At the Masters, against the best golfers in the world, he had virtually lapped the field, winning by a record 12 strokes. He was being hailed as the next Jack Nicklaus, who is considered the greatest golfer of all time.

And now, incredibly, Woods was going to risk it all by overhauling the swing that had brought him to this summit. He told his coach, Butch Harmon, that he wanted to make serious changes in the way he struck the ball. The history of such efforts is not auspicious. Some fine golfers—Ian Baker-Finch, Seve Ballesteros, Chip Beck—have revamped their swing and never returned to their earlier glory. What was Woods thinking?

"I knew I wasn't in the greatest positions in my swing at the Masters," Woods told TIME in 2000, looking back at his decision to alter the fundamentals of his game. "But my timing was great, so I got away with it. And I made almost every putt. You can have a wonderful week like that even when your swing isn't sound. But can you still contend in tournaments with that swing when your timing isn't as good? Will it hold up over a long period of time? The answer to those questions, with the swing I had, was no. And I wanted to change that."

In other words, Woods, already considered the best touring pro by many of his peers, was gambling that he could move his game to a dramatically high-er plane—and was willing to do whatever he thought might help him someday surpass his longtime idol, Nicklaus, as the greatest ever.

Any accounting of the traits and experiences that have shaped Tiger Woods must start with his physical gifts, his exceptional parents and his early start in golf under a series of devoted coaches. He has become, over time, eerily calm under pressure and an obsessive student of the game who reviews videotapes of old tournaments for clues about how to play each hole. He works hard at building his strength and honing his shots. But what is most remarkable about Woods is his restless drive for what the Japanese call *kaizen*, or continuous improvement. Toyota engineers will push a perfectly good assembly line until it breaks down. Then they'll find and fix the flaw and push the system again. That's *kaizen*. That's Tiger. It's also his buddy Michael Jordan, who tells Woods, "Always keep working on your game."

WHAT, ME WORRY? **Faced with the fearsome bunkers at St. Andrews, Woods managed to avoid every single one**

 "YOU DA MAN!" Once reserved and aloof, the new Tiger is more confident in his game—and more open with his fans

When Tiger phoned Butch Harmon after the 1997 Masters and told him he wanted to rebuild his swing, the coach was confident his star pupil could pull it off. But he cautioned that the results wouldn't come overnight—that Woods would have to pump more iron to get stronger; that it would take months to groove the new swing; that his tournament play would get worse before it got better. Both men were aware of how such an apparent slump would be depicted by some golf commentators and fellow pros jealous of Woods' early success and fame. But Woods didn't hesitate. He and Harmon went to work in a *kaizen* sequence of 1) pounding hundreds of practice balls; 2) reviewing tapes of the swing; and 3) repeating steps 1 and 2.

The changes were intended mainly to tame Tiger, who had arrived on the tour swinging full bore on most shots. He would violently rotate his hips and shoulders on his downswing to hit prodigious tee shots. But sometimes his arms couldn't keep up with the rest of his body, and he'd yank the ball into the rough. Harmon had Woods restrict his hip turn and slow the rotation of his torso on the downswing. Tiger weakened his grip slightly, turning the back of his left hand more square to the target. And as he gained more strength in his forearms, Woods held the clubface square to the target line—with his left wrist slightly bowed—for a crucial split second longer through impact. That produced more consistently straight shots than the old swing, in which Woods rolled his wrists earlier.

The new swing is so efficient that Woods can hit the ball as far as before—when he needs to. But one goal of the makeover was to help him control the ball better, even when he dialed down the power. That payoff didn't come quickly. Woods won only one PGA Tour event during the 19 months between July 1997 and February 1999. He often got frustrated and angry—at the rough, where his drives often ended up; at the press; at the demands of his fans and sponsors. After each loss, he said he was "a better golfer" than when he was winning in early 1997. "Winning," he said, "is not always the barometer of getting better."

WOODS SAYS HE FIRST KNEW HE WAS COMING out of the tunnel on a cool evening in May 1999 on the practice ground at the gated Isleworth community where he lives, outside Orlando, Fla. Suddenly, on one swing, he sensed—for the first time in a year—that he had done exactly what he had been trying to accomplish. The motion felt natural and relaxed, and the contact solid. The ball flew high and straight. Excited, he rolled another ball into place but didn't make the same swing. Another ball. Didn't get it. Another ball. Didn't get it. Then he hit another pure shot. A couple of misses. Another pure one. And another. The good swings and shots began coming with greater frequency, like a bag of popcorn taking off in the microwave. "I was able to hit them with different clubs," he recalls, "and different shapes—fades, draws." What's more, each shot with the same club flew at the same trajectory and the same distance. He phoned coach Harmon at his Las Vegas base and said, "I think I'm back."

Woods shot a blistering 61 in the first round of his next tournament. Although he finished tied for seventh, he was thrilled because his swing felt so good. Now he could put his whole game back together: the full swing, the short chips and lobs, the putting. And the victories. He won an extraordinary 10 of 14 events during the rest of 1999 and had eight PGA Tour victories in that year, then won six in a row in late '99 and early 2000. In capturing the career Grand Slam, Woods equaled a feat accomplished by only four other men: Gene Sarazen, Ben Hogan, Gary Player and Nicklaus. And Woods did it at age 24—two years ahead of Nicklaus's pace. Tiger had taped the Golden Bear's career highlights to the headboard of his bed, and kept them in the cross hair of his ambition, since he was 10.

In 2000 Woods simply owned golf. He is now the all-time career money winner, with more than $17 million. As Ernie Els, who finished second in the first three majors this year—and second four times in 2000 to Woods alone—said, "the rest of us are playing one tournament, and there's Tiger, playing a different one."

CAN WOODS BE THE GREATEST GOLFER OF ALL TIME? Well, by the standard measure, he has to win 14 more major tournaments as a pro to pass Nicklaus' record of 18. Nicklaus and Woods say they feel a bond, and the older man has been generous with compliments and advice—for example, counseling Woods against playing so many events that he burns out. But Nicklaus is proud of his records and coy in some of his comments. For one: "Tiger is much like any other player who is at the top of his game." Translation: "Many players have a hot hand for a few seasons and then cool off. It's often a matter not of swing mechanics but of the vagaries of putting, where the eye and the touch can abandon even players with silky-looking strokes."

Adds Nicklaus: "Tiger is better than the other players by a greater margin than I was." Translation: "Who does Tiger have to beat? Els and Vijay Singh, who have won two majors each? David Duval and Phil Mickelson, who have won none? I had to beat Arnold Palmer, who won seven majors; Gary Player, who won nine; Lee Trevino, who won six; Tom Watson, who won eight." Speaking of the seasoned players he was challenged by, Nicklaus says, "I always enjoyed that. Tiger hasn't had that yet—but he will."

After Woods won the U.S. Open, TIME asked golf great Johnny Miller to assess his game. Wrote Miller: "What makes Tiger so good? He possesses a rare combination of strength, talent, brains, will. John Daly hits the ball as far as Tiger. Corey Pavin has shown as much shotmaking skill. Vijay Singh works as hard on his game. Ernie Els has as much poise under pressure. But no one combines these traits like Tiger. His long, high tee shots allow him to sail over the trees, bunkers, ponds and other obstacles that trap or deter lesser golfers. He routinely hits unreachable par-five holes in just two strokes. He can hit a soft, high

nine-iron shot into par-fours where others face more difficult shots with middle and long irons. Unlike many big hitters, Tiger has a delicate touch for the short shots around the green. And he is an excellent clutch putter … He's not just mastering his sport; he's changing the way it's played." In short, Tiger's only competition is that list of Jack's victories that may still be hanging over his bed. ∎

Tiger vs. Jack

Tiger's chasing Jack Nicklaus' records: 70 PGA Tour wins, 18 majors. How they compare at age 24:

Current	As of 1964
TOUR EARNINGS	
$17 million	$1.6 million (adjusted for inflation)
MAJOR TITLES	
5: Masters ('97), PGA ('99), U.S. Open, British Open, PGA ('00)	3: U.S. Open ('62) Masters & PGA ('63)
TOUR WINS	
21	12
U.S. AMATEUR TITLES	
3	2
YEARS ON TOUR	
5	3
TOUR EVENTS	
97	77
SCORING AVERAGE	
67.77	69.96
EARLY 9-HOLE SCORE	
48 (age 3)	51 (age 10)

BUDS **Woods and Nicklaus played together at the PGA**

DARREN CARROLL—SPORTS ILLUSTRATED

Tennis Pays Court to a Sizzling Sister Act

Venus and Serena Williams may dominate the women's game for years to come

ON TOP DOWN UNDER **Venus, left, and Serena cruised to win the doubles gold in Sydney**

GARY M. PRIOR—ALLSPORT

The smashing sibs continued their march to global supremacy in Sydney, where they made up one half of the U.S. women's team, along with Davenport and Monica Seles. The singles gold went to … yup, Venus. The doubles gold went to: Williams & Williams. "The future is now," former player turned pundit Pam Shriver declared. "They could be on top for 10 years."

They truly could be, because neither of the sisters is as good as she's going to get. Powerful as they are, their games are the least complete of any top player's. Consider Venus. Aside from a few deft drop shots against Davenport, who stood a fortnight behind the baseline, Venus' usual strategy is to hit the ball hard, then harder. She can volley but won't come to the net. Her second serve is pudding. She overhits setups and misses too many of them. Still, both sisters boast immense power and glorious athleticism. Venus hit a 121-m.p.h. serve against Serena; Pete Sampras' heater goes about 125.

There's another advantage for the Williamses. Tennis is an individual game, and they come as a team. As Hingis lamented, she often gets softened up by one, finished off by the other. Furthermore, each Williams sister derives an inner strength from being a Williams sister. "Family, religion, education and tennis are the four spokes of this family," said Shriver, who has been Venus' mentor for three years. "Sometimes tennis is fourth on the totem pole, other times tennis moves up—but I think it's in that order."

Amid the universal hosannas, trust supposedly reformed court brat John McEnroe to summon a discouraging word: the senior player, coach and commentator dissed the sisses. A London newspaper published a diatribe in which Mac accused Venus and Serena of being too "cocky" and aloof; he claimed they didn't respect their peers. McEnroe, still agog over Serena's 1999 comment that she would like to play in a men's tournament, restated his belief that many male college players and members of the seniors' tour could defeat the sisters. "Do women golfers say they could go out and beat Tiger Woods?" he asked. "Where's their humility?" Venus declined to return the volley. "I'm always honest," she said, "and the fact is that I'm a good player." Game, set, match—Williams. ∎

VENUS WILLIAMS, 20, WAS BEATING UP ON HER LITTLE sister, which is what big sisters do. But Venus is, it should be noted, a sweeter big sister than most. As she administered the thrashing on a grass court in broadly public view at Wimbledon, she was hardly merciless. She sat on her chair during changeovers and worried, "Does Serena have enough sports drink?"

Guess not. Serena, 18, sagged in the second-set tie breaker and closed with a double fault. Final score: 6-2, 7-6 (3), in a fraught semifinal match marked by mediocre tennis, great theater and almost unbearable intensity. "It's really bitter," said Venus after putting Serena out of the tournament. "But someone had to move on." She did and, in the final, beat another big-hitting Californian, defending champ Lindsay Davenport, 6-3, 7-6 (3).

In 2000 it seemed every important men's golf tournament was won by a guy named Woods, and every important women's tennis tournament went to a gal named Williams. Sure enough, only two months later, there was Venus striking a familiar pose: holding aloft the winner's platter, this time at center court at the U.S. Open. Though the draw had been seeded in hopes of setting up an all-Williams final, it didn't happen: Davenport knocked out Serena in the quarterfinals. In the next round, Venus paid Hingis back for knocking her out of the 1999 Open, shutting her down 4-6, 6-3, 7-5. Once again Venus faced Davenport in the finals, and once again she prevailed, finally picking up the Open title Serena had won the year before.

The World Series Takes the Local

The Yankees and Mets vie for bragging rights in New York City

NEW YORK, NEW YORK! IT'S A HELL OF A TOWN—AS New Yorkers are fond of reminding those poor souls not fortunate enough to dwell in the Big Apple. So when the baseball season ended and the two teams left standing were the New Yawk Yankees and the New Yawk Mets ... well, while Gothamites sank into sepia-toned reveries of the Duke vs. the Mick, Casey Stengel vs. Leo Durocher and Don Larsen's perfect game, Peoria shunned the Subway Series like a Nader-Buchanan debate.

The fall classic may have looked to Middle America like Sodom vs. Gomorrah. But for all sorts of reasons, some of them having to do with baseball, it's too bad these games didn't play west of the Hudson. It's also too bad the lordly Yankees regained their form following a late-season slump and dispatched the Mets in five games, for these two great teams deserved to go seven.

Yankees shortstop and Series MVP Derek Jeter and Mets catcher Mike Piazza are the very definition of franchise players: dramatic and fearless. The Mets' Al Leiter and Mike Hampton and the Yanks' Andy Pettitte, Roger Clemens and Orlando Hernandez are premier starting pitchers in a sport suffering a famine of starting pitchers.

There was lots of gossipy stuff to the Series too. Yankees skipper Joe Torre, who once played for and then managed the Mets until he was canned, is a cancer-surviving father figure no one dislikes—even his meddling boss, George Steinbrenner. Mets manager Bobby Valentine—once fired by George W. Bush as manager of the Texas Rangers—is a self-aggrandizing baseball "genius" few can stand. Jeter (who dates Miss Universe) and Piazza (who dates a bodacious Brazilian Playmate) are high-wattage men about town in the mold of Joe DiMaggio, while Yankees head cases Paul O'Neill and Chuck Knoblauch provided riveting entertainment of another sort: you couldn't take your eyes off them, wondering if they'd blow. (They never did—and O'Neill busted out of a dismal slump in the Series, smacking the ball at a .474 clip.) Pitchers David Cone and Doc Gooden of the defending-champ Yanks were members of the Mets championship team in 1986.

And, oh yeah, there was that little incident in the second game, when Roger Clemens lost it. Fans had been waiting for the first match-up between the Rocket and Piazza, for Clemens, who likes to throw close, had hit the Mets catcher squarely in the head with a pitch during an interleague game in July, and the Mets were spoiling for revenge. But who would have expected Clemens to conclude that the appropriate response upon fielding Piazza's splintered bat ... would be to throw it right back at the unsuspecting Met as he headed toward first? But that's what he did—you could look it up (or *see* Images).

And as for the scores ... well, the Yanks demonstrated their superiority over the Mets right away, taking the first two games at venerable Yankee Stadium in the Bronx.

Game 1 was the Series' best, a 12-inning, 4-3 cliff hanger right up there with Al vs. Dubya. Game 2 was a 6-5 Yankee romp, though the Mets redeemed themselves by coming back to score five runs in the ninth. The Mets took the third game, 4-2, at Mets Central, Shea Stadium in Queens. But after Jeter put the Mets right back in their place with a homer in the first inning in Game 4, the Yanks held on to win, 3-2. In the fifth and final game, the Yanks did what they do best: hang tough and exploit small breaks. With the game tied at 2-2 in the ninth, they converted a walk, two singles and a wild throw into two runs, enough to beat the Mets. The Bronx Aplombers had done it again. ■

PUMPED **Shortstop Jeter led the veteran Yanks to victory**

People

Phil, Shaq and Friedrich

Phil Jackson has always had an appealingly philosophical approach toward coaching basketball, one that helps him coax five NBA-size egos into performing like a marching band at full sprint. His interest in Eastern thought and Native American mysticism have increasingly informed his approach to coaching. Drawing from Buddhism, he speaks often of rejecting selfishness and egotism. In winning six championships with the Chicago Bulls, he emphasized selfless movement without the ball in a pattern known as the triangle offense. The triangle forced defenses to stretch, to cover

JACKSON **Basketball meets Buddhism**

everyone, everywhere—leaving them vulnerable to Michael Jordan.

In his first year as head coach of the long-troubled Los Angeles Lakers, Jackson, 54, faced a squad with self-images large even by NBA proportions and divided in sympathies between overhyped guard Kobe Bryant and overhyped center Shaquille O'Neal. Handing out reading assignments (Shaq got Friedrich Nietzsche's *Ecce Homo*) and urging his men to suck it up for the team rather than for themselves, the 6-ft. 8-in. former Knick brought his mojo to L.A.: at season's end, the philosopher-coach and his newly unified *Uber*-men were NBA champs.

DYNASTY **From left, Richard, Adam and Kyle Petty**

Racing's Royal Tragedy

The world of NASCAR racing can seem regal at times, for there is a long tradition of the father passing his racing smarts—and guts—along to the son. The sport is rich with dynasties, but none is more esteemed than that of Lee Petty and his family. In 1949 Lee ran in the inaugural NASCAR race; in his pit were his sons Richard and Maurice. Richard went on to become racing's king and to father Kyle, who followed his dad and grandfather onto the track. In April Kyle's son Adam became the first fourth-generation NASCAR driver. Days later, Lee Petty died at 86.

Five weeks after the family patriarch's passing, Adam Petty died of head injuries sustained in a crash during practice for a NASCAR Busch Series race at the New Hampshire International Speedway in Loudon. He was 19 years old.

Off His You-Know-What?

January belongs to the iron men of the NFL; most baseball players have the sense to stay out of the headlines. But star Atlanta pitcher John Rocker is not your ordinary player, no indeed. In an unguarded moment, Rocker, whose special nemeses are the New York Mets and their fans, shared his thoughts about New York City with a writer from SPORTS ILLUSTRATED. "Imagine having to take the [Number] 7 train to the ballpark, looking like you're

[riding through] Beirut next to some kid with purple hair next to some queer with AIDS right next to some dude who just got out of jail for the fourth time right next to some 20-year-old mom with four kids. It's depressing."

Soon it was Rocker who was depressed, for SI printed his diatribe and the pitcher found himself Y2K's poster boy for political incorrectness. Major League Baseball commissioner Bud Selig ordered Rocker to undergo psychological counseling. He was suspended for the season's first two weeks, but after he started badly, he was sent to Atlanta's Triple A Richmond team in June. Yet Rocker regained his dominating pitching form by season's end, and the Braves went on to win their division. No surprise: nice guys finish last.

ROCKER **Derided as a bellowing bigot, he fell into a slump**

Images

ARMSTRONG *En famille* in France

Armstrong the Invincible

That which does not kill Lance Armstrong only serves to burnish his legend. In 2000 the cycling champ, who had come back from testicular cancer to win the Tour de France in 1999, won the sport's greatest event for the second year in a row—only to be smacked down by a car on a lonely French road just weeks before he was due to race in the Olympics. He fractured a vertebra in his neck that day. "We were in the middle of nowhere," he said. "The next car to come by was my wife an hour and a half later." At least she didn't run him over.

Cancer helped reshape Armstrong's body and turn him into a much better cyclist. So would his neck injury spur him on for the Olympics? "The accident affected my training, but I'm fit enough," Armstrong said before the cycling time-trial race. "I don't want to use that as an excuse." And he didn't. Armstrong got the bronze in the event, won by Russian Viacheslav Ekimov, who races with Armstrong on the U.S. Postal Team. It was a great race. But Armstrong's is such a rich tale that the final result seemed almost an afterthought.

Encyclopedia Millerannica

What were the network suits to do? Ratings for the war-horse show ABC's *Monday Night Football* were steadily eroding. Loath to satisfy fans' dreams of, say, omitting a few commercials, ABC decided to liven up the play-by-play and hired former *Saturday Night Live* comic and HBO ranter Dennis Miller to join veterans Al Michaels and Dan Fouts in the broadcast booth.

Ratings improved a bit, though the motormouth Miller's hip brand of humor proved so erudite that Britannica.com was soon running a weekly feature parsing his arcane references. In a preseason exhibition game, Miller, a longtime gridiron fan, cooed he was having "so much fun!" Michaels ribbed him, "This is like you won a prize to a fantasy announcing camp, isn't it?"

RANTING Miller with Michaels, left

THE GREATEST SHOW ON EARTH

Ablaze with sport and spectacle, the Olympic Games were tip-top Down Under

Australian sprinter Cathy Freeman, symbol
of her nation's newfound unity, holds aloft the Olympic flame

Greetings from Sydney

The best Olympics ever? That may be more than bluster. Sydney put on a party that caught all the gusto, color and flair of its exuberant hosts. Call 'em the Games of Joy—Oi! Oi! Oi!

1. Sydneysiders paint their harbor with fireworks for the closing ceremonies

2. Canadian synchronized swimmers test the waters. Intriguing—but is it really sport?

3. Aussie athletes join a conga line at the over-the-top closing ceremonies

4. Australia's Brook Staples puts Master Monarch through his paces in the three-day cross-country equestrian event

5. Twist of fate: A drug violation cost Romania's Andreea Raducan her gold medal

6. An athlete makes a spectacle of himself at the closing ceremonies

7. Sailboarders angle to catch a breeze in Sydney's Rushcutters Bay

8. Trompe l'oeil: French athletes become a living mirror image in synchronized diving

9. Men's triathletes take flight in front of the Sydney Opera House

10. Abstract art? No, it's the men's team pursuit event at the cycling velodrome

11. Kick! Women of the U.S. 4 x 100 relay team cheer on a teammate

12. Korea's D.S. Lee goes airborne—and stays there—in badminton's doubles finals

13. Oooof! Spain's Monic Carrio shows the strain in the 75-kg weightlifting event

14. The beach volleyball scene at Bondi Beach was the Games' coolest venue. Aussie Natalie Cook is on her way to gold

15. Horrors! A Frenchman and a Briton form an unseemly tangle in the judo event

16. Let the Games begin: Nikki Webster and Aborigine Djakarporra Munyarrun starred in the opening ceremonies

17. Good on ya! Aussies like these joyous triathlon fans made the Games a carnival

ARNE DEDERT—AFP

Stacy
DRAGILIA

If there seems to be more excitement surrounding women's Olympic events than the men's these days, that may be because women are still in the pioneering stages of some competitions that men have long taken for granted, like the marathon and weight lifting. Another case in point: pole vault, which was contested by women for the first time in Olympic history at Sydney. As women get better and better at this difficult event, which demands a rare combination of speed, flexibility and strength, they are literally raising the bar on the world record almost every time the best of them get together to compete. In the past decade the record has been broken or tied 30 times by six different women.

And the winner of the first Olympic gold in women's pole vault: America's Stacy Dragila, 29, an erstwhile rodeo rider and hurdler who picked up her first pole in 1993—and has set the world record three different times. Battling competition anxiety—and a new, longer pole that had cramped her form—she bested a bevy of blonds and grabbed the gold.

Marion
JONES

Marion Jones, fans say, is one of the world's loveliest women. Indisputably, she is its fastest. In Sydney she was certainly its most ambitious. As some of the best remembered American athletes in history—Spitz, Heiden, Lewis, Blair—had done before her, Jones declared before the Games she intended to win multiple gold medals, five of them, a quest that put her in the center of the Olympic spotlight.

Jones' game plan: gold in the 100-m and 200-m individual races, gold in the 4 × 100 and 4 × 400 relays, gold in the long jump. (She hasn't competed much at the 400-m length, but her one 400 in 2000 produced the second fastest time in the world.) The 5-ft. 10-in. racing machine got off to a strong start, qualifying first in her semifinal heat in her initial event, the 100. The final was exciting only in the way of Secretariat's Belmont win: a superb racer pulled away, showing the audience what fast looks like—and faster. Jones ran a 10.75 and finished 7 m ahead of the rest of the field.

Then reality intervened. Before Jones' next event, the news broke that her husband, 320-lb shot putter C.J. Hunter, had tested positive for using steroids (*see* p. 114). The intensity of the media circus surrounding the star immediately multiplied. Yet she remained calm. In the 200-m run, Jones had to outpace both the controversy and the field, which she did easily. Two golds down.

Jones knew coming into the Games that the long jump posed her biggest challenge. She had not dominated the event during the 2000 season, and has never been especially good at it. In truth, her style on the field is as artless as her form on the track is elegant. In Sydney she crashed out with four fouls in six jumps. Germany's Heike Drechsler took honors, Jones a consolation bronze. Skittish baton passes yielded another bronze in the 4 × 100-m relay, but Jones' sensational leg in the 4 × 400 brought her a third gold medal. Her lofty goal of five golds may have eluded her—but she earned the admiration of a watching world.

ADAM PRETTY—ALLSPORT

Michael JOHNSON

He has always been a sprinter with a split personality. There was the 200-m Michael Johnson, who puts a hoop in his ear, turns up the hip-hop and gets into trash-talk wars with rival Maurice Greene. Then there was the 400-m Michael, who listens to jazz before a race and spends evenings answering e-mail from fans. But berserk Mr. Hyde was sidelined in the Olympic trials, when both Johnson and Greene pulled up with leg troubles. So mellow Dr. Jekyll had extra time in Sydney to make sure his hamstring strain was only a memory—and to defend the Olympic title that he won in 1996 by blowing away the 400 field.

This time around, the 32-year-old world-record holder in the 200 and 400 was eager to burnish his reputation as perhaps the best sprinter ever, but was content to cede the spotlight to Marion Jones while he kicked back with his family, wife Kerry and three-month-old son Sebastian. In the 400 final, his physical superiority was so great he might as well have been the only man on the track. Finishing way out front, Dr. Jekyll calmly collared the gold.

Cathy FREEMAN

Before the race the young star looked anxious, running her tongue over dry lips; as if for protection, she had encased herself, head to toe, in a bodysuit. After the race she slumped exhausted onto the track. In the intervening 49.11 seconds, Australia's Cathy Freeman showed that she is the world's swiftest and most psychologically resilient female 400-m runner.

Few, if any, of the 112,524 fans heard Freeman's name announced before the race—their anticipatory roar drowned it out. In the 10 days since she had lighted the Olympic flame to begin the Games, Australians had come to realize how much they wanted the 27-year-old symbol of her nation's reconciliation with its Aboriginal peoples to win. Her quest for gold had put a knot in the nation's stomach.

As the lead runners entered the final stretch, Freeman was trailing Jamaican Lorraine Graham. Alone on a TV screen, with her muscular thighs and stomach, Freeman looks imposing. In the flesh, however, she's tiny—just 5 ft. 5 in. and 117 lbs. And as she chased the taller, bulkier Graham, the thought occurred that she could not possibly catch her, for this was a girl against a woman. Yet Graham did not have enough to withstand the fast-finishing Freeman, whose victory sparked nationwide jubilation: "Our Cathy" had won.

Konstantinos KENTERIS

Will the Athens Games in 2004 be marked by a sudden ascendancy in Greek athletics? The victory of Konstantinos Kenteris in the 200-m run was so unexpected that the Olympic officials hadn't arranged for a translator for interviews. Kenteris' coach had to step in.

Not that the officials can be blamed. The last time a Greek man won gold in a running event was in the marathon at the very first modern Games in 1896. To find another great Greek sprinter ... well, there's Hermes.

With the field wide open after U.S. stars Maurice Greene and Michael Johnson were injured in the U.S. trials, Kenteris sped past Ato Boldon and Darren Campbell in the last 40 meters to win. Yet the only person who seemed unsurprised was the victor. "I felt I could do something more. That is what I tried in the final," he said.

Dot
RICHARDSON

It wasn't supposed to be this way: the defending Olympic champions on the American women's softball team were heavily favored to enjoy a long, ceremonial stroll to

win the gold in Sydney. But somebody forgot to notify their opponents.

After getting off to a strong start with victories over Canada and Cuba, the American squad went into a slump, losing three games in a row to Japan, China and host Australia. Maybe the U.S. gals were only toying with us: just when things looked bleakest in Mudville, the U.S. rallied to beat New Zealand and Italy (twice) to reach the semifinal round. Then they tasted the sweet joys of revenge, beating China, Australia and Japan to bring home the gold.

Once again the leader of the U.S. squad was the bubbly (to say the least) blond with a medical degree, Dot Richardson, 38, left. This time around, Dr. Dot moved over from shortstop to play second base as her Olympic roomie, California's muscular, 5-ft. 8-in. Crystl Bustos, 23, became the U.S. infield stalwart and cleanup batter. "To play beside her is an honor," said Bustos. It's noisy too.

Tommy
LASORDA

What have previous Olympic Games been lacking? In two words: Tommy Lasorda. The always excitable, often quotable and occasionally lovable former skipper of the Los Angeles Dodgers was the perfect choice to lead a U.S. baseball team made up of former major leaguers and aspiring college kids (although these were the first Games that allowed pro ballplayers to compete, U.S. pros were in the closing weeks of the season and couldn't attend). "Let's put it this way: we're not going 6,000 miles to lose, pal," Lasorda vowed in July. "Those players are gonna … be proud to wear that uniform and … give everything

that they have in them, for the good of the United States of America."

And with Uncle Tommy and Uncle Sam behind them, they did: though the heavily favored Cuban nine marched to the finals by such lopsided scores as 16-0 and 13-5, the Americans whipped them 4-0 to take the gold. Did Tommy cry? You better believe it, pal.

Rulon
GARDNER

It's enough to make you long for the good old days of the cold war: in Greco-Roman wrestling, American Rulon Gardner, 29, an oversize farm boy from Afton, Wyo. who was not even expected to be in medal contention, beat Russian Alexander Karelin, 32, a 6' 3", 286-lb. three-time Olympic champion who hadn't lost a match in 13 years, who had never lost in international competition, and who had not given up as much as a single point in 10 years. Karelin was so intimidating that his last two opponents for a medal in Barcelona in 1992 had rolled over and pinned themselves instead of being pulped by the great Russian.

Gardner's profile makes Rocky look polished. The youngest of nine, he was teased in grade school for his freakish size, even as he gained his strength by working on his father's dairy farm every day after school. "By the end of high school, I was carrying four bales of hay, 100 lbs. each, just walking with them," he said. After making the Olympic squad, Gardner raised some $25,000 from Afton locals for the family's trip to Sydney. And after whipping Karelin, the exuberant new champ celebrated by turning a cartwheel, above.

Alexei NEMOV

RUSSIA

Where have you gone, Mitch Gaylord? A nation turns its lonely eyes to you … for when the gymnastics medals were handed out in Sydney, not a single American—male or female—ascended the podium. The U.S. women's team finished fourth and the men's fifth; no American won an individual medal.

Americans who had learned to love the parallel bars had to content themselves with watching the supremely gifted Russian Alexei Nemov lay claim to being one of the greatest Olympic gymnasts of all time. As he left Sydney, his bags were filled with six medals—the same number he had won in Atlanta. Nemov, a grand old man of the sport at age 24, wasn't sure if he would compete in 2004: "I must take some time off. I'm not a robot," he said. Can you prove that, Alexei?

Womens' SOCCER

NORWAY

You know them: they're the world champions, the team that taught Americans the difference between a corner kick and a penalty kick, whose legendary lineup included Mia Hamm, Julie Foudy and the jersey-doffing star of the World Cup, Brandi Chastain. They weren't supposed to lose in the Olympics— but they did, bowing to Norway in the finals in one of the most thrilling games in soccer history.

Ironically, the U.S. women began the Games by thoroughly whipping the Norwegians, as Hamm and Tiffeny Milbrett scored goals in a 2-0 victory. After tying China 1-1, demolishing Nigeria 3-1 and beating always tough Brazil 1-0 in the semifinals, the Americans felt strong before the final match.

The U.S. struck quickly, as Hamm shook loose to set up a nifty goal by Milbrett only five minutes into the match. Norway came back to tie it up before the half, then took the lead on a header in the 78th minute. The clock ran out with the U.S. trailing 2-1. Despair! But in the final seconds of injury time (extra time at the end of a match to account for stopped play), the ball again came to Milbrett in front of the goal, and her header tied the score. Joy! But the gritty Norwegians hung tough, scoring the winning goal in the 12th minute of overtime. Desolation! Yet both teams could take pride in playing in what Chastain later called "the best game I have ever been a part of."

Eric
THE EEL

Remember Eddie the Eagle—the hilarious British chap who enlivened the Winter Games of 1988 with his earthbound attempts at ski jumping? Well, Eddie … meet Eric the Eel, Sydney's contribution to lovable-loser lore.

Eric Moussambani of Equatorial Guinea had never swum before January 2000. Nine months later, he found himself in an Olympic 100-m freestyle heat before 17,500 cheering fans in Sydney's Aquatic Center. When the two other men in the heat false-started, the 22-year-old Moussambani was left to swim, all alone in a middle lane, two epic lengths of the 50-m pool. The good news: Eric had a free ride to victory. The bad news: he had only trained—one hour a day, three days a week for the past nine months—in a 20-m hotel pool.

Moussambani plowed on, with his head far above the water, turning himself from side to side as he soaked in the applause from the stands. He dog-paddled home—to wild cheers—in 1:52.72, a mere 1:04.88 shy of a world record.

Ian
THORPE

Is Ian Thorpe the most technically proficient swimmer of all time? Probably not. Is he the most physically powerful freestyler there has ever been? No again. Surprisingly, he is unimpressive in the gym and hopeless at ball sports. But at 6 ft. 4 in. and 200 lbs., with natural buoyancy and a basketballer's feet and hands, he can move water like the moon. His cartoon elasticity, combined with the longest stroke in swimming, makes "Thorpedo" all his nickname suggests: sleek, smooth, strangely beautiful and, to the competition, lethal. "If you were going to do a Frankenstein," said Brian Sutton, coach of nine of the Australian Olympians, "if you were going to put a swimmer together from scratch, you'd build Ian Thorpe."

He is just 17 years old and has swum the 200 m and 400 m faster than anyone else in history. He fascinates rivals, coaches, sports scientists and fans, who know a lot about him—from his shoe size (17) to his taste in music (grunge).

Thorpe came into the Games carrying a burden of expectations equal to those of Marion Jones and Cathy Freeman. But he rose to the task: in his specialty race, the 400 m, he beat his world record and won by what seemed a couple of hours (actually, by 2.81 sec.). For dessert, he took silver in the 200 m, then anchored the Aussies' winning team in the 4 × 100 freestyle relay.

Lenny
KRAYZELBURG

All but one of the Olympic swimmers in Sydney were competing for one country: Lenny Krayzelburg was representing one and a half. The handsome backstroker wore the uniform of the U.S., but beneath the red, white and blue was a splash of the Soviet Union's red and gold. Krayzelburg, 24, called on both aspects of his past to win three gold medals: the 100-m and 200-m backstroke and a leg in the medley relay.

The "born backstroker" with the long, lean body and the seemingly double-jointed elbows joined the Soviet sports machine in 1984 but emigrated to Los Angeles in 1989 after his parents saw the Soviet system was declining. At what should have been the peak of his career, Lenny was struggling to learn a new language and earn a living—and swimming only a few hours each week.

After Lenny found his way to Mark Schubert, the masterly swim coach at the University of Southern California, he broke the world records in the 100-m and 200-m backstroke. "The thing about America is … anything is possible," Krayzelburg said. Even a Soviet boy's becoming an American Olympic hero.

SERGEI GUNEYEV FOR TIME

Men's 4x100
FREESTYLE

No, the Sydney Olympics did not include an air-guitar event. The blokes doing the strumming are the Aussie men's 4 × 100 freestyle relay team, who had just won the biggest grudge match of the Games. It all began when U.S. sprinter Gary Hall Jr. boasted that he and his teammates would not only beat the Australians but also "smash them like guitars." Ouch! The U.S. men hadn't lost the 4 × 100 freestyle since forever, and with a sprinter (Hall) up against a middle-distanceman (Aussie hero Ian Thorpe) at anchor, they didn't figure to lose now. But "Thorpedo" was special. He had the lead, he lost it, he found it again with his very last stroke. Thorpe's swim was, instantly, the greatest in Australian history. As his mates serenaded Hall with a little air guitar, the natatorium rocked with cheers: Oi! Oi! Oi!

HEINZ KLUETMEIER—SPORTS ILLUSTRATED

AL BELLO—ALLSPORT

Jenny
THOMPSON

Swimming is a solo sport. Sure, there are relay teams, but the glory is in personal triumph, as in the indelible image of all those gold medals dangling from Mark Spitz's neck. You don't need to remind Jenny Thompson of that. She is America's best sprint swimmer and the most decorated female swimmer of the 1990s. No other American, male or female, has dominated swimming in the past decade like Thompson, who swims the butterfly and freestyle. Since she started at age 8, Thompson has broken more swim records, won more international championships and held more college titles than anyone else who has dipped a toe in the water.

Yet as she embarked for Sydney, Thompson had never won an Olympic gold medal in an individual event. The 27-year-old New Hampshire native already had five gold medals, albeit all from relay teams in the 1992 and '96 Games—yet her main memories were of failing to win individual gold in Barcelona ("I choked big time," she says) and failing even to make the U.S. team in individual events in 1996. The bad news: Thompson didn't achieve her goal of individual gold in Sydney—she tied for a bronze in the 100-m freestyle. The good: she added three more relay golds to her haul, making her the most-decorated Olympic woman in U.S. history.

Camilla MARTIN

Several sports in Sydney had an Anna Kournikova type in the draw—a real looker—but none had anyone to equal badminton's Camilla Martin of Denmark. To say she was smashing is not just to describe her game. But her game, as it happens, was indeed smashing. At 5 ft. 9 in., she was usually taller than her foe, often a woman from China, Indonesia or South Korea, the countries that dominated the sport until the Danes came along. Martin thrashed them all before losing in the finals to China's top-seeded Gong Zhichao.

Martin is lithe on the court and uses her reach to pick a shuttlecock from the floor or violently put it away from on high. Badminton is an astonishing sport: fast and furious, nothing like the gentle game of July cookouts. If anyone can raise its profile, it's this darting Dane.

Tara NOTT

When the women's version of weight lifting debuted as an Olympic sport in Sydney, tiny Tara Nott became the first U.S. athlete in 40 years to win gold in the event. Nott's achievement came at the expense of Bulgarian lifter Izabela Dragneva, who initially won the gold but was disqualified after failing a doping test. Thus Nott, 28, who had won the silver in the 106-lb. class with a total lift of 407¾ lbs., became the Olympic champion.

Nott, who at 5 ft. 1 in. and 105 lbs. looks more like a pixie gymnast than Barbell Barbie, claims she was not interested in competing as a weight lifter. But the accomplished gymnast and soccer player (who also stands out in football and basketball) got hooked when she won the nationals a mere eight months after her introduction to the barbells. "It just came naturally to me," she says. The next question: Can she name a sport that doesn't?

Battle for the Gold Medal—in Excuses

NO ONE KNEW IF MARION JONES WOULD WIN FIVE, IF THE U.S. would rule the pool, if the sun would shine on the beach volleyballers. But heading into Sydney, everyone knew drugs would have a big impact on the Games. Did they ever. The news that C.J. Hunter—a sidelined shot putter who is much better known as Marion Jones' husband—had recently tested positive for nandrolone, a banned steroid, became an overshadowing story. Hunter, a 320-pounder who usually avoids the media like a diet, summoned the press to assert, tears flowing, that he would never do anything to hurt his wife. He claimed, unconvincingly, that he had ingested nutritional supplements that had somehow become tainted, boosting his nandro level to 1,000 times the allowable limit.

Hunter's was not Sydney's only drug case, and his explanation wasn't even the most dubious. In competitions from race walking to hammer throwing, no fewer than three dozen athletes and coaches were removed for using or supplying banned substances. Dozens more had withdrawn before the Games because they would have been nailed. Among those who tested positive for banned substances were Latvian rower Andris Reinholds, who said his nandrolone came from a Chinese herbal supplement, and German runner Dieter Baumann, who said a rival had spiked his toothpaste with steroids. Uzbekistan track coach Sergei Voynov claimed he had brought a large quantity of human growth hormone into the country to help with his hair loss. The I.O.C. was toughest on 16-year-old Romanian gymnast Andreea Raducan, who lost her gold medal after being given a cold medicine by the team doctor. Drug abuse in sport is ugly; crackdowns are uglier.

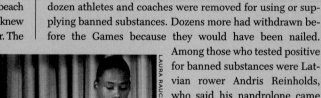

ON THE SPOT **Hunter and Jones meet the press**

WHO GARNERED THE GOLD?

SYDNEY 2000

A highly selective list of the winners of major individual events at the Sydney Games

TRACK AND FIELD

Event	Winner	Country
100 m	MAURICE GREENE	U.S.A.
	MARION JONES	U.S.A.
200 m	KONSTANTINOS KENTERIS	Greece
	MARION JONES	U.S.A.
400 m	MICHAEL JOHNSON	U.S.A.
	CATHY FREEMAN	Australia
800 m	NILS SCHUMANN	Germany
	MARIA MUTOLA	Mozambique
1,500 m	NOAH NGENA	Kenya
	NOURIA MERAH-BENIDA	Algeria
5,000 m	MILLON WOLDE	Ethiopia
	GABRIELA SZABO	Romania
10,000 m	HAILE GEBRSELASSIE	Ethiopia
	DERARTU TULU	Ethiopia
Marathon	GEZAHGNE ABERA	Ethiopia
	NAOKO TAKAHASHI	Japan
High jump	SERGEY KLIUGIN	Russia
	YELENA YELESINA	Russia
Long jump	IVAN PEDROSO	Cuba
	HEIKE DRECHSLER	Germany
Triple jump	JONATHAN EDWARDS	Britain
	TEREZA MARINOVA	Bulgaria
Pole vault	NICK HYSONG	U.S.A.
	STACY DRAGILA	U.S.A.
Shot put	ARSI HARJU	Finland
	YANINA KOROLCHIK	Belarus
Discus	VIRGILIJUS ALEKNA	Lithuania
	ELLINA ZVEREVA	Belarus
Hammer	SZYMON ZIOLKOWSKI	Poland
	KAMILA SKOLIMOWSKA	Poland
Javelin	JAN ZELEZNY	Czech Republic
	TRINE HATTESTAD	Norway
Decathlon	ERKI NOOL	Estonia
Heptathlon	DENISE LEWIS	Britain
Triathlon	SIMON WHITFIELD	Canada
	BRIGITTE MCMAHON	Switzerland

WOMEN'S GYMNASTICS

Event	Winner	Country
All-around	SIMONA AMANAR	Romania
Vault	ELENA ZAMOLDTCHIKOVA	Russia
Uneven bars	SVETLANA KHORKINA	Russia
Balance beam	LIU XUAN	China
Floor exercises	ELENA ZAMOLDTCHIKOVA	Russia
Trampoline	IRINA KARAVAEVA	Russia

MEN'S GYMNASTICS

All-around	ALEXEI NEMOV	Russia
Floor exercises	IGORS VIHROVS	Latvia
Pommel horse	MARIUS URZICA	Romania
Rings	SZILVESZTER CSOLLANY	Hungary
Vault	GERVASIO DEFERR	Spain
Parallel bars	LI XIAOPENG	China
Horizontal bar	ALEXEI NEMOV	Russia
Trampoline	ALEXANDER MOSKALENKO	Russia

SWIMMING AND DIVING

50-m freestyle	ANTHONY ERVIN	U.S.A. (tie)
	GARY HALL, JR.	U.S.A. (tie)
	INGE DE BRUIJN	Netherlands
100-m freestyle	PIETER VAN DEN HOOGENBAND	Netherlands
	INGE DE BRUIJN	Netherlands
200-m freestyle	PIETER VAN DEN HOOGENBAND	Netherlands
	SUSIE O'NEILL	Australia
400-m freestyle	IAN THORPE	Australia
	BROOKE BENNETT	U.S.A.
800-m freestyle	BROOKE BENNETT	U.S.A.
1,500-m freestyle	GRANT HACKETT	Australia
100-m backstroke	LENNY KRAYZELBURG	U.S.A.
	DIANA MOCANU	Romania
200-m backstroke	LENNY KRAYZELBURG	U.S.A.
	DIANA MOCANU	Romania
100-m breaststroke	DOMENICO FIORAVANTI	Italy
	MEGAN QUANN	U.S.A.
200-m breaststroke	DOMENICO FIORAVANTI	Italy
	AGNES KOVACS	Hungary
100-m butterfly	LARS FROELANDER	Sweden
	INGE DE BRUIJN	Netherlands
200-m butterfly	TOM MALCHOW	U.S.A.
	MISTY HYMAN	U.S.A.
200-m IM	MASSIMILIANO ROSOLINO	Italy
	YANA KLOCHKOVA	Ukraine
400-m IM	TOM DOLAN	U.S.A.
	YANA KLOCHKOVA	Ukraine
Springboard	NI XIONG	China
	FU MINGXIA	China
Platform	TIAN LIANG	China
	LAURA WILKINSON	U.S.A.

Science

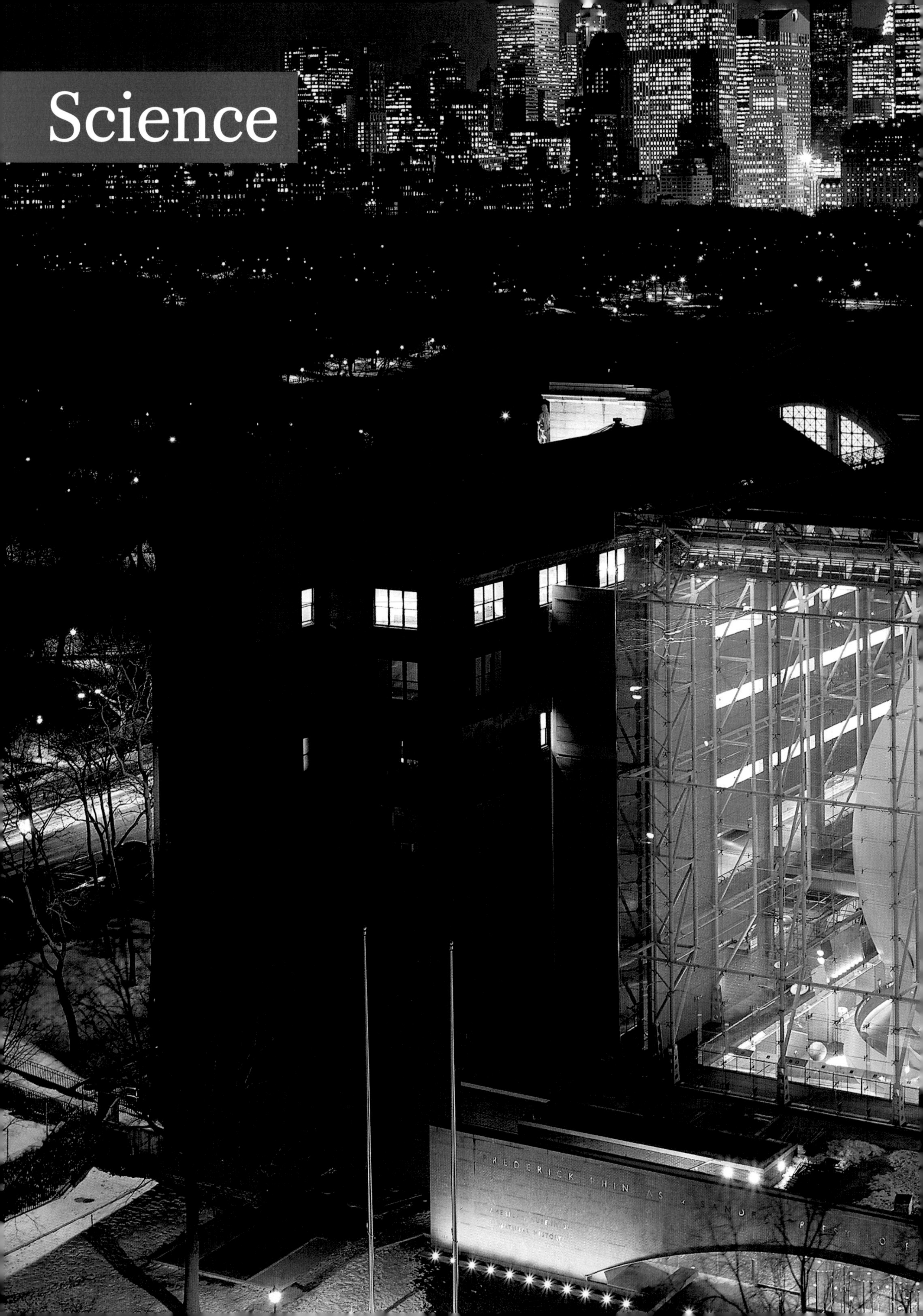

ROOM WITH A VIEW: Working magic with two simple forms, architect James Polshek reimagined the Hayden Planetarium as an 87-ft. aluminum sphere floating within a luminous cube in his design for the $210 million Rose Center for Earth and Space at New York City's American Museum of Natural History

Ted Thai for TIME

TRUCE Longtime rivals Collins, left, and Venter agreed to cooperate

DECODING THE GENOME

In a historic milestone, competing groups unite to decipher the book of life

AFTER MORE THAN A DECADE OF DREAMING, planning and heroic number crunching, two groups that had been locked in a bitter race to unlock the mystery of human genetics concluded their contest amicably on June 26, 2000, with the joint announcement that they had deciphered essentially all the 3.1 billion biochemical "letters" of human DNA, the coded instructions for building and operating a fully functional human. The competitors—the Human Genome Project, funded by the U.S. and British governments and headed by Dr. Francis Collins, and the private firm Celera Genomics, headed by controversial researcher Dr. Craig Venter—were brought together after a White House diplomatic effort. The two groups reached, if not a meeting of the minds, at least a workable understanding—and a framework for the historic joint announcement.

It is impossible to overstate the scientific significance of this achievement. Armed with the human genetic code, researchers can start teasing out the secrets of human health and disease at the molecular level—secrets that will lead at the very least to a revolution in diagnosing and treating everything from Alzheimer's to heart disease to cancer and more. In a matter of decades, the world of medicine may be utterly transformed, and history books will mark the year 2000 as the ceremonial start of the genomic era.

Why the fuss? The genome is a sort of autobiographical record, written in "genetish," of all the vicissitudes and inventions that have characterized the history of our species and its ancestors since the dawn of life. Genes have already told us that we are the closest relatives of chimpanzees; that the common ancestor of fruit flies and people was a 600 million-year-old segmented worm with the ability to learn; that the Basques are as unrelated to other Eurasians as their language implies and may be descended from indigenous European hunter-gatherers. Genes can even tell us a bit about "LUCA," the Last Universal Common Ancestor of all life, a single-celled microbe that lived about 4 billion years ago.

Unlike other autobiographies, the genome contains stories about the future as well as the past. Among the genes are clear messages about what will happen to your body as you age, a few of which we can already read. There is a gene, for example, that can alter one's susceptibility to Alzheimer's disease elevenfold, depending on whether its 334th letter is G or A.

The idea of the genome as a book—longer than 800 Bibles yet so small that there are trillions of copies inside each one of us—is not a metaphor. It is literally true. A book is a piece of digital information, written in linear, one-dimensional and one-directional form and defined by a code that transliterates a small alphabet of signs into a large lexicon of meanings through the order of their groupings. So is a genome. And the decoding of this book should give scientists a tool that will transform the way humans understand and protect their health.

The two organizations approached their decoding work in very different ways. The HGP scientists broke their DNA samples into segments of about 150 million letters long (the overall genome has some 3.1 billion letters). These were subdivided into segments of about 6,000 letters each, which were read by sequencing machines. In the final step, the pieces were reassembled into their original order on the chromosomes.

Venter and the scientists at Celera, by contrast, took a more radical approach, smashing the DNA into millions of pieces, then feeding each piece into new high-speed robotic sequencers. By the end of March, Celera had all of them read, though they were not reassembled for another six weeks. So the announcement of the mapping, while historic, was a murky milestone, for the work is not yet really complete. What the scientists at Celera have done is sequence about 97% of the genome, and the remaining 150 million or so letters won't be deciphered anytime soon. The HGP is even further behind; unlike Celera, it hasn't put its strings of letters into proper order yet. This loose end should be cleared up in a year or two, but even then the so-called book of life will remain unreadable.

Molecular biologists still know so little about the human genome that nobody has even a ballpark figure for how many genes humans have. Before the June announcement, the betting ranged from as few as 28,000 to as many as 140,000. Now it looks more like 50,000.

Beyond that, knowing the code for a gene doesn't mean you know what protein it produces in the body, or what that protein does, or how it interacts with other proteins—vital information if you want to know how the genetic code locked in our cells ends up constructing and maintaining a fully functioning human being.

GIVEN THIS OVERWHELMING IGNORANCE, WHY did everyone make such a fuss? Because laying out the biochemical code for all our genes, however many there turn out to be, and locating them within the 23 chromosomes in the human genome may be the necessary first step to solving many more medical mysteries. The hope is that the completed genome will enable scientists to lay bare the genetic triggers for hundreds of diseases—from Alzheimer's to diabetes to heart disease—and to devise exquisitely sensitive diagnostic tests. It will help pharmaceutical companies create drugs tailored to a patient's genetic profile, boosting effectiveness while drastically reducing side effects. It could change our very conception of what a disease is, replacing broad descriptive categories—breast cancer, for example—with precise genetic definitions that make diagnosis sure and treatment swift.

And while it's true that researchers can and have sequenced individual genes, they had to use a process that was expensive and terribly laborious—like writing your own reference book before you can start any real experiments. Having the sequences laid out in advance gives the scientific world an enormous head start.

Those sequences are so useful, in fact, that re-

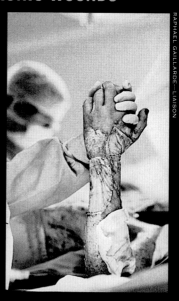

HEALING CHRONIC WOUNDS

WHAT ARE THEY? Burns and ulcers of the skin, mouth and intestines that just won't heal

WHAT CAUSES THEM? Infection, pressure, irritation, extreme temperature, as well as diabetes and chemotherapy

HOW MANY PEOPLE DOES IT AFFECT? About 7 million in the U.S. and Europe

HOW DOES GENOMICS HELP? Scientists isolated the genetic blueprints for 10 proteins active when wounds heal, then eliminated the nine that may also promote cancer. For the 10th, they isolated the protein, called repifermin, and began clinical trials. Nearly 100 skin-ulcer patients are now trying it, with promising results. If things go well, burn patients could also get the protein, and so could victims of smoke inhalation and ulcerative colitis

RAPHAEL GAILLARDE—LIAISON

searchers started tapping into the data long before they were complete. Scientists at drug firms, biotech companies and university labs have taken hundreds of baby steps into the era of genomic medicine using an impressive array of powerful new tools: DNA chips and microarrays that let scientists see at a glance which of thousands of genes are active in a given tissue sample; sophisticated software that can organize gigabytes of genetic data; huge databases of genes, disease-tissue samples and mRNA—the

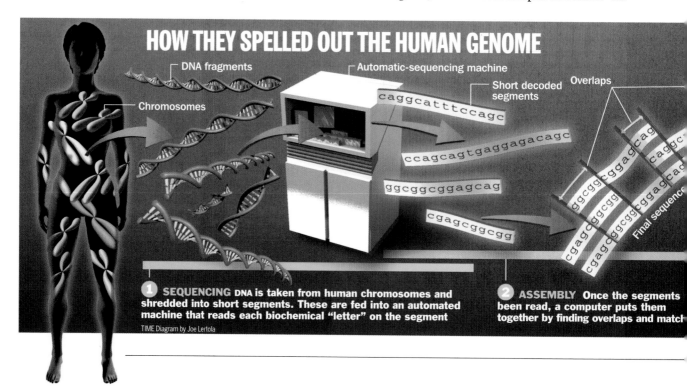

HOW THEY SPELLED OUT THE HUMAN GENOME

DNA fragments

Chromosomes

Automatic-sequencing machine

Short decoded segments

Overlaps

caggcatttccagc

ccagcagtgaggagacagc

ggcggcggagcag

cgagcggcgg

Final sequence

1 SEQUENCING DNA is taken from human chromosomes and shredded into short segments. These are fed into an automated machine that reads each biochemical "letter" on the segment

TIME Diagram by Joe Lertola

2 ASSEMBLY Once the segments been read, a computer puts them together by finding overlaps and match

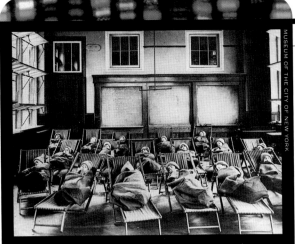

NEW DRUGS TO FIGHT TUBERCULOSIS

WHAT IS IT? An infection that primarily strikes the lungs and can affect other internal organs and bones

WHAT CAUSES IT? An airborne bacterium

HOW MANY PEOPLE HAVE IT? About 2 million people worldwide. Tuberculosis is the most widespread infectious disease on earth

HOW DOES GENOMICS HELP? By looking at the genes turned on in infected cells, researchers learned that the bug disables a gene that makes an immune-system-alerting protein. The protein is used as a drug for other diseases—but nobody knew it could be useful in the fight against TB

molecules that initiate the actual construction of working proteins. "The announcement of finishing the genome is to us a mini-event," says Allen Roses, worldwide director of genetics for pharmaceutical giant Glaxo Wellcome. "We've been making use of the information as it has become available, and we've already done some proof of the concept that finding genes for disease and developing the right drug for the right patient will actually work."

Researchers at Stanford are also harnessing genomic

medicine. They've been studying liver, breast, prostate and lung cancers for clues to their telltale molecular fingerprints. Using microarrays to sense which genes are turned on in sample tissues, says geneticist Charles Perou, the Stanford team has discovered that most of the genes expressed by both normal breast cells and primary-breast-cancer cells are similar, and so are cells for normal and cancerous lung tissue, normal and cancerous prostate tissue, and so on—which should ultimately give doctors biochemical identifiers to guide their treatments.

THESE SORTS OF TIGHTLY FOCUSED STUDIES ARE already beginning to make cancer treatment more effective. "Right now," says Stanford biochemist Patrick Brown, "it's like watching a movie on TV a few pixels at a time and trying to figure out the overall story. Having the complete genome sequence is something categorically different, like going from 100 scattered pixels on your screen to having the whole image. There will be a substantial increase in the rate at which discoveries are made."

Maybe too much of an increase, argues Tom Delbanco, chair of general medicine at Harvard Medical School. "Discovery is intoxicating," he says. "But the consequences of discovery are often complex, and instead of progress, it can lead to disaster." Delbanco is worried that the revolution in genetic medicine may further drain the limited amount of time that physicians have to spend with patients and add even more costs to America's already expensive health-care system.

Yet while Delbanco's fears may be justified—and while the genetic revolution has raised plenty of other troubling issues—its promise is so huge that putting on the brakes may be impossible. The age of genomic medicine is here; the sequencing of the human genome simply marks its ceremonial beginning. ∎

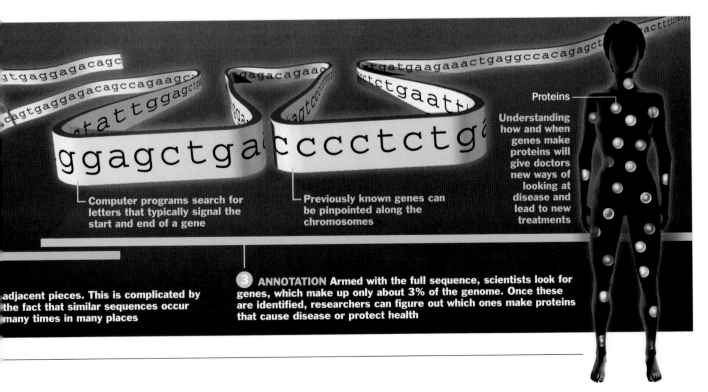

Proteins

Understanding how and when genes make proteins will give doctors new ways of looking at disease and lead to new treatments

Computer programs search for letters that typically signal the start and end of a gene

Previously known genes can be pinpointed along the chromosomes

adjacent pieces. This is complicated by the fact that similar sequences occur many times in many places

3 ANNOTATION Armed with the full sequence, scientists look for genes, which make up only about 3% of the genome. Once these are identified, researchers can figure out which ones make proteins that cause disease or protect health

TREASURES OF THE TOMBS

A rich new find in the "Valley of the Golden Mummies" opens a window onto Egypt's days as a province of the Roman Empire

SUPERSTITIOUS? IT'S HARD NOT TO BE WHEN YOU spend your life excavating Egyptian tombs. But even Zahi Hawass, one of Egypt's leading archaeologists, was not prepared for the apparition that visited him one night in the spring of 2000, shortly before he entered the tomb of the most powerful governor of the Bahariya Oasis during the 26th dynasty, Zed-Khonsu-efankh. In the dream, Hawass was trapped in a large room filled with dense smoke. He tried to call for help, but no one heard him. Suddenly, a man's face—looking for all the world like a carving from a sarcophagus—came swimming at him through the haze. Hawass cried out and forced himself awake.

ANCIENT GOSPEL A worker cleans the Book of the Dead

MORTAL PORTAL Archaeologist Hawass paused in the tomb's antechamber, unaware that the governor's sarcophagus was beyond

Hawass is not the only explorer haunted by the tombs of Bahariya. The sleepy backwater 230 miles southwest of Cairo was largely overlooked by archaeologists before 1996. That's when a donkey belonging to an antiquities guard fell into a hole that led directly to an undiscovered tomb filled with gold-covered mummies. Since then, Hawass and his team have been digging extensively in Bahariya, turning up hundreds of mummies and treasures beyond imagination. Some of their findings appear in Hawass's *Valley of the Golden Mummies* (Abrams; $49.50; 224 pages), a richly illustrated text that was published in 2000. Others, unearthed after the book was finished, appear on these pages.

The bulk of the tombs in Bahariya represent one of two periods: the 26th dynasty (6th century B.C.), when the town first became an important trading and agricultural center; and the 1st and 2nd centuries A.D., by which time Egypt was ruled by Rome. The Zed-Khonsu-efankh site,

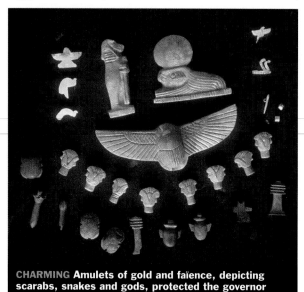

CHARMING Amulets of gold and faïence, depicting scarabs, snakes and gods, protected the governor

ARTIFACTS FROM THE ROMAN ERA

REALISM This pottery mask portrays a curly-haired Bedouin woman

which Hawass opened in April, hails from the earlier era and took even him by surprise. Beginning his dig in a tomb that others had already explored, Hawass spied an opening in a chamber wall. When he and his team excavated the rubble that lay beyond, they found anterooms filled with paintings of religious scenes and inscriptions from the Book of the Dead. In the adjacent burial chamber, which swirled with a yellow powder reminiscent of Hawass's dream, they discovered a limestone sarcophagus. When they dusted off the lid and uncovered the famous name Zed-Khonsu-efankh, Hawass recalls, "we all screamed."

Less ancient but more glamorous wonders are being unearthed in 1st and 2nd century tombs. Seven tombs opened in 2000 revealed 102 more gilded or painted remains. Copper bracelets, obsidian decorations and even what appears to be gaming pieces and dice have been uncovered as well. All told, more than 10,000 mummies may be buried in the ancient necropolis. Thoroughly exploring the site, Hawass estimates, will take at least 50 years—an archaeologist's dream. ■

ETERNAL EMBRACE
A mummified child rests on the body of his father

SHOWING THE WAY A guide leads the dead to the afterlife at an ornate tomb

MASS GRAVE Families were often buried together; this site yielded 41 mummies

Images

POLAR PERIL
Scientists continued to find proof of possible global warming as climatic changes steadily reworked the far north. In the past 20 years, average annual temperatures have risen as much as 7°F in Alaska, Siberia and parts of Canada. Sea ice is 40% thinner and covers 6% less area than in 1980. Permafrost (always frozen subsoil) is proving less than permanent. Tardy formation of winter ice is changing animals' routines. And retreating coastal ice is forcing walruses to dive ever deeper for meals.

Mammals on Death Row

As far as we know, no primate became extinct during the 20th century. That's an impressive record, since the world loses about 100 species a day. But luck may soon run out for the animal order that includes humans. As more and more habitats are destroyed by human population growth, dozens

A rare golden lion tamarin

of our closest relatives—from the gorillas in the mists of East Africa to the wise-looking orangutans of Sumatra—are on the brink of oblivion. As the new century began, Conservation International, a private environment group, and the Primate Specialist Group of the Species Survival Commission of IUCN/World Conservation Union, an international alliance of public and private organizations, compiled a list of the 25 most endangered primates. The list included the golden lion tamarin, left, and other simians, a few so rarely seen that no photos of them exist. Some may be gone before we get a good look at them. Others, the scientists warned, may disappear before we ever knew they existed.

Catch a Wave—on Mars

Once upon a time, Mars had water on its surface. Billions of years ago, however, the low-gravity planet had both its air and water

MARS **Water left the dark streaks**

leak away, causing it to become the dead, freeze-dried place it is today. That's what scientists thought— until June, when NASA released a flurry of new images from the Mars Global Surveyor spacecraft showing water channels that look as fresh as the day they were formed—a day that may have been very close to the present one. The pictures suggest that even today, water may be flowing up from the Martian innards and streaming onto its surface—dramatically increasing the likelihood that at least part of the planet is biologically alive.

PICTURE CREDIT

BLASTOFF The space-station crew

The No-Space Station

Critics argue that the International Space Station is a hole in the sky into which nations (chiefly the U.S.) continue to pour money. In July the Russian space agency finally launched into orbit the 22-ton Zvezda service module—the latest, $320 million addition to the much delayed station. But Russian officials soon conceded a goof: though the school-bus-size pod would be home to three astronauts for four months at a time, it had been outfitted with only two tiny sleeping berths. In November, the first occupants arrived: Russians Sergei K. Krikalev and Yuri P. Gidzenko and American William M. Shepherd. NASA was mum on whether they drew straws for the bunks.

No Horns, No Dilemma

Ravagers, despoilers, heathens, pagans—such epithets pretty well summed up the Vikings for those who lived in the British Isles

HUBERT JOSSE

AT SEA The Bayeux Tapestry depicts a Viking fleet

in medieval times. But that view is wildly skewed. The Vikings were indeed raiders, but they were also traders whose economic network stretched from today's Iraq all the way to the Canadian Arctic. They were democrats who founded the world's oldest surviving parliament. They were master metalworkers, fashioning exquisite jewelry from silver, gold and bronze. Above all, they were intrepid explorers whose restless hearts brought them across the Atlantic to North America some 500 years before Columbus.

Setting the record straight was a rich exhibition, "Vikings: The North Atlantic Saga," that opened in Washington, then traveled to New York City. Shattering pop mythology, the exhibit argued that the Vikings didn't even wear horned helmets. Is nothing sacred?

NANCY PERKINS—CARNEGIE MUSEUM OF NATURAL HISTORY

EOSIMIAS Twixt man and monkey?

A Primate Missing Link?

The chap above is Eosimias, the "dawn monkey." He lived 45 million years ago, weighed no more than a handful of peanuts and flitted about the treetops of humid Asian rain forests. In March paleontologists disclosed new fossil evidence from digs in China placing the little animal at a significant branching of the evolutionary tree— one limb led to lower primates, like lemurs, and the other to the anthropoids, or higher primates, such as monkeys, apes and humans.

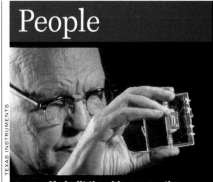

TEXAS INSTRUMENTS

People

KILBY He built the chip on vacation

Maestro of the Microchip

When Jack St. Clair Kilby, a 34-year-old electrical engineer, began working at a fledgling Dallas company called Texas Instruments in May 1958, he didn't yet qualify for the annual two-week summer vacation. So, when co-workers cleared out, he used the lab to test an idea: Why couldn't all those tiny components—transistors, resistors, capacitors—in TI's electronic gadgetry be created out of a single block of material instead of separately wired parts? By September, he had a prototype of just such an integrated circuit, or microchip. In 2000 Kilby's long-ago summer's tinkering won science's ultimate accolade: a Nobel Prize for Physics.

Kilby, now 76, was surprised by the belated honor. "The integrated circuit didn't have much new physics in it," the 6-ft. 6-in., plainspoken inventor told reporters, with a shrug. But the Swedish Royal Academy of Sciences didn't agree. In awarding Kilby half the physics prize (total value: $915,000), it noted that his chip is at the heart of today's electronic world, from computers to smart toasters to talking Barbie dolls. The other half of the prize, fittingly, went to Zhores Alferov of St. Petersburg's Ioffe Physico-Technical Institute and Herbert Kroemer of the University of California at Santa Barbara. They pioneered the lightning-fast chips widely used in satellite links, cell phones and CD players.

If the Nobel were awarded posthumously, Kilby might be sharing his with Robert Noyce, who died in 1990. Working just after Kilby, Noyce developed a chemical etching technique to print transistors on silicon wafers directly and also lay down the connecting tracks between them, simplifying the chips' manufacture and increasing their speed.

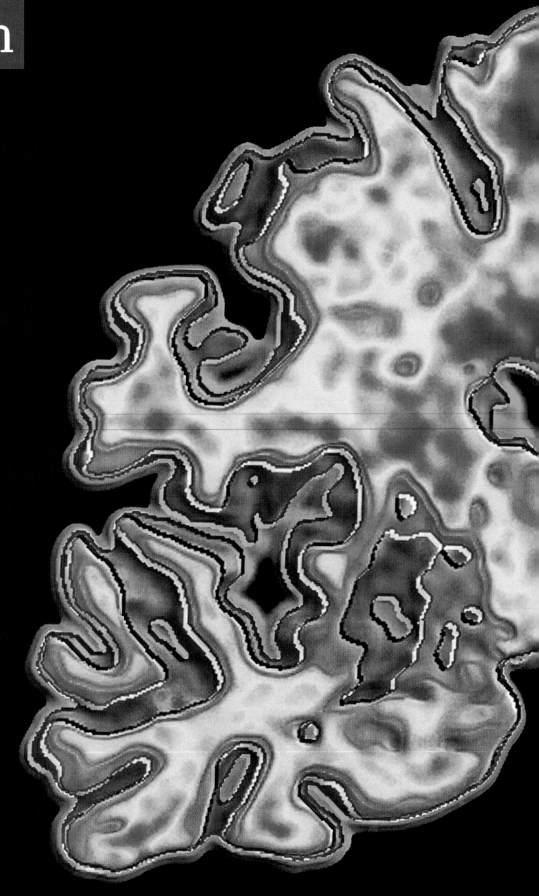

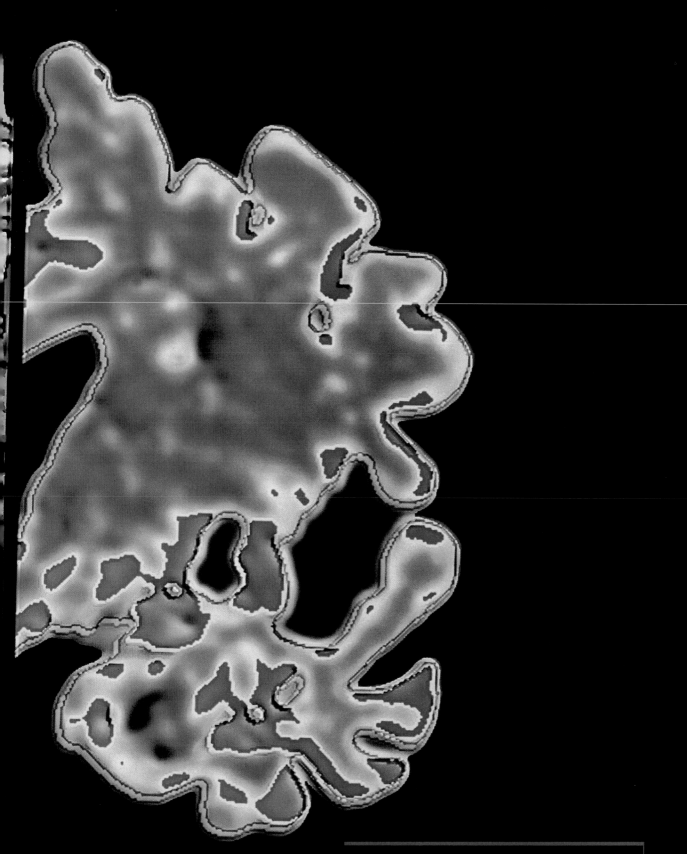

BRAIN DRAIN: These computer images show a vertical slice through a normal brain, left, and the brain of an Alzheimer's patient, right, which is shrunken due to the degeneration and death of its nerve cells. Scientists are developing drugs that may slow, even halt, the progress of the disease

Alfred Pasieka—Science Photo Library—Photo Researchers

KATIE'S CRUSADE

When popular *Today* show host Katie Couric lost her husband to colon cancer, she vowed to spread the word: get tested now ... and you may save your life

KATIE COURIC'S HUSBAND JAY MONAHAN DIED OF colon cancer at age 42 in 1998. Looking back, the popular co-host of NBC's *Today* show recalls that the only clue they had that anything might be wrong was that Monahan, who worked as a TV legal analyst, often felt tired and achy. That wasn't too surprising. He'd been busy covering O.J. Simpson's civil trial for MSNBC, shuttling between California and the home he shared in New York City with Katie and their two young daughters. Says Couric: "We thought it would get better when his schedule improved."

It didn't. After the trial ended in January 1997, Monahan's fatigue persisted. A few months later, doubled over with abdominal pain, he went to a doctor. A series of X rays and other scans revealed that Monahan was suffering from advanced colon cancer—so advanced that the disease had spread to his liver. He died two weeks after his 42nd birthday.

Like most Americans, Couric and Monahan had never thought much about colon cancer. Why should they? Monahan was young and healthy and had never smoked. There was no history of colon cancer in his family. Until her husband became sick, Couric didn't realize how common cancers of the large intestine, which includes the colon and the rectum, are. Or how deadly. Or how preventable.

WIDOW Couric with husband Jay Monahan, who died at 42

ROBIN PLATZER—TWIN IMAGES

Colorectal cancer strikes 130,000 men and women each year in the U.S., according to the American Cancer Society. Although it's more common after age 50, younger people are also affected. Over the next 12 months, more than 55,000 Americans—a quarter of them under 50—will die of the disease, making it the second leading cause of death due to cancer, after lung cancer.

It doesn't have to be this way. Provided it's caught in its earliest, most treatable stages, colorectal cancer can be cured more than 90% of the time. If more people underwent routine screening to find small tumors, experts estimate, the death toll would drop 50% to 75%, saving some 30,000 to 40,000 lives a year. And there's more good news about the disease—early detection works, treatment is improving, and proper nutrition and exercise can dramatically reduce your chances of developing it.

Leading the charge to spread that news is Couric, who was host of a week-long series about the disease on the *Today* show in March. In what must have been a television first, she broadcast footage of her own intestine, taken during a recent colon exam. (She was fine.) Couric has also joined longtime friend and cancer activist Lilly Tartikoff (whose husband Brandon died of Hodgkin's disease in 1997) to finance a public-education campaign and urge more aggressive research into colon cancer.

Before you start thinking, "Just what we need, another gimmicky disease of the month," stop to consider how much good such a campaign can do. There are probably more myths and misconceptions about colon cancer than about any other killer disease. Young people think only old people get it. Women think only men get it. African Americans think only whites get it. (In fact, American blacks are at greater risk than whites, and the disease strikes men and women, young and old.)

And the rest of us—mired in inhibitions that date back to our toilet training—don't even want to think about it. Potty talk is for two-year-olds, not grownups. The idea of a full-scale colon exam (You're going to stick that thing where?) scares most Americans away from the very screening test that could save their life. That sort of reticence proved deadly for Charles Schulz, beloved creator of *Peanuts* (*see* Milestones), who resisted being tested despite the fact that his mother, two uncles and an aunt died of colon cancer. By the time physicians discovered his tumor in the fall of 1999, it had spread to his stomach lining, and there was little they could do.

Even when our own doctor tells us to get our colon checked, we don't always listen. In 1998 Florence Seguin, 73, of Williamsburg, Va., shrugged off her physician's recommendation that she undergo a colonoscopy, a procedure in which a doctor inserts a flexible lighted tube into the colon to look for abnormal growths. Seguin knew that one of her brothers had died of colon cancer, but it wasn't until she saw an article about Couric and Monahan that she stopped procrastinating. Fortunately, the tumor that her doctors found was still small enough to be surgically removed. Says Seguin: "I don't know how many more times I would have canceled or postponed the colonoscopy if I hadn't read that article."

ADVOCATE **Couric filmed her own colonoscopy and showed it on TV**

If you're serious about protecting yourself and your loved ones against colorectal cancer, it will help to know something about the disease. Nearly all colon cancers start as polyps, tiny grapelike projections that sprout on the inside of the large intestine. Most of the time these growths are benign, but occasionally a collection of cells—through a series of genetic mishaps—will get bigger and bigger until it turns into a tumor. About 25% of these malignant growths are triggered by a genetic predisposition. The rest of the time, normal genes become damaged with age or exposure to the toxic brew of wastes that collect in the colon.

Surgery is still the front line of defense against colon cancer, and it is highly effective against small tumors. (Better techniques mean that fewer than 2% of all colorectal-cancer patients now undergo a colostomy, in which the large intestine is rerouted to a hole in the abdomen and emptied into a bag. That's down from as many as 20% two decades ago.) Larger or more aggressive tumors usually require chemotherapy.

Your best bet to overcome colon cancer today is to catch it early—and that means regular screening. It would help if there were just one screening test and some simple rules to follow about when to get it done, but that's not the case. So pay attention to the following guidelines:

First, a warning. If you experience any symptoms—especially bleeding from the rectum, unusual constipation, abdominal cramping or a narrowing of the feces—talk to your doctor immediately about taking a peek inside your colon. All other things being equal, you should start screening by age 50. (Some doctors lean toward 40, but more on that later.) If you have a family history of the disease, particularly among your siblings or parents, you may need to start in your 30s or 40s. A good rule of thumb is to begin getting tested 10 years before the youngest age at which colon cancer was diagnosed in any member of your family.

It's a good idea to keep track of other diseases that have affected your family. There's growing evidence that uterine and ovarian cancers may be genetically related to colon cancer. So if your Aunt Mary died of uterine cancer, don't assume you're in the clear if you've had a hysterectomy or if you're a man. You could be at greater risk of colon cancer as well. The same holds true if you suffer from inflammatory conditions of the intestines, like Crohn's disease or ulcerative colitis.

That's the "when" part of the equation. Now for what you should do. There are three different ways to get screened for colon cancer. Which method you choose depends a lot on your wallet—and the level of risk you're willing to live with.

If you go for the least expensive method—because it's the one most often covered by insurance—make sure you get both parts: a stool test, which looks for the presence of hidden blood, and a flexible sigmoidoscopy, in which a lighted tube is inserted into the lower third of the colon. The stool test should be repeated annually, since only 1 out of 3 tumors bleeds enough to be picked up by the test

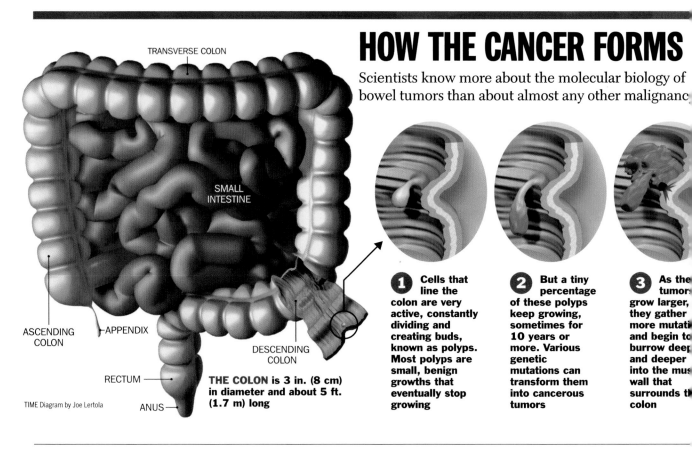

TRANSVERSE COLON

SMALL INTESTINE

ASCENDING COLON

APPENDIX

RECTUM

ANUS

DESCENDING COLON

THE COLON is 3 in. (8 cm) in diameter and about 5 ft. (1.7 m) long

TIME Diagram by Joe Lertola

HOW THE CANCER FORMS

Scientists know more about the molecular biology of bowel tumors than about almost any other malignanc

1 **Cells that line the colon are very active, constantly dividing and creating buds, known as polyps. Most polyps are small, benign growths that eventually stop growing**

2 **But a tiny percentage of these polyps keep growing, sometimes for 10 years or more. Various genetic mutations can transform them into cancerous tumors**

3 **As the tumor: grow larger, they gather more mutati and begin to burrow deep and deeper into the mus wall that surrounds t colon**

and then usually only after it's grown in size. The "flex sig" should be performed every five years, provided there's no change in symptoms or family history. Cost over five years: $100 to $200.

If you're not satisfied with checking out only part of your colon, you have two other options. Both require going on a liquid diet for 24 hours before the procedure and involve flushing the colon ahead of time. But they give more of the big picture.

In a double-contrast barium enema, a technician coats the inside of the intestine with the metallic dye and pumps the colon full of air. Then an X ray of the large intestine is taken, allowing doctors to visualize the outline of most abnormal growths. Provided the colon is free from disease, a barium enema should be repeated every five to 10 years. Cost: $200 to $400.

The other option is a colonoscopy, the procedure Couric underwent for the *Today* show. At $1,000 or more a pop, it's both expensive and invasive. Under normal circumstances you have to do it only once a decade.

"The prep is a pain," Couric admits. The colonoscopy itself is conducted under a mild sedative. "I was chatting the whole time," Couric recalls, "bossing my camera crew around." There is a risk, albeit a small one, that the device can slip and punch a hole in the intestinal wall. Yet a colonoscopy offers a distinct advantage in that the doctor can remove any small precancerous polyps as soon as they are found, making it the only screening test that can prevent cancer, not just detect it. That is why some doctors

and activists are lobbying to make colonoscopy the test of choice. However, most insurance companies won't pay for the test unless you have a family history or symptoms.

In the meantime, try making a few changes in your lifestyle. Start by eating at least five servings of fruits and vegetables a day (a serving consists of a medium-size banana, apple or orange, half a cup of solid vegetables or a full cup of lettuce). There's evidence that natural compounds found in fruits and vegetables can help protect against colon cancer. Besides, fruits and vegetables lower your blood pressure and help preserve your heart.

If that's too difficult, consider adding a multivitamin with 400 micrograms of folic acid (one of the B vitamins) to your breakfast routine. And don't forget to exercise. Joggers in particular seem to have a lower rate of colon cancer, but any physical activity is beneficial.

Whatever you do, don't let embarrassment stand in the way of your health. When Brenda Billingsley of Wilmington, Del., developed abdominal pains in 1998 at age 48, she told her doctors about most of her symptoms. But she never talked about the way her stools had changed shape (and she wasn't asked). The pains must be menopause, the doctors decided. Then in 1999, during a flexible sigmoidoscopy, a physician discovered a tumor the size of a golf ball that had begun to spread. Aggressive treatment seems to have left Billingsley cancer free. Now she's on a mission to persuade family and friends to be screened. "I just goad them until they do it," she says. Katie Couric would be proud. ∎

... AND HOW TO SPOT IT

Once the cancer ades the od and ph systems, lignant cells break off spread to er organs, h as the r, lungs and mach

SIGMOIDOSCOPY
A flexible tube is inserted into the lower third of the colon; repeat every five years, in conjunction with annual stool test

BARIUM ENEMA
Intestines are coated with liquid so that abnormal growths show on X ray; repeat every five to 10 years

COLONOSCOPY
Flexible tube reaches full length of large intestine; can remove small growths; repeat every 10 years

COLONOSCOPE
The handle stays on the outside; the thin part goes in

ACTUAL SIZE
The diameter of a typical colonoscope

THE LIVES IT HAS TOUCHED

From Hollywood to the White House, colon cancer strikes without warning

Audrey Hepburn
Our Fair Lady suffered from stomach pain that was initially misdiagnosed

Darryl Strawberry
While fighting to control his substance abuse, the Straw beat a colon tumor

Ruth Bader Ginsburg
Acute diverticulitis was diagnosed first, but colon cancer was later detected

Ronald Reagan
A routine physical turned up polyps in his colon; one of them was malignant

FOOD CHAIN In San Francisco opponents of genetically modified organisms chant "Hey, hey, ho, ho—GMOs have got to go!"

Frankenfood Hits the Front Burner

The debate over genetically modified food comes to your local grocery store

IT WAS THE SORT OF KITSCHY STREET THEATER YOU EX-pect in a city like San Francisco. A gaggle of protesters in front of a grocery store, some dressed as monarch butterflies, others as Frankenstein's monster. Signs reading HELL, NO WE WON'T GROW IT. People in white bio-hazard jumpsuits pitching Campbell's soup and Kellogg's corn flakes into a mock toxic-waste bin.

But just as the California activists were revving up in July, similar rants and chants were reverberating in such unlikely places as Grand Forks, N.D., Augusta, Maine, and Miami—19 U.S. cities in all. This was no frolicking radical fringe but the carefully coordinated start of a nationwide campaign, the Genetically Engineered Food Alert, to force the premarket safety testing and labeling of GMOs, or genetically modified organisms. Seven organizations, in-cluding such media-savvy veterans as the Sierra Club and Friends of the Earth, were launching the million-dollar, multiyear organizing effort that will put pressure on Con-gress, the Food and Drug Administration and individual companies, one at a time, starting with Campbell's soup.

The offensive represents the seeds of what could grow into a serious problem for U.S. agribusiness, which had been betting that science-friendly American consumers would remain immune to the "Frankenfood" backlash that has been growing in Europe and Japan. After all, this is (mostly) U.S. technology, and it has spread so quickly and so quietly that the proportion of U.S. farmland planted in genetically altered corn now stands at nearly 25%. Some 70% of processed food in American supermarkets, from soup to sandwich meat, contains ingredients derived from transgenic corn, soybeans and other plants.

The issue that is now on the front burner dates back to 1992, when the FDA decided that biotech ingredients did not materially alter food and therefore did not require la-beling. Nor, the agency declared, was premarket safety testing required; biotech additives were presumed to be benign. In March the Center for Food Safety and 53 other groups, including the Union of Concerned Scientists, filed a petition to force the FDA to change its policy.

Meanwhile, the issue has some support in Congress, where safety and labeling bills have been introduced. Sur-veys indicate that between two-thirds and three-quarters of Americans want biotech food to be labeled. Then why not do it? Because companies fear such disclosure could spell disaster. "Our data show that 60% of consumers would consider a mandatory biotech label as a warning that it is unsafe," says Gene Grabowski, spokesman for the Grocery Manufacturers of America. Will the companies succumb to the pressure, as they have in Europe? One thing is certain: the war over GMOs has just begun. ∎

The Abortion Pill Arrives in America

The FDA approves a new way to end unwanted pregnancy. Will women use it?

THE LANDSCAPE OF ABORTION IN America may have changed forever on Sept. 29, 2000, the day the Food and Drug Administration approved the sale of the abortion pill mifepristone—long known as RU 486—and put fewer restrictions on its use than anyone had expected. Virtually any family doctor or ob-gyn can now prescribe it as part of a two-drug regimen, provided he or she has some surgical backup arrangement if it fails to end the pregnancy or there are side effects. The result for women: no more abortion clinics; no more waiting until pregnancy is far enough along for surgical abortion. Just a series of pills taken over a period of days to induce a miscarriage. Pro-choice advocates hailed the decision as a breakthrough equal to the Pill.

Not to be confused with the morning-after pill, which doctors believe prevents a fertilized egg from implanting in the uterine wall, mifepristone causes miscarriage by blocking the hormone progesterone, which is needed to maintain a pregnancy. Mifepristone is followed 48 hours later by a second drug, called misoprostol, which forces the uterus to contract; the fetus is expelled several hours later. When taken within 49 days of the last period, the two-drug combination is 95% effective.

A big advantage of the two-drug combo is that it can end an unwanted pregnancy earlier than most surgical procedures, and with a lower risk of infection. Yet there are drawbacks. Some women can suffer excessive bleeding, nausea or diarrhea. Indeed, for many, surgery is less complicated—and quicker than the three-office-visit protocol required for the new pills.

The FDA's rules are actually less restrictive than many of those found in Europe. In Britain the pills are available only in licensed abortion facilities—usually clinics and National Health Service hospitals—and must be taken on the premises. Similar regulations exist in France, which requires four visits over a period of three weeks to a licensed hospital or clinic. Dr. Elizabeth Aubeny, one of the first physicians to test mifepristone, at the Broussais Hospital in Paris, argues there should be more flexibility in allowing women to take misoprostol at home, if they choose. Still, she says, "there are a lot of women who prefer to stay

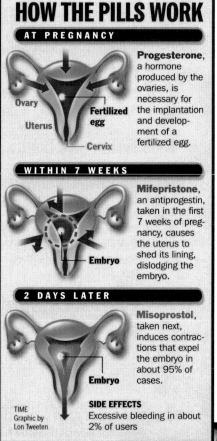

HOW THE PILLS WORK

AT PREGNANCY

Ovary
Uterus
Fertilized egg
Cervix

Progesterone, a hormone produced by the ovaries, is necessary for the implantation and development of a fertilized egg.

WITHIN 7 WEEKS

Embryo

Mifepristone, an antiprogestin, taken in the first 7 weeks of pregnancy, causes the uterus to shed its lining, dislodging the embryo.

2 DAYS LATER

Embryo

Misoprostol, taken next, induces contractions that expel the embryo in about 95% of cases.

SIDE EFFECTS
Excessive bleeding in about 2% of users

TIME
Graphic by
Lon Tweeten

in the hospital for three hours. They are afraid to be alone, afraid of the bleeding. For many it's psychological; they feel more reassured in a hospital than they do at home."

Women who opt for the abortion pill must make up their minds very quickly. Since conception occurs about 14 days after a menstrual cycle begins, they actually have 35 days from the time they miss their period to suspect they are pregnant, decide to abort and set up the appointments. (Home-pregnancy tests will help.) But once they do, many women find the process oddly comforting. Although they expel the fetus, all they see is a bloody mass that's unrecognizable. The nausea passes soon after the expulsion, and they can go on with their lives.

Some doctors hope the new procedure will offer a psychological advantage by giving patients the sense that the process is more natural because their body is doing the work, not a surgeon's vacuum. But that's not to say the drug makes abortion morally simple. In fact,

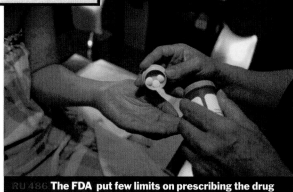

RU 486 **The FDA put few limits on prescribing the drug**

some doctors argue the opposite. Carole Joffe, a sociologist of reproductive health and visiting professor at Bryn Mawr college, believes mifepristone could make abortion "more emotionally wrenching because women who take [it] experience something like a miscarriage, where they have to confront the product of conception." Abortion foes vowed they would target the doctors who prescribe the drug and challenge the conscience of those who might use it. ∎

People

The Rice Man Cometh

For more than a decade, Swiss professor Ingo Potrykus dreamed of creating a "golden rice" that would improve the lives of millions of the poorest people in the world. At their core, these grains wouldn't be pearly white, like ordinary rice, but a very pale yellow—courtesy of beta-carotene, the nutrient that serves as a building block for vitamin A. He had pictured small children consuming the golden gruel their mothers would make, knowing it would preserve kids' eyesight and strengthen their resistance to infectious diseases.

POTRYKUS **Exit frying pan, enter fire**

After succeeding in creating the golden rice in 1999, Potrykus faced a new challenge: getting it accepted. For in addition to a full complement of genes from *Oryza sativa*—the most commonly consumed species of rice—the golden grains also contained snippets of DNA borrowed from bacteria and daffodils.

The new rice was the first compelling example of a modified crop that may benefit not just the farmers who grow it but also the consumers who eat it, including at least 1 million children who die every year because they are weakened by vitamin A deficiency and an additional 350,000 who go blind. Still, Frankenfood critics cried foul when Potrykus and a fellow scientist struck a deal with London-based food giant AstraZeneca to market the rice. As the Frankenfood debate ratchets up,the golden grains may become ground zero in the war over gene-modified food.

DOCTORS WISH **you'd eat more fish**

Gone Fishin'—for Health

Cardiologists have long known that eating fish helps protect against heart disease, but they didn't know why. For years they figured it was a simple question of substitution: folks who replace red meat with fish are naturally cutting down their intake of saturated fat, which the body easily converts into artery-choking plaque. But studies released in 2000 suggest there's something special about fish: the nutrients called omega-3 fatty acids (abundant in species like sardines, salmon and mackerel) seem to promote cardiovascular health. People who eat a lot of fish (think Greenland Eskimos and the Japanese) have relatively low rates of heart disease. The American Heart Association issued new recommendations that everyone eat two 3-oz. servings of fatty fish a week.

In the Testosterone Zone

The hot product for many men in 2000: testosterone supplements. About 4 million men in the U.S. whose bodies don't make enough of the male hormone take a doctor-prescribed synthetic version, mostly by self-injection. They were joined by growing numbers of men looking to bulk up or increase sexual drive, especially when a new, easy-to-apply testosterone ointment, AndroGel, became generally available for the first time by prescription during the summer. Experts cautioned that abuse of testosterone can cause liver damage and accelerate prostate cancer.

BODY SHOPPING **A real-life Popeye checks out supplements in New York City**

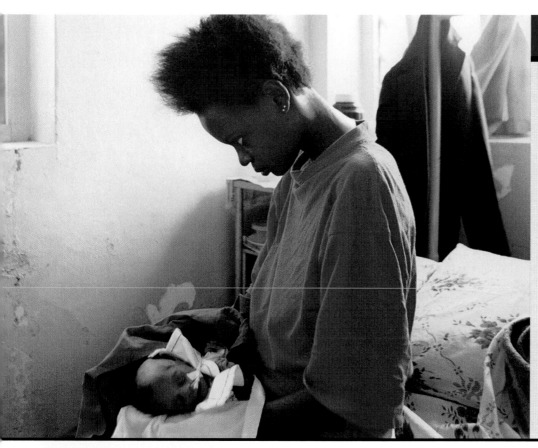

Images

AFRICA'S TRAGEDY
A 2000 U.N. study found that 15-year-olds living in sub-Saharan Africa have a fifty-fifty chance of getting the AIDS virus. African women ages 15 to 24 are two to three times as likely as young men to be HIV-positive, owing to their having sex with older male partners, a heavily infected population in Africa.

Uganda, the first African country to promote safe sex with condoms, has seen its HIV-infection rate among teenage girls drop from almost 5% in 1990 to 1.5% today.

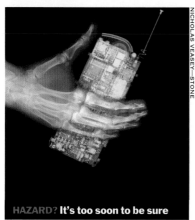

HAZARD? **It's too soon to be sure**

Are Cell Phones Safe?

In the fall, Motorola, Nokia and all other cell-phone makers bowed to mounting concerns about safety by disclosing just how much radiation their phones emit. The once hard-to-find data—measured in specific absorption rates—was on some phones by Christmas. The Federal Communications Commission said all phones below an SAR level of 1.6 are equally safe. (An SAR measures the energy in watts per kilogram that one gram of body tissue absorbs from a cell phone.) The big busy signal is that scientists still haven't reached any definitive conclusions about cell-phone radiation. Studies attempting to prove a much-publicized link between cancer and cell-phone use proved inconclusive. Yet many experts caution that it is far too early to give the handy phones a clean bill of health.

New Target: Ministrokes

According to a 2000 study, the number of strokes—in decline for decades—is rising again. In 1999 alone there were 750,000 full-fledged strokes in the U.S. and half a million transient ischemic attacks, or ministrokes, which are drawing new attention owing to the stealth of their damage and the effectiveness of timely treatment.

Ministrokes result from temporary interruptions of blood flow to the brain. Unlike major strokes, they last anywhere from a few seconds to 24 hours. They rarely cause lasting damage, but often precede a serious stroke. Signs to look out for:
• Numbness or weakness in the face, arm or leg, especially on one side of the body
• Trouble seeing in one or both eyes
• Confusion and difficulty speaking or understanding
• Difficulty in walking, dizziness or loss of coordination
• Severe headache with no cause.

If you experience any of these symptoms, call your doctor at once. The call could save your life.

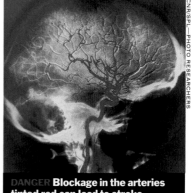

DANGER **Blockage in the arteries tinted red can lead to stroke**

The Arts

BYE BYE BAUHAUS: Architect Frank Gehry brought the mind-bending, shape-shifting, titanium-sheathed style of his Guggenheim Museum in Bilbao, Spain, to the new Experience Music Project in Seattle

Gregory Heisler—Corbis Outline for TIME

WE LIKE TO

The summer smash *Survivor* leads television into *terra incognita,* as America eyeballs a strange new breed of voyeuristic entertainment

J EEPERS CREEPERS—WE'RE ALL PEEPERS! IN THE summer of 2000, something strange happened in America's living rooms: VTV—voyeur television—became the rage. Sure, we'd learned to love seeing real people buck the odds in unscripted fashion on ABC's hit 1999 show, *Who Wants to Be a Millionaire?* But the offering that took reality TV to a new level and hooked Americans on the format was the CBS castaways-themed blockbuster, *Survivor.* This outlandish sibling of *Gilligan's Island,* adapted from a hit European show, "stranded" 16 everyday Americans on a South Pacific island, divided them into "tribes," put

them through some silly contests, then had them convene each week in a tribal council to vote one person off the island. The last person standing received a check for $1 million.

Survivor hit the horse latitudes of summer television like a tsunami. The first week the Pulau Tiga–based game show aired, ABC scheduled the virtually unbeatable *Millionaire* against it. *Survivor* won in almost every audience category, as 15.5 million people tuned in. The second week, *Survivor* won hands down. By the third week, *Millionaire* host Regis Philbin, monochrome outfit in tatters, slunk away from the time slot to lick his wounds, leaving *Two Guys and a Girl* and *Norm* to take his butt whuppin' for him. Soon *Survivor* was attracting 24.5 million viewers each week. Its penultimate episode drew an audience 23% larger than the combined household audience of its five broadcast network competitors—combined. In fact, *Survivor* became the most-watched summer series in TV history, swamping *Millionaire's* record 1999 ratings. CBS sold its 30-second spots on the show's final episode for $600,000 each, more than those on *E.R.,* NBC's top-rated hospital drama.

When 50 million viewers tuned in on that final night, only four of the program's original 16 contestants

remained in the running for the big payoff: Richard Hatch, 39, a corporate trainer from Rhode Island; Kelly Wigglesworth, 23, a white-water guide from Las Vegas; Rudy Boesch, 72, a retired Navy SEAL; and Susan Hawk, 38, a truck driver from Wisconsin. Though taping of the show had ended months before, CBS had managed to keep the eventual winner of the show secret. In an example of the group dynamics that kept viewers glued to their sets, the foursome had teamed up earlier in a loose "alliance" to vote others off the island. The alliance was led by Hatch, an openly gay puppetmaster who held the show together entertainment-wise with his catty punditry, villainous wit—and penchant for walking the beach sans sarong while pro-

SOLE SURVIVOR Winner Hatch savors his paycheck

claiming himself a "fat naked fag." Sure enough, when the last vote was taken, Hatch was pronounced the game's winner, took home the check—and became an instant American celebrity.

What explains the incredible appeal of *Survivor*? For starters, there was the gladiatorial concept: abandoning people on a tropical island to scrabble for food and shelter, all for the delectation of sluggards licking Cheetos dust off their fingers in their air-conditioned living rooms. Then there was the Machiavellian twist: having the contestants vote one another off the island in a slow-motion, psychological version of survival of the fittest. It was a recipe for mind games: for suffering, for meanspiritedness, for betrayal and humiliation. Now, that's entertainment!

MEMO TO FOX: DON'T GET REAL!

Look at it this way: people have been married in Las Vegas for dumber reasons. Probably with less knowledge of each other. Maybe with worse odds of their union's lasting. But whatever those drunk, impulsive legions have had to regret the next morning, they, unlike Darva Conger and Rick Rockwell, did not take the plunge in front of their families, a former Miss America and millions of TV viewers. On Feb. 15, Americans—lots of them—tuned in to witness just such a horror show, Fox's *Who Wants to Marry a Multi-Millionaire?* Fifty women, chosen from more than 3,000, competed for the hand of

IMMODEST PROPOSAL **Rockwell pops the question**

Rockwell, a self-proclaimed San Diego multimillionaire, in what amounted to a beauty pageant minus the class and intellectual heft. Ratings for the two-hour special climbed steadily from 10 million viewers the first half an hour to nearly 23 million.

The show ended with a bended-knee proposal and a civil ceremony under a giant floral arch. The "marriage" ended after a honeymoon cruise from hell during which, Conger said, the pair did not consummate their union. Conger, 34, an emergency-room nurse, walked away with more than $100,000 in loot, including an Isuzu Trooper and a $35,000, three-carat diamond ring. And then she walked away from Rockwell.

The entire show was a fiasco. Rockwell turned out to have allegedly abused a former girlfriend, and apparently was no multimillionaire. The marriage was annulled. Meanwhile, Fox executives vowed they would abandon the show entirely, sparing us a planned sequel. Conger, who insisted all along that she was an intensely private person, ended up in the special place reserved for U.S. women of a certain notoriety: as cover girl and star of a 10-page pictorial in *Playboy*.

Despite *Survivor*'s gross-outs (like eating live insects), its dark premise and its wall-to-wall tackiness—the faux–*Lion King* sound track, the "tribal councils" held in what looked like a Holiday Inn Polynesian lounge circa 1963, the somber narration of Jeff Probst, former host of VH1's *Rock 'n' Roll Jeopardy!* and challenger to Regis for luckiest-man-in-America status—despite all this, viewers embraced the desert-island soap with fascination and bemused contempt. Did Dirk have a crush on Kelly? Would Ramona throw up again?

Sipping a Miller Lite at Harry's of Arlington in Arlington Heights, Ill., and watching the third installment of *Survivor*, Christopher Wojcik, 24, declared, "I think it's fixed, and I don't buy any of it." He had not, however, missed an episode. "Don't vote me off the island!" soon rivaled "Is that your final answer?" as a red flag for water-cooler bores. And, in the surest sign of TV success, CBS quickly scheduled a *Survivor* sequel.

The success of the summer series scrambled up the TV industry. Suddenly, tired old CBS was on the top of the heap, with millions of young viewers eagerly voting with their remotes for the network best known for *Murder, She Wrote.* Other reality TV shows were catching the buzz: PBS's *The 1900 House*, the latest season of MTV's *The Real World*, and CBS's other foray into duplicating a European hit, *Big Brother.*

The VTV phenomenon signaled another strange angle in America's fame-fixated culture: through a sudden explosion of new-wave voyeur shows, ordinary people are becoming our new celebrities. The price: living in front of cameras that catch their every tantrum, embarrassment and moral lapse. TV and media critics are conditioned to believe that once people start entertaining themselves by spying on others, we are just scant moments away from grandma porn and ABC's *Monday Night Stoning.* (You could have based a drinking game on how often the Roman Colosseum, the movie *Network* and George Orwell came up in discussions of VTV.) Stuart Fischoff, professor of media psychology at California State University, Los Angeles, cheerfully admitted to enjoying *Survivor* but added, "The downside

It's the suffering, the humiliation, the meanspiritedness—that's what made millions of Americans tune in

that does concern me is the need to get more excessive and extreme. Let's try a public execution. Let's try a snuff film." On the other hand, TV voyeurism also means millions of ordinary folks are making other ordinary folks, without benefit of surgical augmentation, into stars just for being themselves. Can that be so wrong?

Then again, why on earth are so many people willing to let us look? For one thing, our culture is deep into a populist period of personal confession, the First-Person Era. There's the unflagging craze for memoirs—especially ordinary people's tales of woe, like Frank McCourt's

Angela's Ashes and Mary Karr's gripping childhood tale, *The Liars' Club*. Then there's the World Wide Web, the invention that puts the "me" in "medium." No sooner was the Internet opened to home users than its essential text became the personal home page, a document dedicated to the fact that its author exists: Here I am. Here is my dog. Here is my story. And that was before 24-hr. webcams enabled their users to broadcast live feeds from their offices and boudoirs. With so many willing, casual exhibitionists among us, it's less surprising that VTV happened than that it didn't happen sooner.

I S THIS NARCISSISM OR CATHARSIS? IT'S HARD TO TELL the difference nowadays, but several VTV veterans explained their decisions to bare all in the language of therapy and personal growth. *Survivor* contestant Sonja Christopher, 63, was already a survivor—of breast cancer—and signed on as a way of moving on. "I had been through a lot in the past two years," she said. "Following this fantasy, doing this crazy thing, was a way to try to heal myself. It was a survival instinct."

In *Life the Movie: How Entertainment Conquered Reality*, Neal Gabler argues that celebrity culture has created a universal lust for the camera, and he sees these series as a case in point. "Reality has become the greatest entertainment of all," he said. "It's symptomatic of a larger phenomenon that all of life is entertainment." It's a grand argument, appealing to our now conditioned distrust of the fame machine. But in fact, most of us don't want to, in Gabler's words, "get to the other side of the glass," not this way. That's partly why we goggle at these shows, dumbstruck.

For better and worse, VTV provides something many sitcoms and dramas don't. Surprises, for instance. True, arguments over who's hogging the rat meat are probably not what Aristotle had in mind when conceiving the *Poetics*. And producers can contrive conflict, such as *Survivor*'s races and bug-eating contests, not to mention its million-dollar endgame. But *Survivor* functioned as drama, if not art, because we could map its petty squabbles and triumphs onto our own lives. Those mismatched 16 castaways, working together, then looking out for No. 1, could be your co-workers, your family. Moreover, VTV stars offer a feeling of accessibility that traditional TV's Flockharts and Schwimmers, with their phalanxes of publicists and flunkies, don't. Despite the post-production editing, you feel you're seeing, if not the true person, at least a less mediated version.

The criticism that VTV "reality" isn't "real"—it is edited and subjects adopt false faces—is absolutely valid. It is also, by now, a truism, widely acknowledged by viewers and many participants alike. This is part of why we enjoy laughing at these series: they let us feel superior not only to the people on them but also to the medium itself. Helping make their viewers into savvier media critics, these shows teach survival skills for our wired age. ■

DANGER: "REALITY" AHEAD

Don't bother touching that dial: *Survivor's* success was so overwhelming that it may affect your TV set for years to come. Though the other reality TV shows that aired in 2000 failed to match its success, it's an axiom in Hollywood that every hit show is subject to cloning—including *Survivor,* whose sequel is set in the Australian outback. Among the other shows that made 2000 a voyeur's dream:

MONTY BRINTON—CBS

BIG BROTHER If you missed this show—well, as George Orwell said, "Ignorance is bliss." For the record, here's what went on: 10 folks agreed to spend as long as three months sequestered, sleeping in communal bedrooms and living without TV or newspapers in a 1,800-sq.-ft. house with cameras everywhere (yes, including the bathroom)—all for cash prizes. The human hamsters were on TV five nights a week, and on the Internet 24/7. Like the *Survivor* cast, they were whittled off one at a time, by audience vote, until winner Eddie McGee claimed $500,000. Good news: it started strong, then lost ratings.

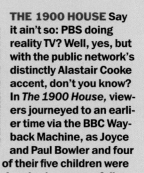

CHRIS RIDLEY—THIRTEEN/WNET TV

THE 1900 HOUSE Say it ain't so: PBS doing reality TV? Well, yes, but with the public network's distinctly Alastair Cooke accent, don't you know? In *The 1900 House,* viewers journeyed to an earlier time via the BBC Wayback Machine, as Joyce and Paul Bowler and four of their five children were plunked into a suburban London home carefully restored to the last year of Queen Victoria's reign. The journey proved fascinating, as the Bowlers and their audience confronted life sans toothpaste, sans washing machine, sans microwave and—ah, the good old days—sans reality television.

THE REAL WORLD MTV kicked off the craze for reality TV in 1992 with its prime-time series *The Real World*. The idea: stick a bunch of nifty-looking coming-of-age kids in a nifty house in a nifty location, wire the place for maximum drama and minimum privacy—then edit the results like crazy. This year, the program's ninth season, the colorful locale was New Orleans.

J. MALECKI—MTV

CHRIS PIZZELLO—AP/WIDE WORLD

Jail Bait ROCK

Music's hot teen stars practice their navel maneuvers as they rise to rule the pop charts

CHRISTINA AGUILERA The 19-year-old singer's body sometimes seems too small to contain her voice. Her bare waist, so thin it might fit between two parentheses, looks too tiny to support the strong, soulful melismata that flow from her lips. In fact, Aguilera's talent seems to require more space than the teen-pop world can provide. Her vocals strain and flutter against the confinement of her songs, a seagull in a parakeet cage. Aguilera, like Britney Spears, is an alumna of Disney's New Mickey Mouse Club; she also sang in Disney's animated hit *Mulan*. Her father is from Ecuador and her mother is Irish American; they divorced when she was seven, and since then she has had little contact with her dad. In 2000 she explored her cultural heritage on the Spanish-language CD *Mi Reflejo*, with translations of five prior pop hits and six original Spanish recordings.

'N SYNC

It was a good year for 'N Sync, *left,* as the boy band's album *No Strings Attached* sold a record-breaking 2.4 million units in its first week in release. 2000 was payback time for the teen idols: the CD had been held up for four months by a $150 million lawsuit filed by Louis Pearlman (the Svengali behind 'N Sync, the Backstreet Boys and LFO) when 'N Sync tried to leave him. After settling out of court, the band signed with Jive Records, also the new home of the Backstreet Boys—who are not exactly in synch with … you-know-who.

VAUGHN YOUTZ—NEWMAKERS-LIAISON

BRITNEY SPEARS Yes, the youngster above, now 19, has the most overexposed belly button in America. Yes, she insists, her breasts are real—contrary to the rumors of implants. ("I would go up to people, and they would stare at [my chest] … and I was like, 'Eeewww!' " she told PEOPLE magazine.) Yes, she is the youngest performer ever to have a No. 1 single and album. And no, despite the hope of adults everywhere, she shows no signs of going away soon.

BACKSTREET BOYS

Omigod! Have the Backstreet Boys passed their sell-by date? Why, it was only back in September '99 that the Fab Five appeared on the cover of pop mag ENTERTAINMENT WEEKLY under a headline declaring, "It's the Backstreet Boys' World: We Just Live in It." Well, in 2000 somebody else moved into their world—yes, it was their bitter rivals, the evil clones of 'N Sync … and don't forget those fast-rising wannabes, 98°. In the harsh realm of kid pop, idols date faster than hairdos. Next!

People

Strutting, Fretting, Selling

One critic called him a "moronic, slime talking, homophobic, pornographic, hate-meister misogynist." But in certain circles—mainly white male teens with money to spend on CDs— that list might be a job description for the new breed of superstar exemplified by the leader of the white rap movement, Eminem, a.k.a. Slim Shady, a.k.a. Marshall Mathers. The Detroit-reared rapper, 27, created a media-ready outsize racial persona— dyed blond hair, played-up trailer-trash roots—to compete with the over-the-top ghetto style of black gangsta rappers.

It worked. Eminem received two Grammy Awards in 2000: Best Solo

EMINEM His whiter shade of rap hit big

Performance for his single *My Name Is* and Best Rap Album for *The Slim Shady L.P.,* both from 1999. The hits kept coming: Eminem's *The Marshall Mathers LP* was released in May 2000 and debuted at No. 1 on the Billboard charts, selling just shy of 1.8 million copies in its first week of release.

All in all, it was a good year for the high-school dropout, by his criteria: in June he was arrested twice on felony weapons charges; in July his wife Kim attempted suicide (in one new song, he rapped of kidnapping her and slashing her throat); and in August the bitter superstar filed a petition for divorce. A bad career move? His Anger Management tour featured a segment in which he beat up a dummy labelled "Kim." Who'll be his designated victim now?

THE CHICKS **Not Nashville enough?**

Hicks Nix Chicks' Mix

Their overnight success took many moons. For nearly a decade the Dixie Chicks played grange halls and coffeehouses and toured from their native Texas to Alaska, without corralling the interest of a Nashville record company. It wasn't until Sony Nashville highlighted the Dixie Chicks' sassy sauciness that the group became the thing du jour, selling albums like hot cakes and earning a bushel and a peck of Grammys. The Chicks are no three-headed blond joke: lead singer Natalie Maines won a scholarship to the Berklee School of Music, Emily Erwin (now Robison) plays a mean banjo, and her sister Martie Seidel is a classical violinist turned fiddler. But the group's mainstream success, along with that of fellow crossover queens Faith Hill and Shania Twain, spurred a Nashville backlash. One anti-crossover song title declared, *I'd Give My Right Nut to Save Country Music.*

WEST WING **A success, even sans sex scandals**

Celestial Trio

For cynical movie buffs who enjoy a good big-budget flop, the signs were promising for Columbia's remake of the '70s TV show *Charlie's Angels:* casting dramas and on-set tensions turned the filming into the most troubled, most chronicled production since *Titanic.* The studio spent some $90 million and deployed an army of 17 writers in hopes of creating a box-office halo for new Angels Cameron Diaz, Drew Barrymore and Lucy Liu.

TIME's critic Richard Schickel concluded, "The film is essentially about displaying the Angels in ways that are titillating to adolescent males, yet give their dates the impression that something inspiring is being said about female empowerment. It is, on both counts, just a tease." But then, he

ANGELS **Liu, Diaz and Barrymore rule**

wasn't the target audience. The film was a hit, joining Jim Carrey's *The Grinch* to give Hollywood its biggest Thanksgiving ever.

Tonight—Farm Subsidies!

With television's best recent drama series, NBC's Emmy-winning saga of the presidency *The West Wing,* creator and writer Aaron Sorkin proved that TV can deal with public policy and still earn good ratings. His characters—President Josiah Bartlet, a liberal Democrat played by Martin Sheen; chief of staff Leo McGarry, played by John Spencer; and a clutch

Images

WIZARD WANNABES
A few seconds past the witching hour of midnight on July 8, a huge, unnecessary marketing blitz culminated with the release of J.K. Rowling's *Harry Potter and the Goblet of Fire,* fourth in the British author's series involving life in a boarding school for wizards-to-be. The big buildup was pure Hollywood, so it was refreshing to recall that kids like this pair of Ohio boys were dressing up to salute Harry's latest adventures not on the screen, but in the 734 dense pages of ... a book.

of earnest young staff members— wrestled with school vouchers, the Pentagon's "Don't ask, don't tell" policy on gays, even the debate over using statistical sampling to improve the Census.

The program's topical wrangles hew closely to Washington realities instead of Hollywood's usual cartoon version of them. "The farther you get away from the truth of those debates, the softer the drama is going to be," said Sorkin, who relies on consultants like former Clinton press secretary Dee Dee Myers to keep things real. Sorkin's unusual approach, said Myers, is, "Give me a really boring issue and let's have a fight about it."

Who Let the Fad Out?

Call 2000 the Year of the Woof, for people seemed to be barking a lot. Kids across the U.S. were woofing it up. Sports fans too. David Letterman and his crew were barking on *The Late Show.* Blame it on the Baha Men.

Their unavoidable hit, *Who Let the Dogs Out* (the title of the album as well as the single), was a mix of calypso-inflected insults ("Get back, you flea-infested mongrel!") set to a dizzy beat. In the great hook, the singer shouts, "Who let the dogs out?" The reply: a male chorus of "Woof! Woof! Woof! Woof! Woof!"

The ditty sprinted up the charts and into the Top 10 faster than Marion Jones. A fixture on MTV and Nickelodeon, the tune excited kids, annoyed parents and was chanted at sports venues across the land. It was the first major U.S. hit for the band, long stars in their native Bahamas. Call it revenge: their last U.S. CD had sold a grand total of 700 units. Now, that was a dog.

BAHA MEN **Rising from a setback, they put their doggone hit atop the charts**

THE BEST OF
2000
CRITICS' CHOICES

WE LOOK BACK ... WELL, WHY DO WE look back? The technological revolution has no rearview mirror. We have not only seen the future, we've moved into it. Yesterday is history. Familiar forms are beginning to disappear. Who needs fiction when we have *Survivor* and the Florida Supreme Court? New formats are already transforming what designer Bruce Mau calls "the global image economy." Soon the multiplexes will go digital; "films" will no longer exist. We're already consuming e-books, e-movies, e-music. E-nough!

Why look back? Because the past, as recalled and reshaped through art, is the wisest guide to what lies ahead. Thus we codify the year's pleasures in 10 Best lists, to determine which artifacts in the hall closet of recent memory are worth saving.

Not just technicians but creators have that retrospective spirit. Fully half of our cinema entries are set in the past, from a decade ago back to World War II and into the mythical mists of the Qing dynasty. Some of our top CDs are replays of Shostakovich and Django Reinhardt. The hip place for Londoners to see modern art is in a revamped old power station. The best of theater includes a Trojan War epic and something called *Hamlet*. And on our fiction list, No. 4 is ... *Beowulf*!

So everything old is new again. And the new? If it's good, it will age very nicely.

FROM HIGHBROW ART TO MASS-MARKET gewgaws, transparency—a visual trend popularized earlier by Apple's coveted iMacs—was the year's clear (*ahem*) buzz word. Some of the year's most notable buildings played with teasing, gauzy see-through effects, and you could scarcely buy consumer goods not skinned in Technicolor plastic: the Handspring Visor personal digital assistant, the Power Mac G4 Cube, translucent trash cans and toilet-brush holders from the likes of Ikea and Target. And magazines and books were rife with die-cut covers. The luminous transparent artifacts of 2000 thrummed with Jell-O-colored energy, as if so jazzed they could hardly contain their insides. Now you see it. And you don't.

THE ROSE CENTER
FOR EARTH AND SPACE

(1) The new planetarium addition to New York City's Museum of Natural History is a 21st century update of an 18th century dream. Architect James Stewart Polshek's simple design, a metal sphere set in a mostly glass cube, is a homage to the unbuilt ball that Etienne-Louis Boullée conceived in 1784 as a memorial to Sir Isaac Newton. It tells of the grandeur of the universe itself, speaking in the language of both classic modernism and very high tech.

Polshek's forms operate on our deepest fantasies about the order of the cosmos. His sphere is covered with steel panels that inscribe it with meridians and latitude lines, so it stands in easily for the earth. But see it from the side, within sight of the floating models of Jupiter and Saturn, and it's the sun. Get underneath, next to the giant tripod that supports it, and it's the underside of a sci-fi space pod. Stand back in a properly reflective mood, and it suggests the expanding bubble of creation itself.

2 HET OOSTEN PAVILION As the clouds pass over Amsterdam, colors shimmer and shift subtly on the surface of architect Steven Holl's magnificent yet playful cube. This riverside structure, built for a Dutch corporation, looks less as if it was made from glass and perforated metal than from the surrounding water and light.

3 THE TATE MODERN An ingenious appropriation took a former London power station and cranked up its wattage. The design team, led by Jacques Herzog and Pierre de Meuron, has provided natural illumination for 20th century classics and warehouse-scale space for contemporary artists.

4 THE OKLAHOMA CITY NATIONAL MEMORIAL The Butzer Design Partnership honored the 168 people killed in the 1995 bombing with a pavilion containing bronze and glass chairs—one for each victim—that recall the innocent dead while offering figurative comfort to the living (see pp. 84-85).

5 PS1'S TEMPORARY DUNESCAPE OUTDOOR SUMMER PAVILION Architect firm SHoP's temporary "urban beach" in Queens, N.Y., became a breezy, inviting summer sensation. Made from 6,000 2-in. by 2-in. boards that rolled, twisted and slid about, it offered wet and dry places for visitors to bask, wade and escape the sun. It was an architectural drawing suddenly come to life.

6 HEADBLADE A fashionably shaved head is either the ultimate in minimalist

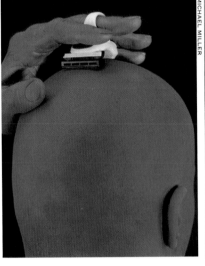

dandyism or the 21st century version of the comb-over. HeadBlade's power razor has a form as curvy and clean as Patrick Stewart's pate. Nestle it in your palm and "comb" yourself bald. It's shear elegance.

7 LIFE STYLE Design guru Bruce Mau argues passionately that form is inextricable from mes-

sage. Nowhere is that truer than in his 624-page book, part portfolio, part manifesto, urging readers to become alert to

the meanings transmitted in "the global image economy."

8 DUCATI SPORTS BIKE MH900e Like a futurist painting, this sensuously sleek Italian motorbike, designed in honor of champion racer Mike Hailwood, seems to move while standing still. And did it ever move! Just after midnight on New Year's Day, it sold out its first year's entire production at the Ducati website in 31 minutes flat.

9 DESIGN CULTURE NOW This sprawling exhibit at New York City's Cooper-Hewitt Museum, the first of what is planned

to be a triennial event, epitomized Americans' rising interest in design. The show celebrated contemporary work in an accessible frame that laid plain the degrees of separation—and connection—between Frank Gehry's buildings and Martha Stewart's merchandise.

10 THE NIKE iD Here's a nifty thing to Just Do: Nike allows Worldwide Web surfers to customize this sneaker online. You can select the style, colors and lace types, even stamp the shoes with your personal ID code. Any bets on how long until you can pick your own sweatshop worker online?

THIS WAS THE YEAR MUSIC LOST ITS SHAPE. For more than a century, musical performances have been contained: on piano rolls, on vinyl, on compact discs. With the rise of online music, the art form became free: songs could be zipped from fan to fan across continents, acts were able to reach fans directly. Much has been made of online music's economic threat (even though artists from Scott Joplin to TLC have faced money woes doing things the old way), but the Net is also changing music's sound: rare tracks, remixes and material too strange for stores are now just a click away.

② RADIOHEAD *Kid A* (Capitol). Well crafted and inscrutable, this deceptively mellow CD has the haunting power of a dream remembered. Tinged with electronica, bursting with restless creativity, it delivers both rock's elegy and its *raison d'être*.

③ SINEAD O'CONNOR *Faith and Courage* (Atlantic). This time around, the defiant Irish singer and gadfly delivers not a sermon of fire but a psalm of forgiveness. Her pop songs may bear weighty spiritual messages about loving one's self, but they carry themselves lightly, as if lifted by seraphim's wings.

④ THE EMERSON QUARTET *Shostakovich String Quartets* (DGG). Shostakovich turned Stalin's Great Terror into art in his 15 string quartets, a laceratingly vivid document interpreted here by America's greatest quartet.

⑤ SADE *Lovers Rock* (Epic). The soulful singer returns with a solemn CD that was worth the eight-year wait. These elegant songs explore heartbreak, yes, but racism as well. On each cut, Sade's lovely, melancholy voice blossoms like a blue bruise.

⑥ SHELBY LYNNE *I Am Shelby Lynne* (Island). Is it country? Is it soul? Maybe the words rhythm and bluegrass best capture the revelatory jolt

D'ANGELO VOODOO

① Slick as chicken grease. Hotter than summer asphalt in Nevada. D'Angelo summoned old ghosts—Jimi and Marvin—and woke up a new artistic spirit in R. and B. *Voodoo* (Virgin) is a ménage à trois of soul, hip-hop and jazz, all tangled up like lovers caught in the act. Even as D'Angelo pays homage to music's past, he proves the future is in good hands.

of songs with which Lynne, a Nashville expatriate, bends two great rivers of American music into a pool brimming with fresh ideas.

⑦ SARAH HARMER *You Were Here* (Zoe). Harmer, a Canadian singer-

songwriter, has a voice with some of the sublime charm of Dido's and writes erudite but colloquial lyrics that evoke the folksy smarts of the Indigo Girls. This is the year's best debut, with honorable mention going to Nelly Furtado's blithe set *Whoa, Nelly!*

⑧ MARIA SCHNEIDER *Allégresse* (Enja). Schneider's big band paints musical landscapes full of glowing

pastel harmonies and sharp-angled rhythms. Listen to her sweepingly ambitious compositions and hear the next wave in jazz taking shape before your very ears.

⑨ JAMES CARTER *Chasin' the Gypsy* (Atlantic). This tribute to Django Reinhardt offers more than covers of the Gypsy guitarist's songs. Carter also serves up involving originals inspired by Reinhardt and, in doing so, establishes himself as one of the premiere saxophonists in jazz. The chase is on, and Carter is closing in.

⑩ WYCLEF JEAN *The Ecleftic: 2 Sides II a Book* (Columbia). While other hip-hoppers just lay tracks, Wyclef writes songs. No topic, from romance to the Amadou Diallo killing, is beyond his range, and no musical style, from reggae to country, is beyond his grasp. Political, comical, unpredictable—Wyclef is simply the most inventive male performer in rap.

"REAL PEOPLE SHOULD NOT BE ON TELEVISION," host Garry Shandling declared at the Emmys, to cheers from the nervous actors. Reality TV dominated 2000, providing some of its best shows (*see* No. 1) and ickiest lows (remember Rick Rockwell?). TV had other fantasy-reality conflicts: CBS's *Early Show* digitized its logo onto video of Manhattan; and then there was election night. At the Emmys, reality lost out. There's no award for nonscripted shows, and *The West Wing's* airbrushed depictions of our better angels beat the *The Sopranos'* gritty realism. Sometimes fantasy still bites.

2 MALCOLM IN THE MIDDLE (Fox). More lovable than Raymond, more destructive than the Ebola virus, the sugar-buzzed *Malcolm* dropped a firecracker down the shorts of the family-sitcom genre. Jane Kaczmarek, as ferocious, loyal Lois, is not just a mom but the life force.

3 THE LEAGUE OF GENTLEMEN (BBC America, Comedy Central). Part *Monty Python*, part *Blue Velvet*, this macabre British comedy introduced viewers to the murderous town of Royston Vasey (slogan: "You'll never leave!") and three gifted sketch comics who played more than 60 bizarre but richly defined characters.

4 GILMORE GIRLS (The WB). Planned as family-friendly TV, *Gilmore* was meant to be Good and ended up good. A charming story of a happily unwed mom and a brainy teen whose life isn't defined by boys, it shows that feminism and family values don't have to be mutually exclusive.

5 THE TALLY HASSLE IN TALLAHASSEE After TV fumbled its Florida projections, it landed a tailor-made story. The recount saga stripped the election of those pesky issues, leaving what 24-hr. news covers best: raw politics and lawsuits. At last, a story that cable couldn't blow out of proportion.

6 WONDERLAND (ABC). TV loves shootings and heart attacks but has ignored mental illness. The best medical show in years dared to go inside a psychiatric hospital with clear-eyed compassion and depth. Two ill-rated airings later, ABC, like society, chose to look the other way again.

7 FIRST PERSON (Bravo). Filmmaker Errol Morris beautifully shot these profiles of odd obsessives (a squid hunter, an abattoir designer). In his trademark style, he had his subjects tell their stories gazing straight into the lens; their eyes were windows to the surreal.

8 THE TOM GREEN CANCER SPECIAL (MTV). In the Year of Celeb Health— Dave's heart, Michael's Parkinson's—Green's testicular cancer was the most creatively rewarding affliction. Green took his gross-out comedy to a new level on an unflinching show that took quite a pair to make.

9 THE CORNER (HBO). The addicts and pushers in this miniseries would have been anonymous, two-dimensional perps and problems on a cop drama, but here they swelled to life fully realized and unromanticized. Khandi Alexander gave TV's performance of the year.

10 DARK ANGEL PILOT (Fox). Although fun and stylish, the weekly series sometimes bogs down in ill-wrought slang and a creepy fixation on young star Jessica Alba's curves. But the 2-hr. opener of movie wizard James Cameron's first-ever foray into televised sci-fi—sleek, explosive, sexy and packed with stunning, sweeping visuals—was simply postapocalyptastic.

SURVIVOR (CBS)

1 When **16 people battled on hot Pulau Tiga for a cool million, the "snakes and rats" proved Sartre right: Hell is other people.** The biggest prime-time soap since *Dallas* was an addictively tacky social chess game, full of societal metaphors and water-cooler fodder. It achieved everything good TV (and bad TV) should.

I F ACADEMY MEMBERS WERE LIMITED to Hollywood fare when filling out their ballots for the Best Picture of 2000, they might enter NONE OF THE ABOVE. It was that kind of year for mainstream films. Some made money (*Mission* this, *Perfect* that), but few were as good as their marketing campaigns. When Hollywood makes good movies, we'll let you know. But there are wonderful films made all over: in Asia, Europe and independent America. Next time, check out a film like these ten. The most satisfying movie adventure can be in choosing a film you never knew you'd love.

② YOU CAN COUNT ON ME A roughneck wanderer (Mark Ruffalo) drops in on his staid, small-town sister (Laura Linney) and incidentally makes a man of her overprotected son. Writer-director Kenneth Lonergan's film is a rueful, truthful study of heartland heartache.

③ GEORGE WASHING-TON Poor kids in rural North Carolina face a drab life and sudden death with varying degrees of grownup perplexity, anger and idealism. From these convulsions of preadolescent yearning, auteur David Gordon

Green, 25, weaves a rich, rapturous tapestry of images and emotions.

④ SUNSHINE Three generations of a Hungarian-Jewish family endure 20th century tyrannies: imperialism, Nazism, Stalinism. Ralph Fiennes plays all three central victims in director Istvan Szabo's vast yet intimate tale of failed compromises, grim diminishments, brutal loss.

⑤ CHICKEN RUN "*The Great Escape*—with feathers" is how co-director Nick Park described this nifty comedy-adventure about a heroine hen spurring her balky brood to freedom. A triumph of stop-motion animation and a hymn to plucky sisterhood.

CASTLE ROCK

⑥ BEST IN SHOW Patient doggies and their frenzied owners compete for a top kennel-club prize in this wicked but unpatronizing comedy. Improvised by a maniacally alert cast under the supervision of director Christopher Guest, it is the year's most original and delirious laff riot.

⑦ THE COLOR OF PARADISE A blind boy with a consuming love of nature struggles to love a father who is blind to his

son's gift for wonder. Majid Majidi's Iranian drama has enough incident for an action movie and the soul of a child who is himself a glorious force of nature.

⑧ NURSE BETTY Addled by her husband's vicious murder, a waitress (Renee Zellweger) hits the road for L.A. to embrace a more pleasing life inside her favorite soap opera. Director Neil LaBute's film is a hilarious, touching meditation on fantasy and reality in media-mad America.

UNIVERSAL

⑨ PROOF OF LIFE Isn't the phrase "intelligent thriller" an oxymoron? Not this season: a political-ransom action movie can also be a complex romantic triangle, with Russell Crowe, Meg Ryan and David Morse all excellent. It's *Casablanca* with heavier firepower.

⑩ EAST-WEST After World War II, a Russian-born doctor and his French wife accept an invitation to help rebuild the U.S.S.R.—and enter into decades of police-state agony. Director Regis Wargnier's film is a great, gray epic of despair and survival.

CROUCHING TIGER, HIDDEN DRAGON

① In Ang Lee's martial-arts enthraller, two mature warriors (Chow Yun Fat and Michelle Yeoh) are challenged and imperiled by a willful young beauty (Zhang Ziyi). A lovely melancholy anchors the buoyant fight scenes that exceed expectations even as they defy gravity. The result—magic, not trickery—should leave the viewer gasping—for breath and in awe.

SONY PICTURES CLASSICS

For BROADWAY THEATER, the new millennium has started on a note of musical diminuendo. With the demise of *Cats* and the soon-to-be-missing *Miss Saigon*, the era of the Brit-generated mega-musical seems all but over. Happily, straight plays seem to be filling the gap. Demanding dramas like Michael Frayn's *Copenhagen* have become unlikely Broadway hits, while off-Broadway's Manhattan Theatre Club transferred two strong works, *Proof* and *The Tale of the Allergist's Wife*, to the main drag this fall. With regional theaters thriving, the American stage is alive and bustling.

② COMIC POTENTIAL
Alan Ayckbourn, a prolific British delicacy long underappreciated in the U.S., gets treated right in this deft off-Broadway production of his London hit. Janie Dee is brilliant as a robot actor of the future, in a comedy whose laughs are more than skin deep.

③ AIDA Disney faces a *Lion King* problem—how can anything measure up?—but this kid-friendly version of the opera, with Elton John and Tim Rice replacing Verdi, has pleasures aplenty. Heather Headley is a knockout, and Bob Crowley's colorful, inventive sets will do until the next Julie Taymor comes along.

④ FULLY COMMITTED
A frazzled afternoon with the reservations clerk for a hot-hot-hot Manhattan restaurant. Becky Mode's one-actor play

(a hit off-Broadway and now in Los Angeles) is a tart and hilarious send-up of the social feeding frenzy.

⑤ THE LARAMIE PROJECT
The brutal murder of gay student Matthew Shepard in Wyoming was the impetus for Moisés Kaufman's unique stage docudrama, constructed entirely from interviews with locals, witnesses and participants. A pioneering work of theatrical reportage and a powerful stage event.

⑥ TANTALUS British theater titans Peter Hall and John Barton use the mythic Trojan War as the centerpiece of their adventurously scaled, sharply written satire of modern politics. This 10-hour marathon, which premiered in Denver, bristles with enough back-stabbing drama to keep the slack moments few.

⑦ PROOF David Auburn's intriguing mix of memory play and math lesson concerns a professor's daughter who may or may not have solved a famous math enigma. Of the year's two brainy science plays (the other: *Copenhagen*), this is the one that touches the heart.

BOY GETS GIRL

① With *Spinning into Butter*, a provocative play that explored race relations on campus, Rebecca Gilman gave notice that she was a playwright to watch. And with this intense drama of a woman's encounter with a stalker, she became a playwright to hail. First produced by Chicago's Goodman Theatre, it's more than just a gripping play—it's also an important one.

⑧ DINNER WITH FRIENDS Two couples see their friendship go sour when one of them gets

a divorce. Donald Margulies' perceptive, well-crafted, very contemporary play won the Pulitzer Prize and is already popping up on the regional circuit.

⑨ SEUSSICAL: THE MUSICAL The critics were grinches, but this musical of Dr. Seuss stories is surprisingly charming, with popsicle-colored sets, a tuneful Lynn Ahrens-Stephen Flaherty score and an irresistible cast. Even the mishmash of Seuss-iana goes down easy. *Green Eggs and Ham* as a marching chant? We like it, Sam-I-am.

⑩ HAMLET The most controversial production of Shakespeare all year was Andrei Serban's brash, sometimes wacky (three ghosts of Hamlet's father) but always engrossing off-Broadway update. And Liev Schreiber in the title role was a charismatic and memorable Dane.

HISTORIANS MAY LOOK BACK ON THIS YEAR as the thin edge of the e-publishing wedge, the moment when books made of paper and ink began sliding into digital obsolescence. But those not yet ready for the brave new reading world can mark 2000 by the extraordinary output of new fiction from big-name veteran authors, all producing energetic work at age 60 or older: Margaret Atwood, Saul Bellow, Doris Lessing, Joyce Carol Oates, Edna O'Brien, Philip Roth, Susan Sontag, John Updike. The millennium has so far been generous to readers. In with the new! In with the old!

FICTION

THE BLIND ASSASSIN

1 Margaret Atwood's novel is one part family saga, one part social history, one part suspense tale and altogether captivating. As its elderly narrator, Iris Chase, looks back on her life—and some mysterious deaths—she evokes not only a tangled past but a luminous fictional realm.

KEVIN KELLY

2 THE AMAZING ADVENTURES OF KAVALIER & CLAY Michael Chabon's serious but never somber tribute to the Golden Age of American comic books leaps 600 pages in a single bound. The title characters create an imaginary pulp icon while they live through a vivid, unsettling era of real-life melodramas from the 1930s to the '50s.

3 RAVELSTEIN Much ink was spilled wondering how much Saul Bellow's novel t of the real lif of his deceas friend Allan Bloom. Such waste of ene gy. What ma ters is that the author, 85, produced another brainy, complex and cantankerous hero to add to his gallery of memorable fictional beings.

4 BEOWULF The Anglo-Saxon epic, the bane of English majors, looks brand new and thrilling in a verse translation by Nobel laureate Seamus Heaney. The ancient tale may still strike readers as bloodthirsty, but Heaney's language evokes Beowulf's tragic stature, his helplessness to avoid—and his bravery while facing—the dictates of his fate.

5 WHITE TEETH Zadie Smith's miraculous first novel takes place in a tumultuously multicultural London where unlikely friendships and even more unlikely romances rule. Much of the novel's action is comic, but even at their most foolish, Smith's characters are both fascinating and admirable.

---

2 ROBERT KENNEDY Evan Thomas calls his superb biography "the story of an unpromising boy who died as he was becoming a great man." Bobby's well-documented life and legend are re-examined here with moral clarity, psychological subtlety and a bracing dramatic pace.

3 A HEARTBREAKING WORK OF STAGGERING GENIUS Dave Eggers tricks out his riveting

memoir with an ironic title and a surplus of literary gamesmanship, but the story he tells is indeed heartbreaking: the death of his parents and his subsequent guardianship of his younger brother. His book

NONFICTION

NOTHING LIKE IT IN THE WORLD

1 Veteran historian Stephen Ambrose writes at full throttle about the construction of the transcontinental railroad during the 1860s. This compelling tale of high finance, low finagling and workers hacking through 2,000 miles of challenging terrain is magnificently told.

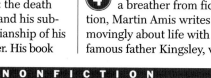

shows how laughter is sometimes the only medicine.

4 EXPERIENCE Taking a breather from fiction, Martin Amis writes movingly about life with his famous father Kingsley, who

died in 1995. The book hums with the same antic prose and looping comic riffs that characterize Martin's novels, along with a surprising admixture of familial tenderness.

5 IN THE HEART OF THE SEA In 1820 the Nantucket ship *Essex* was rammed and sunk in the South Seas by an angry whale. This event, which inspired Melville's *Moby Dick*, is thrillingly retold by Nathaniel Philbrick.

NOBEL PRIZES

Peace
Kim Dae Jung, President of South Korea, for "his work for democracy and human rights in South Korea and East Asia"

Literature
Gao Xingjian, China, "for an œuvre of universal validity, bitter insights and linguistic ingenuity"

Chemistry
Alan J. Heeger, Alan G. MacDiarmid and Hideki Shirakawa, for developing conductive polymers

Physics
One-half to Zhores I. Alferov and Herbert Kroemer, for work in developing semiconductor structures, and one-half to Jack S. Kilby, for inventing the integrated circuit

Economics
James J. Heckman and Daniel L. McFadden, for work in the statistical analysis of human behavior

Physiology or Medicine
Arvid Carlsson, Paul Greengard and Eric Kandel, for work in signal transduction in the nervous system

SPORTS CHAMPIONS

Baseball
- *World Series*
  New York Yankees
- *College World Series*
  Louisiana State Tigers

Basketball
- *NBA*
  Los Angeles Lakers
- *NCAA Women*
  Connecticut Huskies
- *NCAA Men*
  Michigan State Spartans

Football
- *Super Bowl XXXIV*
  St. Louis Rams
- *Collegiate champions*
  Oklahoma Sooners

Hockey
- *Stanley Cup*
  New Jersey Devils

Horse Racing
- *Kentucky Derby*
  Fusaichi Pegasus
- *Preakness Stakes*
  Red Bullet

- *Belmont Stakes*
  Commendable
- *Breeders' Cup Classic*
  Tiznow

Golf
- *Masters*
  Vijay Singh
- *LPGA*
  Juli Inkster
- *U.S. Open*
  Tiger Woods
- *U.S. Women's Open*
  Karrie Webb
- *British Open*
  Tiger Woods
- *PGA*
  Tiger Woods

Tennis
- *Australian Open*
  Lindsay Davenport
  Andre Agassi
- *French Open*
  Mary Pierce
  Gustavo Kuerten
- *Wimbledon*
  Venus Williams
  Pete Sampras
- *U.S. Open*
  Venus Williams
  Marat Safin

TELEVISION

1. *Who Wants … Millionaire* (Tuesday), ABC
2. *Who Wants … Millionaire* (Thursday), ABC
3. *Who Wants … Millionaire* (Sunday), ABC
4. *E.R.*, NBC
5. *Friends*, NBC
6. *Monday Night Football*, ABC
7. *Frasier*, NBC
8. *Frasier* (9:30), NBC
9. *60 Minutes*, CBS
10. *The Practice*, ABC

TONY AWARDS

Play
Copenhagen

Musical
Contact

Actress, Play
Jennifer Ehle, *The Real Thing*

Actor, Play
Stephen Dillane
The Real Thing

Actress, Musical
Heather Headley, *Aida*

Actor, Musical
Brian Stokes Mitchell
Kiss Me, Kate

THE OSCARS

FOR THE RECORD 2000

Picture
American Beauty

Actress
Hilary Swank
Boys Don't Cry

Actor
Kevin Spacey
American Beauty

Supporting Actress
Angelina Jolie
Girl, Interrupted

Supporting Actor
Michael Caine
The Cider House Rules

Director
Sam Mendes
American Beauty

Cinematography
American Beauty

Foreign Film
All About My Mother

LAURA CAVANAUGH—GLOBE PHOTOS

BESTSELLERS

1. *Harry Potter and the Goblet of Fire*
   J.K. Rowling
2. *Harry Potter and the Prisoner of Azkaban*
   J.K. Rowling
3. *Harry Potter and the Chamber of Secrets*
   J.K. Rowling
4. *Harry Potter and the Sorcerer's Stone*
   J.K. Rowling
5. *Who Moved My Cheese?*
   Spencer Johnson
6. *Body for Life*, Bill Phillips
7. *The Brethren*, John Grisham
8. *The Poisonwood Bible*
   Barbara Kingsolver
9. *Eating Well for Optimum Health*, Andrew Weil, M.D.
10. *The Bear and the Dragon*
    Tom Clancy
11. *Rich Dad, Poor Dad*
    Robert T. Kiyosaki
12. *The Greatest Generation*
    Tom Brokaw
13. *The Beatles Anthology*
    The Beatles

14. *The Indwelling*, Tim F. Lahaye, Jerry B. Jenkins
15. *Tuesdays with Morrie*
    Mitch Albom
16. *Flags of Our Fathers*
    James Bradley
17. *The O'Reilly Factor*
    Bill O'Reilly
18. *From Dawn to Decadence*
    Jacques Barzun
19. *It's Not About the Bike*
    Lance Armstrong
20. *Relationship Rescue*
    Philip C. McGraw

HOLLYWOOD FILMS

1. *How the Grinch Stole Christmas*
2. *Mission Impossible 2*
3. *Gladiator*
4. *The Perfect Storm*
5. *Meet the Parents*
6. *X-Men*
7. *Scary Movie*
8. *What Lies Beneath*
9. *Dinosaur*
10. *Erin Brockovich*

SOURCES. NOBELS: THE NOBEL PRIZE INTERNET ARCHIVE. SPORTS: THE NEW YORK TIMES. TELEVISION: NIELSEN MEDIA RESEARCH ('99-'00 SEASON). TONYS: THE AMERICAN THEATRE WING. BOOKS: AMAZON.COM. DOMESTIC FILMS: BOX OFFICE ONLINE.

GOOD GRIEF: Charles Schulz, creator of Charlie Brown, Snoopy, Lucy, Linus and the rest of the gang of little losers at *Peanuts,* **perhaps the world's most beloved cartoon, died at 77 of colon cancer—on the eve of the publication of his final Sunday strip**

John Burgess—Santa Rosa *Press-Democrat*—Liaison

ENRIC MARTI—AP/WIDE WORLD

Hafez Assad: 1930-2000

■ **THE SPHINX: Syria's inflexible boss was an austere enigma**

FOR THREE DECADES, HAFEZ ASSAD RULED SYRIA—AND confounded the world. Six American Presidents found him frustrating, remote; he was dubbed the Sphinx. The onetime air force pilot seized power in a coup in 1970, then took his poor nation of 17 million and made it a pivotal player in the Middle East—though it remained poor.

The austere Assad neither smoked nor drank. He would summon aides at all hours to discuss an issue, then closet himself for days before abruptly announcing a decision. He never came to America; from Nixon to Clinton, U.S. leaders either traveled the road to Damascus or met him in neutral Geneva. They worried about elections and deadlines; a dictator, he never worried about the clock ticking. He was legendary for his marathon negotiating sessions and infuriating intransigence. But it was his actions that so befuddled American leaders. Syria helped lead the 1973 Yom Kippur War against Israel; in 1976 it marched into Lebanon and never left. Assad's Syria has been a stalwart of the State Department's terrorism list since its inception in 1979—but the country was also part of the anti-Iraq coalition that fought in the Gulf War.

Assad was, in some ways, a good foe to have: smart, reliable in his opposition. Though in 1973 he sent hundreds of tanks swarming toward Israel on the Jewish Day of Atonement in a concerted effort with Egypt to regain Arab territory, once he'd lost the war, he scrupulously kept to the truce. Coming soon after the death of Jordan's King Hussein, Assad's passing (at 69) marked a changing of the guard in the region as leaders like Egypt's Hosni Mubarak, the P.L.O.'s Yasser Arafat, and Saudi Arabia's King Fahd—all in their 70s—grow old. Syria's parliament named Assad's son Bashar, 34, to take his place. ■

LES STONE—CORBIS SYGMA

John Cardinal O'Connor: 1920-2000   ■ MAN OF GOD: He led by example, not fiat

WHEN POPE JOHN PAUL II NAMED THE LITTLE-known bishop of Scranton, Pa., to lead the New York diocese as archbishop, big-city Catholics were wary. John O'Connor's prize credential was his 27 years of service as a military chaplain—and he was known to be a strong conservative on such divisive issues as abortion and homosexuality, hot-button topics in New York City. But when O'Connor succumbed to cancer at 80 in May, he was mourned by Americans of many faiths and from many regions. TIME invited Mario Cuomo to explain why:

"I was Governor [of New York] in 1983 when AIDS suddenly struck like a plague and our great New York City nearly panicked. People thought to be suffering from AIDS were treated as pariahs; it was difficult to get beds for the victims, or doctors and nurses to treat them. With no need for prodding, John Cardinal O'Connor made St. Clare's Hospital in Manhattan a haven for AIDS victims, and that example helped encourage the city's aggressive response to a uniquely severe crisis. For many years after that, without publicizing it, the Cardinal visited AIDS patients, sought to comfort them and even changed bedpans.

"Cardinal O'Connor was best known as one of the Vatican's favorite conservative dogmatists. Most New Yorkers, however, had scant knowledge of his equally vigorous struggle for the traditional Catholic social-justice agenda. His New York archdiocese has educated, housed and cared for hundreds of thousands of Catholics and non-Catholics. He was a proud advocate of workers' rights and a supporter of unions. And his insistent importunings have advanced ecumenism, particularly with the Jewish community. He was an extraordinary prince of the church but always a priest first."   ■

NIGEL PARRY—CPI

John Gielgud: 1904-2000

■ **TRIPPINGLY ON THE TONGUE: His voice was the century's best**

AS SINATRA WAS TO POPULAR MUSIC, SO JOHN GIELGUD was to theater: the Voice. It could draw a word out into a long cello note or quaver like the lead fiddle in a Victorian melodrama. It made Shakespeare's verse immediately comprehensible and ethereal: perfectly articulated, beautifully felt. For nearly 80 years in theater, film, radio and TV, Gielgud, who died in May at 96, gave such passionately acute readings in works sublime and not so; what other actor would be pleased both to be the definitive romantic Hamlet, which he acted some 500 times, and to lend regal pedigree to Bob Guccione's pornific *Caligula*? Who else could earn critic Kenneth Tynan's prickly compliment "the finest actor on earth, from the neck up"?

The actor was virtually born one: great-nephew of actress Ellen Terry and second cousin of designer Gordon Craig. By 21, in Chekhov and Coward, he was a London fixture. He directed and starred in the renowned 1935 *Romeo and Juliet* (the cast included Peggy Ashcroft, Edith Evans and Alec Guinness), advancing Laurence Olivier's career by swapping roles (Romeo and Mercutio) in mid-run. Later Gielgud championed such bold young playwrights as Tennessee Williams and Edward Albee.

He even got on with film, logging some 130 credits in movies and TV, most of them after he turned 75. He won an Oscar as the proper, patient butler in *Arthur*, but his great turns are in Alain Resnais's *Providence*, as a novelist with nightmares, and in Peter Greenaway's *Prospero's Books*, in which he played his favorite Shakespearean magician and appeared nude! Outlasting the century he brilliantly ornamented, Gielgud will live longer still, as long as the melody of his voice and vision resound in films, recordings and grateful memories. ■

Alec Guinness: 1914-2000

■ **MASKED MAN: He mastered the art of disguise**

CRITIC KENNETH TYNAN NAILED IT: "ALEC GUINNESS," he wrote admiringly, "has no face." So true. Sir Alec, who died at 86 in August, was the most self-effacing screen actor imaginable, often retreating under a mountain of makeup. He borrowed the props of anti-Semitism to concoct a monstrously engaging Fagin for *Oliver Twist*. He found the proper wigs and noses and shadings for each of the eight doomed D'Ascoynes, one of them a woman, in the elegant high comedy that was *Kind Hearts and Coronets*. He searched the globe for new accents and characters: Bedouin (*Lawrence of Arabia*), Japanese (*A Majority of One*), Russian (*Doctor Zhivago*), Indian (*A Passage to India*). His transparency made it easy for him to incarnate specters; he was Marley's Ghost in *Scrooge* and Obi-Wan Kenobi in *Star Wars*—the role that heaped on him the annoyance of multigenerational fame.

The camera was delighted to find the young Guinness popping into *Great Expectations* as the giddily genial Herbert Pocket. It embraced him, in Guinness's grand postwar decade of Ealing Studios comedies—both as that Candidean innocent, the creator of a miracle fabric in *The Man in the White Suit*, and as the mousy banker who nearly pulls off the legendary Eiffel Tower paperweight caper in *The Lavender Hill Mob*. It saw him locate the suicidal pride of the colonel in *The Bridge on the River Kwai*. The camera may even have captured an on-the-fly self-portrait when the older Guinness sat, purring and omniscient, for the role of George Smiley in the two '80s mini-series *Tinker, Tailor, Soldier, Spy* and *Smiley's People*. Perhaps, in the sum of these men, we caught a profile of the composite Guinness character: he defined what it meant, at the sunset of the empire, to be an Englishman. ■

PEGGY SIROTA—CORBIS OUTLINE

Walter Matthau: 1920-2000

■ **DOUR POWER: The serial grump struck a pose in 1995**

WALTER MATTHAU MADE MOVIEGOERS LAUGH AT their own venality—or make that humanity. A deft character actor with star quality, he was the ideal mouthpiece for the wisecracks of Neil Simon (*The Odd Couple, The Sunshine Boys*) and Billy Wilder (*The Fortune Cookie*). Born Walter Matuchanskayasky, he grew up in the pressure cooker of Manhattan's mostly Jewish Lower East Side; his Russian father deserted the family when Matthau was learning to walk. His life was shaped by the tough years of the Depression, when he began acting in New York City's Yiddish theaters. After a stint as a radio operator and cryptographer in World War II Britain, he returned to America, studied acting on the G.I. Bill and became a familiar presence on Broadway in supporting roles until his 1965 breakthrough as the slovenly Oscar Madison (against Art Carney's tidy Felix Unger) in *The Odd Couple.*

Matthau didn't need good writing to be funny. He had a posture designed by Rube Goldberg and a lovely snarl of a voice that cut like a foreclosure notice. That got him small, dark roles (he beat up Elvis Presley in *King Creole* and took a shot at the sainted Audrey Hepburn in *Charade*) until Wilder and Simon put him above the title. Then he suavely juggled two genres: romantic comedy (*A New Leaf, House Calls*) and 32 years of grumpy-buddy movies with Jack Lemmon.

Matthau had a few weaknesses, but optimism wasn't one of them. "I'm a degenerate gambler," he said in 1994. "If I get lucky, I'll die before I go broke." He exited (as a dying meanie in *Hanging Up*) the way he entered: like the sour sage who believes not one thing he hears—or says. If Walter Matthau were to be told that Walter Matthau had died, he'd ask for a second opinion. ■

Tom Landry: 1924-2000

■ TRAIL BOSS: Landry headed up the Cowboys from the get-go

N O ONE EXPECTED HIM TO VANISH FROM THE SPORT. When he lost the Dallas Cowboys, the team he loved, everyone expected Tom Landry to move on to another, to lead a different tribe of men to even more victories, even more Super Bowls. After all, Landry was the third most winning coach in the National Football League, behind Don Shula and George Halas. But following a graceless dismissal in a rebuilding shuffle by Dallas' new owner in 1989, Landry remained a silent, mournful football widower, reproachfully if silently carrying a torch for the team that moved on without him to further victories. At his firing, he shed public tears, which shocked an America that saw him as the faultlessly tailored, taciturn but brilliant sideline tactician. "Fireproof, bulletproof, emotionproof," the writer Pete Axthelm once described him.

Yet the young Landry had been a fiery player on the field. New York City football fans of a certain age recall him as a rough-and-tumble left cornerback for the Brooklyn–New York Yankees of the old All-America conference, then for the Giants. In the late 1950s, when Landry became the Giants' defensive coach, his colleague as offensive coach was Vince Lombardi—a deep bench, indeed.

Landry earned the right to cry when the Cowboys sent him packing. He had been coach since Dallas joined the NFL in 1960 and had nurtured the team from its winless first season through five Super Bowls and two world championships. In Landry's 29 years at the helm, Dallas won 13 division titles and had 20 consecutive winning seasons. His team became America's team. After months of treatment for leukemia, he died in February, at 76. He remains an icon of control and loyalty, a gridiron legend. ■

■ **Steve Allen**

Carl Albert, 91, Oklahoma Democrat and Speaker of the House of Representatives from 1971 to '77. A coal miner's son, he represented Oklahoma's Third District for 30 years until retiring in 1977 and twice stood a heartbeat away from the presidency. A pragmatist, he said, "I like to face issues in terms of conditions and not in terms of someone's inborn political philosophy."

Steve Allen, 78, late-night talk-show pioneer. The first host of NBC's *Tonight* show, Allen went on to star in a string of influential talk and comedy shows. He was also an author, pianist, songwriter (*This Could Be the Start of Something Big*) and, in recent years, vocal crusader against TV sleaze.

Victor Borge, 91, hammy pianist and conductor whose one-man Broadway show, *Comedy in Music*, ran a record 849 performances. Borge, a Jew who fled Europe to escape the Nazis, originally trained as a concert pianist in his native Denmark but eventually began incorporating satire and sight gags into his act.

Gwendolyn Brooks, 83, prolific poet of Chicago's streets and proud voice of black identity who, in 1950, became the first African American to win a Pulitzer Prize.

David Brower, 88, uncompromising environmental activist. Brower helped transform the Sierra Club from a 7,000-member club into one of America's most influential environmental groups. He later founded Friends of the Earth, the League of Conservation Voters and the Earth Island Institute. He resigned in protest from the Sierra Club board several times. "The world is burning," he said, "and all I hear from them is the music of violins."

Don Budge, 84, tennis player who in 1938 became the first to win all four Grand Slam events in a single year, a feat matched by only four players since. One of the sport's greatest figures, Budge pioneered the power game that prevails today and is considered the first to have used the backhand as an attack stroke.

William Bundy, 83, patrician Counsellor to three Presidents who was a pivotal figure in leading America into the Vietnam War along with his brother McGeorge Bundy, National Security Adviser under Kennedy and Johnson. Bundy supported aerial attacks on North Vietnam in 1965 and reluctantly backed the large-scale introduction of U.S. troops. Later he was critical of Henry Kissinger's secretive attempts to disentangle America from the war.

Dame Barbara Cartland, 98, best-selling romance novelist whose 723 books featuring virginal heroines in rococo plotlines sold more than 1 billion copies worldwide. She could write a novel in a week—dictating to secretaries while she reclined on a sofa—thus earning a bejeweled lifestyle, a host of pink gowns and a bit part in a real-life romantic drama: step-grandmother to Princess Diana.

■ **Douglas Fairbanks Jr.**

Ellery Chun, 91, native Hawaiian who created the brightly colored aloha shirt in 1931. The short-sleeved silk shirts, originally decorated with palm trees, pineapples and hula girls, were designed to drum up business during the dark years of the Depression.

Alexander Cohen, 79, voluble Broadway impresario who brought the Tonys to TV and Richard Burton's portrayal of *Hamlet* to Broadway.

Ivan Deblois Combe, 88, body-care Edison who created the acne cream Clearasil, Odor-Eaters foot-care products and Just For Men hair color.

Alex Comfort, 80, aptly named British physician, pacifist and author of the lively 1972 gourmet's guide to the sexual revolution, *The Joy of Sex*.

Anthony (Tony Ducks) Corallo, 87, last of the old-time Mafia dons; he died in prison while serving a 100-year sentence for racketeering. Corallo, former boss of the Lucchese family, was known as Tony Ducks for ducking subpoenas; he also ducked the limelight. His rare slipup: a bugged 1982 talk with his driver on Mob control of New York City's construction industry.

Jimmie Davis, thought to be 101, the "Singing Governor" of Louisiana. Davis, who penned some 400 songs, including *You Are My Sunshine*, served as an ineffectual segregationist Governor from 1944 to '48 and 1960 to '64. "[Davis] served two terms as Governor of Louisiana and was never indicted," said former Governor Edwin W. Edwards (who was). "That's a genuine achievement."

Douglas Fairbanks Jr., 90, dashing star of 75 films and son of silent-screen legend Douglas Fairbanks Sr.

Richard Farnsworth, 80, archetypal movie farmhand and two-time Oscar nominee; he died from a self-inflicted gunshot. Partly paralyzed from cancer, in 1999 he became the oldest leading actor to receive an Oscar bid, for his role in *The Straight Story*. He worked as a stuntman in some 300 films before winning a speaking role in 1976.

Thomas Ferebee, 81, *Enola Gay* bombardier who dropped the atom bomb on Hiroshima in World War II. He retired from the Air Force in 1970, after acting as an observer in Vietnam.

Penelope Fitzgerald, 83, late-blooming, prizewinning British author of *The Bookshop, Offshore* and *The Blue Flower.* She was born into a literary family but didn't begin writing until her 60s. Her subtle, somewhat autobiographical novels often focused on people struggling to cope.

Vittorio Gassman, 77, urbane Italian actor who appeared in hundreds of plays and films, including *The Big Deal on Madonna Street* (1958) and *Scent of a Woman* (1974), which earned him a Best Actor award at Cannes and was later remade in English.

■ **Edward Gorey**

Elmer Gertz, 93, crusading Chicago civil rights attorney who helped Nathan Leopold, accused with Richard Loeb of young Bobby Franks' murder in 1924's "Crime of the Century," win parole in 1958; defended Henry Miller's explicit novel *Tropic of Cancer* against censorship; and overturned the murder conviction of Lee Harvey Oswald's killer, Jack Ruby.

Edward Gorey, 75, author and illustrator of more than 100 morbidly funny books. A former book-jacket designer, he created such macabre classics as *The Gashlycrumb Tinies,* an alphabet book in which *A* stands for "Amy who fell down the stairs." Gorey once said that to take his work seriously would be "the height of folly."

Lou Groza, 76, all-star Cleveland Browns tackle and place kicker known during his 21-year career as "the Toe." His most memorable field goal was a 16-yd. boot with seconds left, to win the 1950 championship over the L.A. Rams. College football's top kicker each year earns the Lou Groza Award.

Gus Hall, 90, four-time presidential candidate who led the American Communist Party for 41 years. Found guilty in 1949 of conspiracy to advocate the violent overthrow of the government, he fled to Mexico but was extradited and spent 5½ years in prison. His subsequent refusal to register with the government as a communist led to the 1965 Supreme Court decision that abolished that law.

R.H. Harris, 84, gospel great and last surviving member of the pioneering Soul Stirrers, the first gospel group inducted into the Rock 'n' Roll Hall of Fame. Harris was a mentor to Sam Cooke; his vocal legacy echoes in Al Greene and R. Kelly.

Screamin' Jay Hawkins, 70, wildly theatrical rock singer. He was best known for his drunken rendition of *I Put a Spell on You* (1956), an underground classic replete with screams, grunts and gurgles.

Doug Henning, 52, tie-dyed Emmy-winning magician who used Broadway rock musicals to revive famous illusions and once performed Houdini's water-torture escape on live TV.

Gil Kane, 73, self-taught comic-book artist whose half-century career included bringing Green Lantern back to life in the late 1950s and the Atom soon after, and reinterpreting other great superheroes, from Spider-Man and the Hulk to Captain America and Conan the Barbarian.

Richard Kleindienst, 76, Richard Nixon's Attorney General who stepped down during the Watergate crisis and later pleaded guilty to a minor charge in an antitrust-scandal.

Reggie Kray, 66, British gangster who in the 1950s and '60s ruled east London with his identical twin Ronnie as

■ **Screamin' Jay Hawkins**

modern-day Robin Hoods, giving money to the poor and hobnobbing with socialites. He died a month after he was released from prison, where he spent 32 years for murder.

Hedy Lamarr, 86, sultry actress. The Viennese-born Lamarr (the star of *Samson and Delilah*) also shared a 1942 patent for a device that prevented radio-controlled torpedoes from having their signals jammed.

Ring Lardner Jr., 85, screenwriter, son of author Ring Lardner. Lardner was the last surviving member of the "Hollywood 10" group of writers, directors and producers blacklisted in the 1940s for refusing to answer questions posed by the House Un-American Activities Committee. He served nine months in prison in 1947 and didn't receive credit for any screenplays until 1965. He won an Oscar in 1942 for *Woman of the Year* and in 1970 for *M*A*S*H.*

■ **Doug Henning**

■ Hedy Lamarr

Chester Lee, 80, NASA mission director who oversaw the return of Apollo 13 after an oxygen tank exploded in mid-flight. The Navy captain helped develop the Polaris missile as well as NASA's shuttle program.

John V. Lindsay, 79, mayor of New York City during the turbulent years from 1966 to '73. Dashing and energetic, he brought people back to the city's parks, walked black neighborhoods to keep the peace after Martin Luther King's murder—and tangled with city unions. The onetime Republican Congressman changed his party affiliation to Democrat and ran for President in 1972, but dropped out after failing to garner support in the primaries.

Julie London, 74, actress and breathy pop phenom whose 1955 song, *Cry Me a River*, sold more than 1 million copies.

■ Patrick O'Brian

Honed in nightclubs, London's hushed, smoked-out voice made hits of *Around Midnight* and *My Heart Belongs to Daddy*. She appeared as nurse Dixie McCall on TV's *Emergency!*

Nancy Marchand, 71, versatile, award-winning actress best known for playing Mob matriarch Livia Soprano on the HBO series *The Sopranos*. A theatrically trained performer, Marchand garnered acclaim on Broadway and in film, and won four Emmys for her role as a newspaper publisher on the television series *Lou Grant*.

Don Martin, 68, *Mad* magazine cartoonist whose wild-haired, flat-faced creations suffered miserable, grotesque, almost palpable fates (Splop! Shklip! Pwang!). Martin influenced scores of young cartoonists.

William Maxwell, 91, author and *New Yorker* fixture who polished the prose of Vladimir Nabokov, John Updike and J.D. Salinger, among other authors. A 40-year veteran of the magazine, Maxwell wrote six novels as well as dozens of short stories, essays and reviews.

David Merrick, 88, ruthless, larger-than-life Broadway producer of nearly 90 plays and musicals. "The Abominable Showman" often tangled with critics but built a string of smashes, including *Gypsy; Fanny; Hello, Dolly; 42nd Street; Promises, Promises; Play It Again, Sam; The Entertainer; Look Back in Anger;* and *Marat/Sade.*

Harold Nicholas, 79, acrobatic tap dancer who with his older brother Fayard helped break the color barrier in Hollywood musicals. The brothers' dizzying footwork and preternatural elegance awed such dance greats as Fred Astaire and Mikhail Baryshnikov, who called them "the most amazing dancers I've ever seen in my life."

Patrick O'Brian, 85, English author of probing, learned novels of the British navy in the Napoleonic Wars. His tales of Captain Jack Aubrey and ship's surgeon Dr. Stephen Maturin showcased his gifts as prose stylist, naturalist, antiquarian and master of nautical arcana. Described in TIME by William

F. Buckley as "the most evocative writer on the sea since Homer," O'Brian was also a translator, linguist, biographer and—it emerged after his death—a masterly dissembler about the facts of his own life.

Anthony Powell, 94, British social-comic novelist whose richly woven 12-volume *A Dance to the Music of Time* chronicles the genteel manners and morals of Britain's upper-middle class from World War I to the 1970s. A 20th century great, Powell was the last of Britain's Brideshead generation of writers, which included Evelyn Waugh, Graham Greene and George Orwell.

Tito Puente, 77, mambo king and extroverted percussionist who made 119 al-

■ Pierre Trudeau

bums during his six-decade career and won his fifth Grammy in 2000. Carlos Santana brought Puente into the mainstream with his '60s smash recording of Puente's *Oye Como Va.*

Zeljko Raznatovic, 47, notorious Serbian paramilitary leader popularly known as Arkan; he died after being shot in the head by unknown gunmen. A close ally of Serbian President Slobodan Milosevic's, Arkan was indicted by the U.N. war-crimes tribunal in 1997, accused of ethnic cleansing during the wars in Croatia and Bosnia.

Steve Reeves, 74, sword-and-sandal-epic actor who pumped his Mr. Universe physique into the popular role of Hercules in a series of films made in the 1950s and '60s.

Maurice Richard, 78, a.k.a. "the Rocket," perennial hockey All-Star who netted eight Stanley Cups during his 18-year career with the Montreal Canadiens and whose name appears on the NHL trophy given each year to the league's top goal scorer.

Jason Robards Jr., 78, gritty stage and screen actor renowned for his performances in such Eugene O'Neill plays as *Long Day's Journey into Night* and *A Moon for the Misbegotten.* He won back-to-back Oscars in the '70s for *All the President's Men* and *Julia.*

Carl Rowan, 75, crusading newsman, syndicated columnist and commentator once dubbed "the most visible black journalist in the country." He rose from poverty in Tennessee to become a gifted reporter and columnist who often wrote on racial issues.

George Segal, 75, American Pop Art icon whose monochromatic sculptures were cast from live models and outfitted with bland commercial products. A so-called New Realist, he evoked the mystery and pathos of human existence in his tableaux.

Robert Trent Jones Sr., 93, golf architect who designed or remodeled more than 450 courses, many renowned for their natural obstacles, which he believed kept golf a challenging game.

Claire Trevor, 91, actress who specialized in playing tough-talking floozies with hearts of gold and won a supporting-actress Oscar for just such a role in *Key Largo* (1948). One of her best roles was opposite John Wayne in the classic *Stagecoach* (1939).

Pierre Trudeau, 80, dashing former Prime Minister of Canada who served from 1968 until '84 (except for nine months when he was voted out of office). Energetic and abrasive, he knifed through dowdy Canadian politics like a downhill skier: he used the army against Quebec terrorists while forcing the English-speaking provinces to make services available in French and also led a rethinking of the constitutional structure of the country and its relationship with Britain.

■ **Gwen Verdon**

Stanley Turrentine, 66, soulful blues-based tenor saxophonist. The three-time Grammy nominee played with Ray Charles, Max Roach, Herbie Hancock and Earl Bostic.

Roger Vadim, 72, French filmmaker whose 1956 debut, *And God Created Woman,* launched wife Brigitte Bardot in film. Vadim won a reputation for making stars out of the stunning women he married (Jane Fonda) or lived with (Catherine Deneuve).

Jim Varney, 50, lovable long-faced comic who made hundreds of commercials and nine movies as the dimwitted bumpkin Ernest P. Worrell, a cult figure in the 1980s famous for his "KnowhutImean?" catchphrase.

Gwen Verdon, 75, Broadway's red-tressed first lady of dance and winner of four Tony Awards. The sultry Lola of *Damn Yankees* married choreographer Bob Fosse in 1960 and was Roxie Hart in his production of *Chicago.* The two separated in 1971 but never divorced.

Edward Craven Walker, 82, unabashed nudist and inventor of the oozing 1960s groovy-soothing Lava lamp. "You can avoid going on drugs," he once said. "If you have a Lava lamp, you won't need them."

Frank Wills, 52, keen-eyed former Watergate security guard who, working the midnight shift, discovered the break-in at the offices of the Demo-cratic National Committee that led to Richard Nixon's resignation.

Joseph Wolfson, 50, legendary surfer who was nicknamed "Dr. 360" after being the first boogie boarder to turn full circle while riding a wave. Surfers rescued Wolfson in 1998 after the lung-cancer patient left a note onshore with $5,000 for a funeral party and paddled out to sea to die.

Loretta Young, 87, the loveliest of Hollywood movie queens of the 1930s and '40s who appeared in 90 films opposite the likes of Clark Gable and Cary Grant. She won an Oscar for *The Farmer's Daughter* (1947); in 1953 she was host and star of TV's *The Loretta Young Show,* creating a trademark entrance in a glam gown. Young, thrice married (and thrice Emmied), all but retired from acting in 1963.

Emil Zatopek, 78, four-time Czech Olympic gold medalist and political dissident. Zatopek won three of his golds at the Helsinki Games in 1952: in the 5,000 m, the 10,000 m and—having never run one before—the marathon. He was dismissed from the military and reduced to manual labor after standing on anticommunist front lines during the 1968 Prague Spring.

Elmo Zumwalt Jr., 79, Chief of Naval Operations during the Vietnam War. A veteran of the Pacific theater in World War II and of Korea, Admiral Zumwalt presided over a major update of Navy personnel procedures. In Vietnam he ordered the use of Agent Orange in combat areas where his son served; his son later died of cancer caused by exposure to the chemical.

■ **Elmo Zumwalt Jr.**

INDEX

fish, in diet, 136
Fitzgerald, Penelope, 165
Flaherty, Stephen, 153
flexible sigmoidoscopy, 132-33
Florida
    Elián González, 4-5, 42-45
    presidential election, 2-3, 20-25
Food and Drug Administration
    abortion pill approval, 135
football, 103
    champions, 155
Foote, Tad, 45
Ford, Whitey, 17
Ford Motor Co., 66-69
Foudy, Julie, 111
Fouts, Dan, 103
Fox, Vicente, 14, 65
Frankenfood, 134, 136
Frayn, Michael, 153
Freeman, Cathy, 104-5, 113
Fujimori, Alberto, 64
Fully Committed (Mode), 153
Fusaichi Pegasus, 155

G

Gabler, Neal, 143
Gao Xingjian, 155
Gardner, Rulon, 110
Garfield, Bob, 17
Gassman, Vittorio, 165
Gates, Bill, 15
Gateway Computer, 71
gay Boy Scout leaders, 49
gay marriage, 48
Gehry, Frank, 138, 149
General Electric, 72
genome, 119-21
Gertz, Elmer, 165
George Washington, 152
Georgia state flag, 16
Gidzenko, Yuri P., 127
Gielgud, John, 160
Gifford, Kathie Lee, 17
Gilman, Rebecca, 153
Gilmore Girls, The, 151
Ginsburg, Ruth Bader, 26, 27, 133
Giuliani, Rudolph, 14, 30
Gladiator, 155
Glaxo Wellcome, 121
global warming, 126
golden rice, 136
Goldman, Jim, 44
golf
    champions, 155
    Tiger Woods, 96-99
González, Elián, 4-5, 15, 17, 42-45
González, Juan Miguel, 15, 43-45
González, Lázaro, 4-5, 43, 44
González, Marisleysis, 43, 45
Gooden, Dwight, 101
Gordon, David, 152
Gore, Al, 15, 16, 17, 28-30, 36
    presidential election, 19, 20-27
Gorey, Edward, 165
Gorton, Slade, 30
Graves, Michael, 92
Green, Tom, 151
Green Party, 29
Greene, Maurice, 113
Greengard, Paul, 155
Greenspan, Alan, 71
Groove, 88, 89
Groza, Lou, 165
Guepiere, Anne, 80
Guest, Christopher, 152
Guinness, Alec, 161
Guzman, Onel de, 81
gymnastics, 111

H

Hagelin, John, 28
Hall, Gary, Jr., 109
Hall, Gus, 165
Hall, Peter, 153
Hallam, Clint, 16
Hamlet, 153
Hamm, Mia, 111
Hampton, Mike, 101
Haram al-Sharif, 54
Harmer, Sarah, 150
Harmon, Butch, 97, 98
Harris, Katherine, 23, 24, 25, 26
Harris, R.H., 165
Harry Potter books, 16, 147
Hatch, Richard, 141
Hawass, Zahi, 123-24
Hawk, Susan, 141
Hawkins, Screamin' Jay, 165
Hayden Planetarium, 116-17
HeadBlade, 149
Headley, Heather, 153, 155
Heaney, Seamus, 154
Heartbreaking Work of Staggering
    Genius, A (Eggers), 154
Heckman, James J., 155
Heeger, Alan J., 155
Henning, Doug, 165
Hepburn, Audrey, 133
Hernandez, Orlando, 101
Herzog, Jacques, 149
Het Oosten Pavilion, 149
Hill, Faith, 146
Hingis, Martina, 100
HIV infection, 137
hockey, 155
Holder, Eric, 45
Holl, Steven, 149
Holyfield, Evander, 103
Home Depot, 71, 72
homosexuality
    Boy Scout leaders, 49
    gay marriage, 48
horse racing, 155
How the Grinch Stole Christmas,
    146, 155
Human Genome Project, 119-21
Hunter, C.J., 112, 114
Hussein, King, 158

I

I Am Shelby Lynne (Lynne), 150
iMac (computer), 91
Immigration and Naturalization
    Service (INS), 43-44
Indianapolis Pacers, 94
Inkster, Juli, 155
Innocence Project, 49
Institutional Revolutionary Party
    (P.R.I.), Mexico, 65
International Monetary Fund, 73
International Space Station, 127
Internet
    computer viruses and, 80-81
    e-commerce, 14, 70-72, 83
    Napster, 77-79
In the Heart of the Sea
    (Philbrick), 154
Iran, 65
Israel, 52-57
iVillage, 73

J

Jackson, Jesse, 24, 25
Jackson, Phil, 102
Jean, Wyclef, 150
Jerusalem, 54, 55
Jeter, Derek, 14, 101

Joffe, Carole, 135
John, Elton, 16, 153
John Paul II, Pope, 14, 64, 159
Johnson, Michael, 113
Jolie, Angelina, 155
Jones, Marion, 14, 112, 113, 114
Jordan, Michael, 28, 97, 102

K

Kaczmarek, Jane, 151
kaizen, 97, 98
Kandel, Eric, 155
Kane, Gil, 165
Karelin, Alexander, 110
Kaufman, Moisés, 153
Kennedy, Anthony, 27
Kennedy, Robert, 154
Kenniff, Sean, 17
Kenteris, Konstantinos, 113
Khatami, Mohammed, 65
Kid A (Radiohead), 150
Kidd, Joanna, 62
Kilby, Jack St. Clair, 127, 155
Kim Dae Jung, 64, 155
Kim Jong Il, 64
King, Larry, 17
King, Stephen, 14, 83
Kiss Me, Kate, 155
Klebanov, Ilya, 61
Kleindienst, Richard, 165
K Mart, 72, 91
Knight, Bobby, 14
Knoblauch, Chuck, 101
Kodak, 92
Kolesnikov, Dmitry, 63
Koppel, Ted, 16
Korea, 53, 64
Kostunica, Vojislav, 58-59
Kozmo.com, 83
Kray, Reggie, 165
Krayzelburg, Lenny, 109
Krikalev, Sergei K., 127
Kroemer, Herbert, 127, 155
Kuerten, Gustavo, 155
Kursk, 60-63

L

LaBute, Neil, 152
Lamarr, Hedy, 165
Landry, Tom, 163
Laramie Project, The (Kaufman), 153
Lardner, Ring, Jr., 165
Lasorda, Tommy, 110
Lazio, Rick, 30
League of Gentlemen, The, 151
Lee, Ang, 152
Lee, Chester, 166
Lee, Wen Ho, 17, 48
Leiter, Al, 101
Letterman, David, 147
Levin, Gerald, 73
Lewis, Terry P., 24
Liars' Club, The (Karr), 143
Lieberman, Hadassah, 15
Lieberman, Joe, 24
Life, the Movie (Gabler), 143
Likud Party, 54
Lindsay, John V., 166
Linney, Laura, 152
Liu, Lucy, 146
Loewy, Raymond, 91, 92
Lonergan, Kenneth, 152
London, Julie, 166
Los Alamos, N.M.
    Wen Ho Lee spy case, 48
    wildfires, 10-11
Los Angeles Lakers, 15, 94-95, 155
Lott, Trent, 15, 17

Louisiana State Tigers, 155
Love Bug computer virus, 80-81
Lovers Rock (Sade), 150
Lyachin, Gennadi, 61
Lynne, Shelby, 150

M

MacDiarmid, Alan G., 155
Madonna, 17
Maher, Bill, 17
Maines, Natalie, 146
Majidi, Majid, 152
Malcolm in the Middle, 151
Mao Zedong, 39
Marchand, Nancy, 166
Margulies, Donald, 153
marriage, gay, 48
Mars Global Surveyor, 126
Martin, Camilla, 114
Martin, Don, 166
Mathers, Marshall (Eminem), 146
Matthau, Walter, 162
Mau, Bruce, 148, 149
Maxwell, William, 166
McCain, John, 28, 29, 69
McEnroe, John, 100
McFadden, Daniel L., 155
McGee, Eddie, 143
McMellon, Edward, 48
MDMA (ecstasy), 87, 88
Medsprout.com, 70, 72
Meek, Erin, 70
Meet the Parents, 155
Mendes, Sam, 155
Merrick, David, 166
Meuron, Pierre de, 149
Mexico, 14, 65
Michaels, Al, 103
Michigan State Spartans, 155
Mickelson, Phil, 99
microchips, 127
Microsoft, 80
Middelhoff, Thomas, 79
Middle East, 52-57, 158
mifepristone, 135
Milbrett, Tiffeny, 111
Miller, Dennis, 16, 103
Mills, Betty, 43-44
Milosevic, Slobodan, 7, 58-59
ministrokes, 137
Mission Impossible 2, 155
Mitchell, Brian Stokes, 155
Moby, 89
Mode, Becky, 153
Monahan, Jay, 131
Monday Night Football, 103
Moore, Mary Tyler, 17
Morris, Errol, 151
Morse, David, 152
Moussambani, Eric, 108
Moynihan, Daniel Patrick, 28, 30
MP3 music software, 78
Mubarak, Hosni, 158
Murphy, Richard, 48
Museum of Natural History, 148
music
    awards, 155
    best of 2000, 150
    kidpop, 144-45
    Napster and, 77-79

N

Nader, Ralph, 15, 29
Napster, 76-79
NASCAR racing, 102
Nasser, Jacques, 69
National Action Party (P.A.N.),
    Mexico, 65